The FIRST
NORTH
AMERICANS

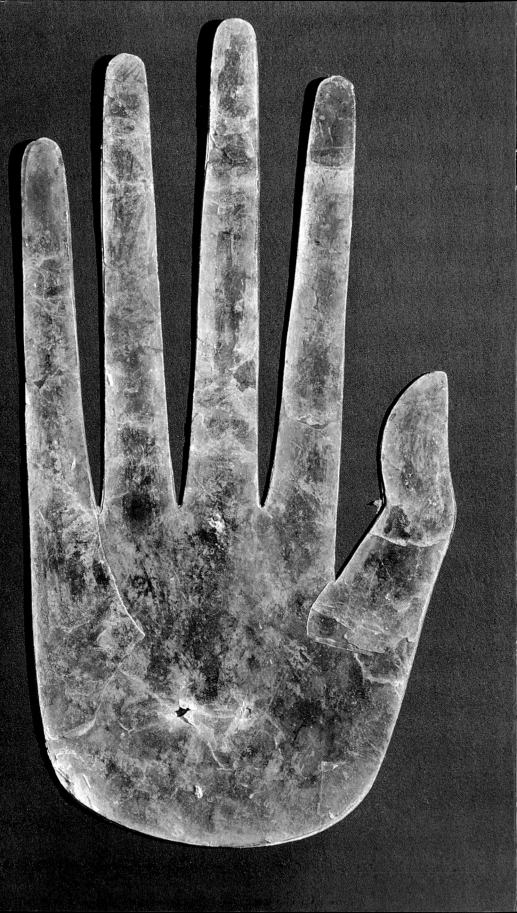

BRIAN FAGAN

The FIRST
NORTH
AMERICANS

An Archaeological Journey

With 190 illustrations, 26 in color

 Thames & Hudson

Ancient Peoples and Places
FOUNDING EDITOR: GLYN DANIEL

For Nadia, with thanks for constant encouragement ... and a big Hee Hee!

Frontispiece: A human hand with elongated fingers cut from a mica sheet, found in Mound 25 at Hopewell in Ohio. Length 11.4 in (29 cm).

First published in hardcover in 2011 in the United States of America by Thames & Hudson Inc., 500 Fifth Avenue, New York, New York 10110

thamesandhudsonusa.com

First paperback edition 2012

Library of Congress Catalog Card Number 2010932490

ISBN 978-0-500-28941-9

Printed and bound in China by 1010 Printing International Ltd

Contents

Part II   APOGEE

Preface

I wrote this book in the belief that the time was ripe for a short, narrative account of ancient North America, from first settlement to the arrival of Europeans in the late fifteenth century AD. Nearly twenty years ago, I attempted a more comprehensive synthesis in *Ancient North America*, which, by the standards of this book, is a truly encyclopedic work. It has stood the test of time well, but there is now a strong case for a shorter volume that summarizes the highlights and is of interest to the general public, to students, and to archaeologists and historians without a specialized knowledge of the subject.

The pace of research has accelerated dramatically in recent years, largely because of numerous cultural resource management (CRM) projects mandated by federal and state law. These have led to some important discoveries, many of the projects involving large-scale surveys and a few big excavations. In recent years, we have also witnessed a revolution in remote sensing and in non-intrusive archaeology, which involves little or no excavation. At the same time, an extraordinary array of scientific tools has come to bear on the past, many of them originating in large-budget CRM projects. Field research is ever more fine-grained, but even more remarkable are the achievements in air-conditioned laboratories, which have yielded fascinating insights into such esoterica as long-distance exchange, sourcing of raw materials, maize cultivation, and human genetics. A revolution in the study of past climate has also given us priceless insights into the ways in which such phenomena as El Niños and prolonged droughts have affected ancient societies. Native American scholars are becoming more involved in North American archaeology and their insights are likely to change many of our views in future years. Our portrait of ancient North America – and the pages that follow are but a snapshot – becomes more detailed and more nuanced every year. I have attempted to navigate between passionate debates, agreements, and disagreements, while concentrating on the basics.

The First North Americans is very much a narrative, focusing on the highlights, on such issues as first settlement, the beginnings of maize cultivation, and the development of more complex societies in the centuries before European contact. Space limitations have forced me to gloss over controversial issues, and sometimes to couch things in more definite terms than might seem justified to a specialist. I do this unashamedly, on the grounds that an overstatement in these pages is easily qualified by further reading or in the classroom. Terminology and the proliferation of cultural labels have also been a challenge in a book this short. I have used boxes and tables to clarify key issues where appropriate. Anyone seriously interested in the intricate culture history of North American archaeology can easily find guidance (and, it must be said, often confusion) in the more technical literature in the Further Reading.

This is not a book about archaeological methods, so there is minimal discussion of them here. Nor have I delved into the complex theoretical approaches that surround North American archaeology, fascinating and important as they are. Readers interested in such topics should consult one of the widely used college textbooks known collectively as "method and theory texts." The narrative in these pages is based on theoretical frameworks of all kinds; there is no overarching theoretical approach here. It simply would not work. I have also omitted any discussion of the colorful history of archaeological discovery in North America, which is effectively irrelevant to my narrative. Again, there are admirable discussions of the subject in easily accessible books, and a summary in my *Ancient North America*.

The book is divided into two parts. Part I, "Foundations," begins with two chapters that cover first settlement and later colonization of North America as a whole. The next five survey early developments in major culture areas up to a somewhat flexible date of about 2000 BC, and in some cases later. Part II, "Apogee," describes the more complex societies that developed in the same culture areas throughout the continent in later times, especially in the 2,000 years before European contact. The story ends in AD 1492, but a short Epilogue highlights some of the developments wrought by European exploration and colonization, notably the holocaust created by epidemic disease. The Further Reading section presents key references for more detailed inquiry.

These pages are the culmination of many years of field research, travel, museum study, and reading, as well as of discussions with more colleagues than I could ever list. I am deeply beholden to them all, and hope that they will take this book as a tribute to their experience and willing cooperation. I am particularly grateful to the following scholars, who kindly read the draft and made insightful, sometimes trenchant, comments: Douglas Bamforth, Christopher Carr, Linda Cordell, Mark Freisen, Lynn Gamble, John Hart, John Hoffecker, Robert Hall, Robert McGhee, Herbert Maschner, George Milner, Vincent Steponaitis, Gwinn Vivian, Greg Wilson, and William Workman. The book is immeasurably better as a result.

I am greatly indebted to the staff of Thames & Hudson in London and New York for their work during the editorial and production stages.

My friend Shelly Lowenkopf was his usual encouraging and insightful self as I grappled with inexorable word limits and issues of readability.

Finally, some conventions that are worth noting:

- All dates after 12,000 years ago are expressed in AD/BC format.
- Where used, radiocarbon dates are calibrated readings in calendar years.
- All cultural, place-name, and other spellings are those most commonly used in the literature.
- Both imperial and metric measurements are given in the text.
- Generally, I have not referred a great deal to researchers by name, not because I don't appreciate their work, but because of space considerations.

I urge anyone with comments or suggestions to contact me via email, at brian@brianfagan.com.

Chronological table of Ancient North American societies

Archaeologists often use three loosely defined cultural terms:
Paleoindian: The first human societies in North America, from first settlement to after 8000 BC.
Archaic: Later hunter-gatherer societies that developed local adaptations after 8000 BC until about AD 1.
Woodland: Hunter-gatherer and agricultural societies in the Eastern Woodlands after 1000 BC.

Dates	Climate	Arctic	West/Southwest	Plains	Eastern Woodlands	Northeast
		H I S T O R I C	P E R I O D			
Historic	LITTLE ICE AGE			Horse introduced	MISSISSIPPIAN	NORTHERN
AD 1500 —		NORSE THULE	HOHOKAM		LATE	IROQUOIANS
	MEDIEVAL WARM		ANCESTRAL PUEBLO		WOODLAND	
AD 1000 —	PERIOD		MOGOLLON			
		DORSET NORTON		Communal bison hunting	HOPEWELL	
			LATE PERIOD		MIDDLE WOODLAND	
· AD 1 —	LATE HOLOCENE		NORTHWEST AND	Important maize farming	ADENA	
			CALIFORNIA			
1000 BC —		PRE-DORSET				
2000 BC —	MIDDLE HOLOCENE	ARCTIC SMALL TOOL	Maize introduced		EARLY WOODLAND	
3000 BC —						
4000 BC —	ALTITHERMAL (climatic optimum)	ALEUTIAN TRADITION		ARCHAIC SOCIETIES		
5000 BC —						
6000 BC —						
7000 BC —		PALEOARCTIC				
8000 BC —	EARLY HOLOCENE			LATER PALEOINDIAN SOCIETIES		
9000 BC —						
10,000 BC —	YOUNGER DRYAS (cold)			CLOVIS		
				FIRST SETTLEMENT		
11,000 BC —						
12,000 BC —						

Chronological tables are intended as a general guide only. Not all sites, phases or cultural terms used in the text appear in these tables. The following key is used throughout the tables:

—————— Well-established chronology. Time span may continue beyond the line.

———————| Limit of the chronology is generally agreed.

- - - - - - - - Chronology doubtful.

CLOVIS A name in capital letters is an archaeological culture, horizon, or tradition.

Meadowcroft A name not in capital letters is an archaeological site.

Part I

FOUNDATIONS

Those who at the First Beginning
Were given the world,
the bushes,
the forest,
we meet them there.

Zuni song, recorded 1929

Chronological table of early settlement of North America

Years before present*	Years BC	Northeast Asia	North America			
			Alaska	West	Plains	Eastern Woodlands
9250 —	7300 —			WESTERN EARLY ARCHAIC	EARLY PLAINS ARCHAIC	EARLY ARCHAIC
9900 —	7950 —	SUMNAGIN CULTURE	PALEOARCTIC TRADITION			
				YOUNGER DRYAS		
12,200 —	10,250 —		NENANA COMPLEX	—— REGIONAL PALEOINDIAN STYLES ——		DALTON
13,450 —	11,500 —			CLOVIS	CLOVIS	CLOVIS
13,950 —	12,000 —					?Meadowcroft
				Monte Verde (Chile)		
15,950 —	14,000 —	DYUKTAI CULTURE	———————— ?? FIRST SETTLEMENT ————————			
16,950 —	15,000 —					
18,000 —	16,050 —		LAST GLACIAL MAXIMUM			

*Present is AD 1950

1 · The Earliest Americans

Between Siberia and Alaska, summer, 15,000 years ago. Imagine flying in an ultralight over a seemingly endless arctic plain. A fierce wind buffets your fragile craft. Gray-brown glacial dust cascades in the breeze, obscuring the far horizon. Strong gusts scurry through the low scrub that hugs the featureless landscape for mile after mile. Then a stretch of meandering green comes into view, a narrow river set in a shallow valley. Some low, windswept arctic willows cling to life along the river banks; small patches of ice linger at the water's edge. It is then that you see a now-rare sight, great beasts browsing on the stunted vegetation – long-haired mammoths oblivious to the cold, their ears flapping at the unfamiliar engine noise. Two musk ox drink in the shallows. Arctic foxes skulk among the trees. And then, at the valley's edge, you spot them: perhaps a dozen fur-clad men, women, and children, walking carefully down a gully. They carry spears and skin bags, tiny figures, alone and dwarfed by the immense, harsh landscape. These few people, and others like them in small family bands, are the first Americans....

Stone projectile points, scatters of toolmaking debris, clay potsherds, burial mounds, and shell middens: the residues of the achievements and history of the first Americans have come down to us in a palimpsest of finds from archaeological sites large and small. The tapestry of written history goes back five centuries, to 1492; Native American oral histories and origin tales speak of infinite timescales, but are documents of an entirely different kind, concerned as they are with defining relationships with the cosmos, with the forces of the supernatural world. Before 1492, a 15,000-year historical landscape looms before us, with only the site, the artifact, and all the awesome panoply of multidisciplinary science to clothe it with people and their deeds.

This is a story teased from thousands of minute clues, many of them startlingly exotic and obscure, but it is a vital history of anonymous people going about their daily lives – negotiating, communicating, avoiding, loving and hating, growing up, getting married, having children, and dying. It's a chronicle of adaptation and opportunism, of emerging diversity, and, above all, of societies where ties of kin were all-important, where close links with the supernatural world were at the core of human existence. Archaeology, which studies the material remains of the past, can reconstruct but a shadow of what happened. However, as archaeological methods improve and multidisciplinary research accelerates, the shadows gradually emerge into full sunlight and we discern more and more as we gaze into what has been called the "mirror of the intangible." All of this history began with a few small hunter-gatherer bands, who crossed from Siberia into Alaska. At the time, Ice Age sea levels were much lower than today. A low plain linked Alaska and Siberia, known as the Bering Land Bridge. Which brings us to perhaps the most fundamental question of all: when and how did the first Americans arrive in their new homeland?

Ultimate origins: genetics, teeth, and languages

The question of "when" has exercised scholars for centuries. By 1900, many had settled on a date of about 4,000 years ago for first settlement, even as ranch foreman George McJunkin discovered sun-bleached bison bones and a stone spear point in a dry gully near the small town of Folsom, New Mexico, in 1908. His finds lay around the ranch house for seventeen years until they reached the desk of archaeologist Jesse Figgins at the Colorado Museum of Natural History. Figgins dug into the Folsom site in 1926 and uncovered stone points in direct association with extinct bison bones. Even then, his colleagues were skeptical, until more discoveries, notably at Clovis, New Mexico, in 1932, confirmed his findings. However, it was not until after World War II that Clovis points with their distinctive fluted bases were shown to underlie Folsom specimens. Thus, Clovis was earlier (a date of about 10,000 years ago was a mere estimate) and people had hunted now extinct animals in North America. Today's calibrated radiocarbon dates place the short-lived Clovis occupation of North America to between 13,050 and 12,800 years ago.

But were Clovis people in fact the first Americans? A scatter of inconspicuous archaeological sites appeared to contain significantly earlier artifacts, extending deep into what became known as pre-Clovis times. How far back did this seemingly earlier settlement extend – 15,000, 40,000 years ago? Everyone agrees that the only humans to settle in the Americas were anatomically modern *Homo sapiens* – people like ourselves. Everyone also concurs that the most likely time frame for first settlement lies between about 50,000 and 15,000 years ago, during, or just after, the last Ice Age glaciation. The disagreement starts when you try and narrow down the time frame within these 35,000 years.

You cannot answer this question without establishing where the first Americans came from. There's practically universal agreement that they crossed from Asia, but can we be more precise as to both place and time frame? Let's turn first to non-archaeological sources, which provide us with a broad-brush perspective.

1 Proof of high antiquity: A Folsom point nestles next to a rib of *Bison antiquus*, Folsom, New Mexico, 1924.

Molecular biology is revolutionizing our understanding of the major population movements of the remote past, most notably the origin and spread of *Homo sapiens* from its tropical African homeland. It has the potential to do the same for the first Americans. Studies of mitochondrial DNA (mtDNA, inherited through the female line) show that 98 percent of all Native Americans share just five mtDNA haplogroups (a group of haplotypes, which share alleles of common genes). This low genetic diversity caused many geneticists to assume that all Indians derived from a single migration from Asia. However, these haplogroups are far from evenly distributed across the Americas. For instance, Haplogroup A is common across the Arctic, occurs along the Pacific Coast, and is also found in eastern North America and into Central America, whereas Haplogroup B is almost absent in the far north and Siberia, but becomes common much further south. These divergences may reflect different migrations, or, perhaps more likely, result from small numbers of migrant groups living very isolated lives, during which genetic drift occurred. Genetically speaking, Native Americans and Northeast Asians are ultimately descended from the same ancient population, but the relationships with modern Asian populations are complex and remain poorly resolved.

The non-combining portion of the Y chromosome, known as NRY, passes down the paternal line and provides another clue. Three major NRY lineages occur in over 95 percent of Native Americans. As with mtDNA, Y chromosome diversity in the Americas is much lower than in Asia, as the ancestral populations departing from Asia brought only a narrow genetic range with them. The closest modern Y-chromosome similarities lie with people living in the Altai Mountains region of Siberia, but, as with mtDNA, we need samples from Ice Age populations there to confirm this. The molecular clock that plots DNA changes places the split from the ancestral population in the range of 18,000 to 14,000 years ago.

Most geneticists agree that today's five mtDNA haplogroups and Y-chromosome groups are the result of a small, closely related founder population that crossed the Bering Land Bridge. How large this population was is a matter of debate and guesswork, with figures ranging from a mere seventy individuals to between 1,000 and 5,400 people. Research is at a very early stage; the samples are few in number and almost all from modern populations. Ancient DNA (aDNA) samples are still extremely rare, but they may reveal that the founder population was both larger and more diverse than is currently suspected, funneled across the bridge from a wide area.

Then there's dental morphology. Biological anthropologist Christy Turner has studied over 200,000 teeth from more than 9,000 ancient and modern people throughout the Americas, China, Siberia, and other parts of eastern Asia. He found that ancient Americans display fewer variables in their dental morphology than do eastern Asians, but their crown- and root-traits are similar to those of northern Asians. He called these characteristics "Sinodonty," a pattern of tooth features that includes incisor shoveling

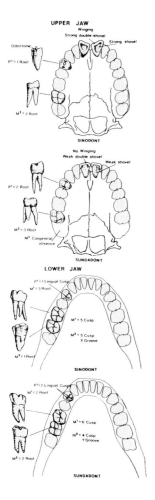

UPPER JAW

LOWER JAW

2 Dentochronology: Sinodonty and Sundadonty. Sinodonts display incisor shoveling (scooping out on one or both surfaces of the tooth), single-rooted upper first premolars, and triple-rooted lower first molars. Sundadonts (Europeans and East Asians) do not display these features, perhaps an adaptation to the extreme cold of the north.

(scooping out on the interior side), single-rooted upper first premolars, and triple-rooted lower first molars, among other features. Sinodonty only occurs in northern Asia and the Americas, not among the people of the Lake Baikal region in western Siberia, or far to the west in Stone Age Ukraine. "Sundadonty," denoting teeth that do not share all these characteristics, is common in Southeast Asia. Turner argued that the northern Chinese may have evolved from a Southeast Asian population, people they resemble more closely than the eastern Siberians and Native Americans, who evolved in turn from the northern Chinese. He used statistical calculations based on dental morphology to date the approximate moments at which Sinodont populations split off from ancestral Asian groups. The first of these divergences, Turner believes, led to the migration of Sinodonts into Mongolia, and across the Bering Land Bridge some time later. Turner guessed at a split between Northeast Asian and American populations at about 14,000 years ago.

Languages change through time, sometimes slowly, often more rapidly. Can one extrapolate linguistic data back to the Ice Age? One school of thought argues that all traces of earlier languages vanish between 8,000 and 10,000 years ago. Another believes that subtle echoes of early languages survive today. The researches of linguist Joseph Greenberg long dominated thinking about the subject. He compared relatively few words across a broad spectrum of languages and identified three language families in the Americas: Eskimo-Aleut in the far north, Na-Dene in the northern interior, and Amerind, the largest of the three, everywhere else. Greenberg believed these were distinct families before people moved to the Americas, with Amerind, the most widespread and diverse, being the oldest, dating to around 11,000 years ago. Greenberg's work unleashed furious criticism from other linguists, who rejected his Amerind family amidst strong condemnation of his methods. They pointed to faulty methodology and to errors in his word lists, accusing him, among other things, of "megalocomparison," of not paying enough attention to detail. A generation of research since Greenberg's work of the 1970s

3 Joseph Greenberg's map of Native American languages, which is considered too simple by most authorities. Eskimo-Aleut and Na-Dene are, however, widely accepted subdivisions.

and 1980s has moved away from his simplistic formulation.

In truth, the great diversity of Native American languages can tell us little about a colonization process well over 12,000 years ago. And beyond general agreement that the Native Americans originated in Asian populations, genetics and dental morphology cannot yet tell us much about the details of first settlement. We must turn, then, to archaeology.

The pre-Clovis question

The search for the very first Americans has been long and frustrating. Canadian archaeologist Richard Morlan once aptly called the quest for the first settlers "a search for a needle in a haystack and a frozen one at that." The hunt for pre-Clovis sites revolves around a putative settlement of the Americas by tiny numbers of people during a period of constant and harsh climatic change. In most cases, all that remains of their passing are mere scatters of often uninformative stone tools that defy precise

3

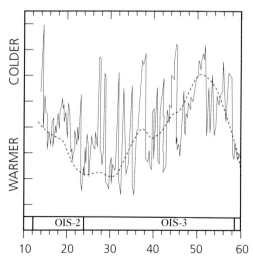

4 Climate change during the late Ice Age. Zigzag climatic shifts from 60,000 to 10,000 years ago, as reconstructed from various sources. A brief warming between 60,000 and 45,000 years ago was followed by irregular climatic shifts, then intense cold. Warming began about 15,000 years ago. The brief cold of the Younger Dryas, starting c. 12,950 years ago, is clearly visible.

dating. Unfortunately, pre-Clovis after pre-Clovis site has failed to stand up to close scrutiny. As David Meltzer remarks in a recent comprehensive survey of the question, almost all pre-Clovis finds "have a shelf-life of about a decade: better than fish and house guests, but ultimately they, too, begin to stink."

No claim of human settlement earlier than 20,000 years ago currently stands. The earliest widely accepted pre-Clovis site comes not from Alaska or North America, but just about as far as one can travel from the Bering Strait, from Monte Verde in southern Chile, some 10,000 miles (16,000 km) to the south. About 15,000 years ago, 31 miles (50 km) from the Pacific, a small group of people camped on the sandy banks of a creek subsisted off game and especially plant foods. They lived in a cluster of near-rectangular huts anchored by wooden stakes extending over a length of about 65 ft (20 m). Traces of mastodon (an extinct form of elephant) and paleo-llama hide are adhered to a number of the posts that covered the structure, some of the cordage still knotted around the wooden pegs. There were communal and individual hearths inside the huts.

If people had settled this far south so early, then the date of first settlement might be considerably earlier. How long would it have taken small numbers of hunter-gatherers to travel this enormous distance? We know that Clovis people spread rapidly over North America, perhaps within

5 Meadowcroft Rockshelter, Pennsylvania, one of the very few possible pre-Clovis sites. An overhead view of the site near the beginning of the excavations in 1973.

6 Paisley Cave, Oregon, in the Cascade Mountains. Human feces from the cave have been radiocarbon dated to about 14,000 years ago, one of the earliest records of human occupation in the Americas.

centuries. Could an infinitesimally small human population have done the same thousands of years earlier? Unfortunately, incontrovertible evidence for pre-Clovis in North America remains elusive. There are some claimants. At Meadowcroft Rockshelter, 30 miles (50 km) west of Pittsburgh, Pennsylvania, James Adovasio excavated 20 ft (6 m) through eleven natural layers containing human occupation. The meticulous excavations yielded fifty-two radiocarbon dates dating back from the eighteenth century AD. A lanceolate-shaped projectile point and other stone tools date to around 14,250 years ago, a time when the huge eastern Laurentide ice sheet was within 30 miles (50 km) of the rockshelter.

Paisley Cave in Oregon's Cascade Mountains has yielded a scatter of human feces that date to about 14,270 to 14,000 years ago. The DNA from the feces matches the DNA haplogroups found in Native Americans. A bone scraper-like tool apparently comes from the same time frame. The list of other potential early sites includes a Paleoindian and later site at Cactus Hill, Virginia, which contains a pre-Clovis occupation dating to about 15,000 years ago or earlier. The few stone tools from this level include two simple points and blades. The Topper site, close to the Savannah River in South Carolina, includes what is said to be a pre-Clovis level dating to about 16,000 years ago.

Thus, the footprint of pre-Clovis colonists in North America is still vanishingly small, which is hardly surprising, considering that the number of people involved was tiny, that they moved all the time, and that the chances of their transitory camp sites being preserved are never high, unless they are deeply buried below later deposits in somewhere like a rockshelter. If Paisley Cave, Meadowcroft, Cactus Hill, and others stand up to further scrutiny, then maybe we can push known North American settlement back to about 15,000 years ago – which is where a now partially vanished Ice Age continent and microblades come in.

Beringia and a tale of microblades   ?15,000 years ago

In 1937, Swedish geologist Erik Hulten used the Soviet term "Beringia" to describe an arctic land that straddled northeastern Siberia and Alaska and shared common fauna and flora. The heart of this expanse was the treeless, sunken Bering Land Bridge, now under the chilly waters of the Bering Strait, buried by rising sea levels at the end of the Ice Age. However, 20,000 years ago, Beringia was a single landmass extending from the Lena River Valley east to the borders of the Yukon. Huge ice sheets mantling northern

7

7 Beringia and the Bering Land Bridge.

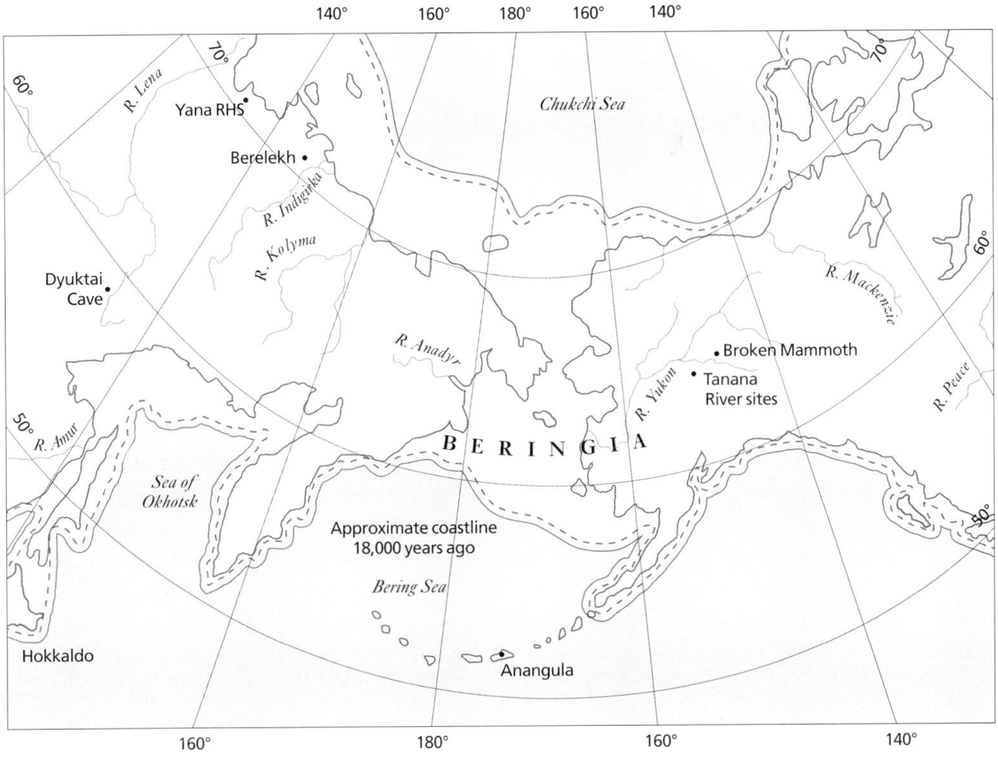

21

North America effectively isolated Beringia from southern latitudes. For many millennia, Alaska was biogeographically part of Siberia.

The story of humans in Beringia begins on the other side of the world, in tropical Africa. *Homo sapiens*, anatomically modern people, evolved in Africa, tall nimble hunter-gatherers who moved out of their homeland into the wider world after about 50,000 years ago. By 45,000 years ago, some of their descendents were living in the brutally cold landscapes of the East European Plain and in southern Siberia. They thrived there, thanks to important technological innovations. These included needles and layered, tailored clothing, effective ways of heating their dwellings, and sophisticated, lightweight weaponry and trapping devices, the latter important for acquiring furs. They lived in highly mobile societies, and their adaptations to open steppe-tundra were honed to perfection. By 30,000 years ago, some of them were hunting seasonally as far north as the Arctic Circle in both Europe and Northeast Asia.

Between about 60,000 and 28,000 years ago, conditions in the north were more temperate, and a few groups moved into extreme northeast Siberia. We know of them from only one location, the so-called Yana RHS sites, some 87 miles (140 km) from the Arctic Ocean on the river of that name. Here, scatters of mammoth, horse, and reindeer bones lie with some stone tools. A rhinoceros horn foreshaft for a projectile point dates to around 30,000 years ago. These may have been summer camps, where people hunted reindeer and some birds, as well as larger animals as part of annual movements that spanned hundreds of miles.

Then, between about 27,000 and 23,000 years ago, the Last Glacial Maximum brought extremely low winter temperatures and much drier conditions. Much of northeast Siberia became a polar desert, with little vegetation, and, from the human perspective, there was a major problem – a lack of firewood needed to kindle hearths fueled with green animal bones. There were still large game animals on the arid steppe, but the harsh realities of the brutal environment appear to have limited human occupation.

Conditions warmed somewhat between 15,000 and 14,000 years ago. Tiny numbers of people moved into the Siberian zone of Beringia once more. Dyuktai Cave in the Middle Aldan Valley contains human occupation dating to about this time – the dates are uncertain. The occupants' tools included stone bifaces (projectile heads flaked on both surfaces), and so-called "microblades," which were probably mounted by their makers in slotted bone or antler points; these were then lashed to wooden shafts.

Microblades were part of a highly effective, lightweight weaponry that apparently came into use in the Gobi Desert and Mongolia at least 30,000 years ago as an adaptation to large hunting territories and very dry conditions. They appeared near Lake Baikal in western Siberia by 20,000 years ago, then passed into Beringia. Making these artifacts required fine-grained rock, also wedge-shaped cores that allowed the stoneworker to remove a series of bladelets from a single face. Microblades are strikingly regular, so much so that they were probably made by supporting the core against an anvil and removing the blades with sharp pressure.

The arid steppe environments of the Late Glacial Maximum had given way to better-watered shrub tundra. Willow and dwarf birch now provided fuel and gradually reached higher elevations. This may have been a critical tipping point, with firewood providing the means to tap the heat that could be generated from burning green bone. It's no coincidence that most of the earliest sites in Beringia have yielded burnt bones. This was still a far from produc-tive environment, so much so that only tiny hunting bands settled in areas to the east of the Lena River. Each must have exploited

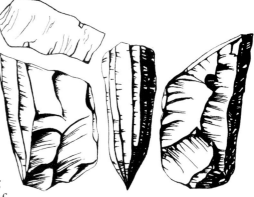

8 A wedge-shaped microblade core from Dyuktai Cave, Siberia, dating to about 15,000 years ago.

large hunting territories, the distances they covered reflected in their light-weight weapons. By 14,000 years ago, some of these small groups had long crossed the Bering Land Bridge into Alaska, not as a deliberate journey into a new continent, but simply as part of their regular migratory lifeway.

What remains of their Beringian homeland is still inhospitable today, a difficult landscape in which to find archaeological sites, so it's hardly sur-prising that we have few traces of their passing. One of the earliest Siberian sites is Berelekh on the Indigirka River near the Arctic Ocean coast, famous as a mammoth cemetery, a place where hundreds of beasts died, perhaps having drowned in spring floods. A scatter of bone and stone tools, also the bones of hares, birds, even fish, came from a nearby site, as if the inhabitants were living off a broad-based diet like that of historic people in the Siberian interior. The camp may date to about 14,200 to 13,300 years ago.

Across the strait, the earliest known archaeological sites in Alaska reveal what archaeologists John Hoffecker and Scott Elias call a "shrub tundra" economy. Much of the diet came from larger animals such as elk and wild sheep, but smaller animals including hares were of great importance, as were waterfowl, a reflection of a rapidly thawing Beringian environment with numerous shallow lakes. The people may have killed the occasional mammoth, but these animals were increasingly rare, and extinct by about 12,000 years ago. They may also have scavenged bones and tusks from long-dead carcasses. In many respects, their subsistence may have resembled that of modern-day northern Athabascans of the Alaskan and Yukon interior.

People were still thin on the ground, their movements governed by seasons of plant foods, game movements, and especially spring waterfowl hunts. We know of them from scatters of tools and from three open-air sites along the Tanana River, about 60 miles (100 km) southeast of Fairbanks.

9 Excavations at Broken Mammoth, 1991, site of some of the earliest human occupation in Alaska.

9   The three locations – Broken Mammoth, Mead, and Swan Point – date to between 14,500 and 13,000 years ago. There are no dwellings, only traces of hearths that have yielded bone fuel and wood charcoal. Swan Point contains the most diagnostic artifacts, which include wedge-shaped cores and microblades just like those at Dyuktai on the Aldan. Obsidian (volcanic glass), out of which razor-sharp tools could be made, came from hundreds of miles away, either obtained by traveling long distances or from extensive trading networks. The stone artifacts from these three sites and other locations are but a tiny part of what must have been a quite elaborate hunting and foraging technology, fabricated in bone, wood, and ivory. Traps for ptarmigan and fur-bearing animals, as well as light weaponry for hunting waterfowl, must have been an important part of toolkits that bore at least some resemblance to those of interior northern groups right into historic times, even if we have no evidence for them.

First settlement in the far north was thus in the hands of mobile, lightly equipped foragers. Theirs was a distinctive adaptation to a new, warming world when settlement of the harsh land that was Beringia became possible for the first time in thousands of years. A chronological baseline for significant human settlement in the far north appears to be around 15,000 years ago.

Climatic changes since the Ice Age

The twelve millennia since the last global cold snap are known as the Holocene, from the Greek *holos*, meaning "entire," and *kainos*, "recent," thus "entirely recent." We are, in fact, in an Ice Age interglacial, but one that shows no signs of ending in another glacial episode, as would occur in the natural order of things. Widespread global warming ensued when the last major cold episode ended about 15,000 years ago. About 12,950 years ago, a 1,000-year-long cold snap, known to geologists as the Younger Dryas, plunged northern latitudes into near-glacial conditions. Temperatures in parts of North America dropped about 9°F (5°C). The continent was generally drier, the Southeast wet and relatively warm: a combination of conditions unknown today.

The Younger Dryas, named after a polar flower, ended as abruptly as it began, ushering in warmer conditions, which persisted until about 5,000 years ago, since when the climate has been slightly cooler and drier. The impact of the cooler conditions of the Younger Dryas on Paleoindian societies is at present unknown. Constant minor fluctuations, known as "Bond events," have brought brief cold periods, roughly every 1,500 years, the most recent marking the Little Ice Age, which peaked in the seventeenth century AD. North American societies adapted to staggering rises in sea levels, changes in forest cover, and rapid shrinking of ice sheets with remarkable flexibility.

The Holocene is conventionally divided into somewhat loosely defined Early, Middle, and Late stages, a terminology we use here (see chronological table on p. 10).

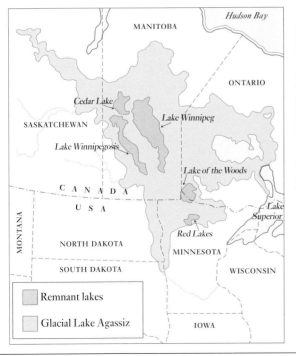

10 Lake Agassiz lapped about 683 miles (1,100 km) of the retreating Laurentide ice sheet 12,000 years ago. When a southward bulge of the ice melted, vast amounts of freshwater flowed down the St. Lawrence Valley into the North Atlantic. The influx shut down the Gulf Stream, perhaps triggering the Younger Dryas.

Remnant lakes

Glacial Lake Agassiz

Moving south   exact date unknown

Any hunting group pushing southward into continental North America faced formidable landscapes – the retreating Laurentide and Cordilleran ice sheets and rapid warming (see box p. 25). Thick ice blocked movement southward except for an ice-free corridor that opened up between the two now separated and shrinking sheets. The only alternative was to use a coastal route along the ice-free and today submerged coastline of south-east Alaska and British Columbia. Much of this coastline was ice free by 16,000 to 14,500 years ago.

No question, some groups moved into the heart of North America through the widening corridor, but significant numbers may also have passed down the Pacific Coast. The shoreline as we know it today bears little resemblance to what it did then. There is no theoretical reason why people should not have moved southward there, either hunting on exposed conti-nental shelf covered with shrub tundra, or by hugging the shore in canoes. Evidence for human occupation is thin on the ground. On-Your-Knees Cave in southeast Alaska was visited by humans some 10,000 years ago. Human occupation of the Queen Charlotte Islands in British Columbia goes back at least 10,000 years; earlier settlement certainly lies below modern sea levels.

Reality was, of course, much more complex than that conveyed by simple lines on a map. The dynamics of hunter-gatherer life drove all population movements – the migrations of favored prey like the caribou and elk, salmon runs along coasts in spring and fall, the distribution of plant foods and game across dynamic, changing landscapes. Then there were the ten-sions and constant social fluidity of hunter-gatherer life – hunting accidents that killed all the males in a band, sons splitting off and settling in the next valley, quarrels that caused people to move away, and so on. All of these real-ities, and others, contributed to a constant ebb-and-flow of people across uninhabited landscapes.

The world of Clovis   13,050 to 12,800 years ago

A few sites, most little more than artifact scatters, mark the arrival of human settlers south of the ice sheets, but the real population explosion began with the Clovis people. Clovis appeared suddenly and flourished for only around 250 years, between about 13,050 and 12,800 years ago. There is some controversy over the chronology, with some experts believing that Clovis began several centuries earlier. Thanks to their distinctive fluted projectile points, we know that their technology spread rapidly across North America, if the radiocarbon dates are to be trusted. These peripatetic hunter-gatherers dropped, at recent count, at least 4,400 points at numerous locations. They camped on low terraces along rivers and streams, in places

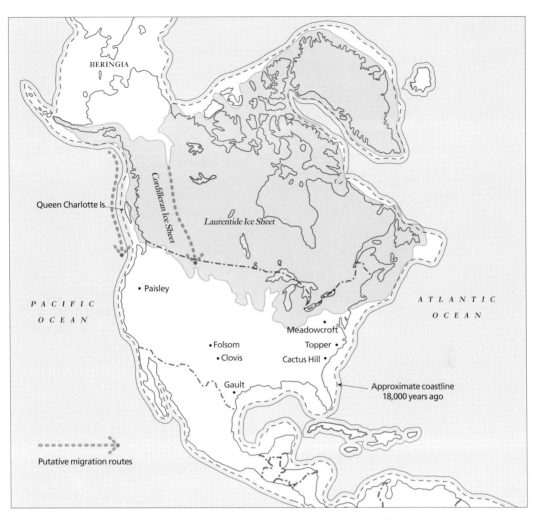

11 Putative migration routes of the first Americans. Two huge ice sheets, the Cordilleran, centered on the Rocky Mountains, and the Laurentide, which covered central and eastern Canada, mantled the landscape as far south as the Seattle region and the Great Lakes. Much of Alaska was ice-free.

where game came to feed and plant foods were abundant. The densest concentrations lie around the Cumberland, Tennessee, and Ohio River valleys in the east, where stone outcrops were commonplace. Fewer finds occur elsewhere, but everywhere population densities were low, which is what one would expect of mobile people who preferred areas where food resources were locally abundant. Many bands may have lived on coastal plains – now sunken continental shelves – where, conceivably, they relied heavily on marine resources. Inland, a few Clovis sites, like the much-visited Gault location in central Texas, reached a considerable size. The site covers about 40 acres (16 ha) at the head of a small valley where water and good toolmaking stone were abundant, and was occupied from around 13,000 years ago into later times. 12

12 Excavations at the Gault site, Texas, showing excavation in progress along the south edge of the site near a spot where Clovis points were found in association with mammoth bones. The lowest, pale zone contains numerous Clovis artifacts, also bison, horse, and mammoth bones, dating to 12,900 to 13,600 years ago.

13   Fluted Clovis points are one of the iconic artifacts of ancient North America, but their makers remain something of an enigma. They were clearly versatile hunter-gatherers who could kill animals of all sizes, as well as subsisting off plant foods and perhaps fish near lakes and coasts. Bringing 14 down a large beast like a mammoth was probably a rare event, perhaps experienced but once in a lifetime.

The fluted point itself may be a local invention that developed on the Great Plains or in the Southwest. Such examples that occur in Alaska are later in date, perhaps introduced by people moving northward in pursuit of bison. The Clovis toolkit, which included bone, ivory, and probably hunting nets and bags, generally reflects a mobile lifeway, where everything had to be carried on one's person, including large bifaces, which served as a kind of "savings bank" from which one could strike blades or blanks for projectile points.

Clovis stoneworkers cherished fine-grained toolmaking stone, relying heavily on high-quality chert, jasper, and obsidian, hard rocks that were ideal for making weapons. They knew their sources and traveled considerable distances to obtain raw material. In one well-known example, Clovis points left in a cache in northeastern Colorado were made of dolomite from the Texas Panhandle, 364 miles (585 km) away. At least twenty Clovis caches are known, the most famous of them from the Richey-Roberts site near East

13 Clovis points from Lehner, Arizona, and Blackwater Draw. Length of Lehner point *c.* 3.5 in (9 cm). Classic Clovis points were ground along the base and part of the sides, presumably to reduce wear on the shaft binding. Fluted points vary considerably because of "cultural drift" as people spread across the continent.

14 Clovis points found with the Naco mammoth kill, Arizona. The beast had eight Clovis points in its carcass, four times more than any other known kill. Perhaps it escaped wounded, only to die later. If each point belonged to an individual hunter, then at least eight men attacked the beast or four if each fired off two spears.

Asteroids and *Sporormiella*

One flamboyant megafaunal hypothesis envisages a great asteroid, at least 2.5 miles (4 km) across, hitting earth during Clovis times. No one has found the impact crater; the evidence for it is a carbon-rich black layer, known as the Black Mat, found at Clovis sites. It contains high concentrations of iridium, titanium grains, glass-like carbon, also soot and charcoal – said to be from catastrophic brush fires after the impact. Few archaeologists believe that an asteroid wiped out humans and animals during the Younger Dryas. There is, for instance, no evidence for a human population crash – quite the contrary. Numerous later Paleoindian societies rapidly succeeded Clovis.

Sporormiella further undermines the asteroid theory. This exotic fungus passes through an animal's digestive system to complete its life cycle, so its spores appear in animal dung. By examining the number of these spores in cores taken from an Indiana lake, biogeographer Jacqueline Gill showed

15 *Sporormiella* fungus.

that there was a steady disappearance of large animals between 14,800 and 13,700 years ago. As the spores disappeared, so pollens of new plants like oaks appeared. Established vegetation emerged as grazing by large animals ceased. This unusual research – still, it should be stressed, from only one location – documents the disappearance of megafauna before Clovis people hunted in the region and before the putative asteroid.

PL. I Wenatchee, Washington, including some of the largest Clovis points ever found, 9⁹⁄₁₆ in (23.3 cm) long. Perhaps caches were a product of hunting in new territories, often far from known stone outcrops, the dumps being a form of insurance against running out of raw material for weaponry.

Mass extinctions

Ice Age North America was dominated by the megafauna, mammoths, and other large mammals such as steppe bison. But what happened when temperatures rose and human hunters were added to the equation? It makes for a compelling image: small bands of predatory big-game hunters bursting into an uninhabited continent teeming with large Ice Age mammals. Armageddon ensues. Slow breeding, lumbering mammoth and other prey fall before the hunters' spears. Soon the ancient megafauna are but a distant memory. By an intriguing coincidence, Clovis people appeared about 13,050 years ago, at approximately the same time as the extinctions. A generation ago, geoscientist Paul Martin of the University of Arizona unleashed a long-lasting controversy when he argued that Clovis hunters devastated the megafauna with promiscuous hunting, then suffered a population crash themselves. Martin's premise has not withstood close scrutiny. Not only was there no dip in human population, but new research and more precise chronologies tell us that the extinctions may have resulted, at least in part, from climate changes before and during the Younger Dryas. Those 1,000 years of much colder conditions that arrived without warning, perhaps within a few generations, may have contributed to mass extinctions among animals that had survived previous Ice Age fluctuations unscathed. In recent years, new theories have proliferated, among them claims for an asteroid impact and an ingenious proxy – spores that thrive in animals' digestive systems (see box opposite).

The debate continues. What role humans played in the extinction equation remains uncertain, but it seems increasingly unlikely that it was a large one. Human predators may have accelerated extinction by preying on slow-breeding animals like mammoth, but there were certainly not enough of them to wipe out an entire megafauna within a few centuries.

At the beginning of the Younger Dryas, some 12,950 years ago, the short-lived Clovis tradition began to rapidly diversify into numerous local lithic and cultural traditions. Between 12,800 and 12,000 years ago, scattered human populations thrived across the continent's diverse landscapes. As temperatures warmed after the Younger Dryas, so North America's biotic communities gradually assumed their modern configurations, a process that was over by about 5,000 years ago. Meanwhile, human populations increased; extinction was no longer a possibility. Knowledge of the land and its flora and fauna became ever more encyclopedic and ways of wresting a living from diverse environments stabilized for thousands of years.

16 Major culture areas of North America, as commonly used by archaeologists and in this book.
The Eastern Woodlands are divided into the Northeast and Southeast (including Florida).

2 · After Clovis

What happened as the North American climate warmed up after 10,000 BC, with the end of the Younger Dryas? Accelerating warming brought dramatic changes in rainfall patterns, sea levels, and vegetation. Temperate woodlands spread northward as the great ice sheets continued their retreat. Continental shelves vanished inexorably as the Atlantic and Pacific rose. Aridity in the west intensified. Greater environmental diversity throughout North America presented profound challenges to Paleoindians living in isolated bands with little contact with other humans. How did the North Americans adapt to these changed circumstances? Their varied responses and brilliant opportunism laid the foundations for the great diversity of North American societies in later millennia.

16

Hell Gap   *c*. 9000 to 5500 BC

Our story begins at Hell Gap, a small valley near Guernsey, southeastern Wyoming. Paleoindians camped at four locations here repeatedly between about 9000 and 5500 BC. No other Paleoindian location contains such a long record of Plains peoples after Clovis times. Discovered and excavated during the 1960s, Hell Gap vanished into archaeological obscurity until the 1990s, when new excavations brought an impressive team of specialists to the site. We now know that the Hell Gap Valley was wetter in Paleoindian times, with cooler temperatures than today. This was not a kill site, but a place where people processed hides and parts of bison carcasses brought back to camp. We can imagine hunters hefting complete bison limbs into the valley from a nearby kill. They throw them on the ground, then deftly disarticulate them and break the bones to get at the rich fatty marrow within. Meanwhile, other members of the band stagger under the weight of a bison hide. They unroll it, and then peg it out on the ground. Scrape, scrape: the sound of the women working over the hide with stone scrapers continues for hours on end. So does the sharp clicking noise of stoneworkers roughing out blanks for stone projectile points from chert and quartzite outcrops conveniently nearby.

17

18 Some major Plains Paleoindian point forms.

The first Hell Gap visitors arrived at a time of profound change. Clovis people and their contemporaries had lived in tiny bands dispersed over enormous hunting territories. Now human numbers rose gradually, breaking down the extreme isolation of earlier times. For the rest of pre-Columbian times, human populations expanded and contracted, adapting to a broad variety of environments in many ways. We still know little of the initial stages of these contractions and expansions.

A well-watered valley close to good toolmaking stone: Hell Gap was an idyllic location for generations of Paleoindians, chronicled mainly by superimposed projectile point forms. Goshen, Folsom, Midland, and so on – each point style has a hidden meaning, even if the basic adaptation to bison hunting remained much the same over the centuries. What do these changes mean? Entire archaeological careers have thrived on projectile points, on the fluted, stemmed, lanceolate, and other forms that proliferated after Clovis times. Some of the changes may represent different groups, others random 18 shifts or more efficient weaponry. There are never sharp boundaries between the disappearance of one form and the appearance of another. Many just represent changing fashions, which were just as volatile then as they are today, but spread over hundreds of years. The proliferation of different spear points reflects a major turning point – a time of better-defined hunting territories. These tended to be large in the arid west, much smaller in the east, where numerous local point variations reflect a multitude of local foraging strategies.

Bison hunting on the Plains   9000 to *c.* 6000 BC

By around 9000 BC, grassland extended from the frontiers of Alaska to the shores of the Gulf of Mexico. This was the "Great Bison Belt," which lay in the rain shadow east of the Rocky Mountains. Spring and early summer rains supported, and still support, short grasses that keep much of their biomass beneath the surface. Such grass retains moisture at the roots, so grazing animals can find high-quality nutrients in the dry autumn. Bison succeeded where other Ice Age animals failed: they became short-grass

17 (*Opposite*) Excavations at Hell Gap, Wyoming.

feeders as this type of grassland expanded during and after the Younger Dryas. By 8500 BC, the Plains Paleoindians had narrowed much of their hunting to bison, deer, pronghorn antelope, and a few other animals.

As Clovis vanished, so Folsom hunters, also using fluted points, but of different design, pursued bison over a wide area. One prime bison parkland habitat was at Folsom, New Mexico, itself, where a group of hunters worked a steep-sided arroyo and a small tributary in about 8500 BC. Here they killed thirty-two members of a cow-calf herd in peak condition during the autumn. They then butchered the animals, carrying off many of the rib racks, leaving the butchered carcasses in the arroyo, where they were soon buried under windblown sand. After staying for several days, the group departed. No trace of their camp has come to light despite an intensive search. While much hunting preyed on single animals, occasional mass drives of bison herds involving several bands yielded great quantities of meat and other products. These must have been memorable events and involved driving the beasts over cliffs or into narrow defiles, where they could be killed in large numbers.

Conducting bison drives is a difficult art, especially on foot. Most likely, a combination of solo and cooperative hunting ensured a regular supply of bison flesh. When left alone, bison soon become less fearful of humans. Subjected continuously to pursuit, however, they become unpredictable and far harder to drive. The hunters were probably careful to pursue the herds intermittently, driving them small distances, giving them time to calm down. Modern bison can be moved a mile or so without trouble; then they start to break and run, when it is almost impossible to stop them. Thus, large-scale game drives probably required careful organization; witness a successful hunt at Olsen-Chubbock, Colorado, in about 7400 BC (see pp. 38–39).

19 Excavations at Folsom, New Mexico.

A skilled group of hunters could subject a quarry herd to gentle influences over periods of days, moving them a little way in the right direction when conditions were favorable. They would line the approach with decoys, with shouting men and women, while hunters dressed in bison hides would approach the unsuspecting animals. Once the drive began, the hunters would run and shout, even wave skins at the thundering herd. Clouds of dust rose from the plain as the sheer mass and weight of the herd forced the leaders into a narrow gully to their deaths. At Casper, Wyoming, in about 8000 BC, the hunters used a parabolic sand dune with steep, loose sides to trap a herd of about 100 bison in late autumn, then killed them as fast as they could, each hunter or group of hunters selecting an individual beast, then spearing it through the heart.

It would be misleading to think of these Plains societies as pure bison hunters. Like all foragers, they were opportunists, who, as well as taking deer and other animals, also, on occasion, took fish and mollusks, while plant foods were a staple. They would return again to the same locations over many generations, those where a wide range of foods could be found.

The western interior   10,000 BC to modern times

The men removed the dried fish from the seemingly ordinary food cache in the cave the evening before. Then they rummaged below the false bottom of the storage pit and lifted out their precious feathered duck decoys and snares. They carefully cleaned the bone tubes that would serve as snorkels in the hours ahead. Long before dawn, they crouched in the reeds around the lake, pushing their decoys out in the still water, wearing some of them on their heads. A few of the hunters slipped into the lake, leaving not even a ripple, moving silently toward the sleeping waterfowl. Imperceptibly, the human "birds" approached their prey, breathing carefully through their snorkels. Suddenly, a duck would vanish below the surface, grabbed by the legs, its neck wrung in seconds, the still twitching prey quickly pushed into a netting bag. Decoys looking just like real birds moved quietly among the ducks, thinning them one by one.

Dry caves and rockshelters in the arid landscapes of the west document a way of life that changed little over thousands of years. Enormous tracts of the Great Basin and the California deserts receive little rainfall. These arid and semi-arid lands encompass great environmental diversity – high mountains and intervening valleys, some lakes and wetlands in valley bottoms, and huge tracts of desert land. Environmental zones are stacked vertically and intermittently from the deepest dry valleys and others with lakes and wetlands to the wetter, climatically more complex mountain peaks. Rainfall varies greatly from year to year, so much so that a wet year could produce six times more plant food than a dry one. Everyone in the western interior subsisted on a very broad range of food. To do otherwise was to invite disaster.

22

The Olsen-Chubbock bison kill

20 The Olsen–Chubbock bone bed.

We can imagine the dust and confusion, the galloping bison, the dust rising high above the short grassland on a fine day. The Olsen–Chubbock site, 16 miles (26 km) southeast of Kit Carson, Colorado, records a Paleoindian bison hunt of about 7400 BC. The hunters stampeded a small herd into a dry gully. The leading bison arrived at the steep edge and then tottered over, swept on by the animals behind them. About 190 beasts were immobilized, trampling one another to death. The hunters cut up the carcasses at the arroyo edge, or in the defile.

Excavator Joe Ben Wheat estimated that 150 to 200 people participated in the hunt. The Olsen–Chubbock hunters butchered 75 percent of the animals they killed, acquiring about 54,600 lb (24,750 kg) of meat in the process. Wheat estimated that it would have taken ten men less than three days to butcher or partially butcher the 140 carcasses. They also obtained 5,400 lb (2,450 kg) of fat and 4,000 lb (1,800 kg) of edible internal organs as well. While some of the flesh was consumed immediately, most of it was probably dried for later use. The meat from this ancient hunt may have sustained over 100 people for a month or more.

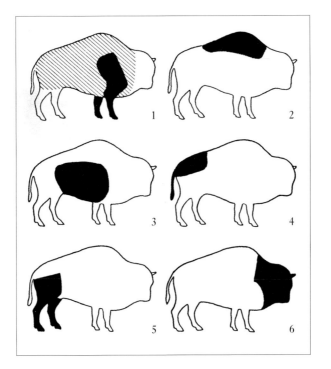

21 Paleoindian butchery. The hunters skinned the bison down the back to get at the tender meat below (hatched area). Then they cut free the forelegs and shoulder blades (1), also the hump and rib meat and inner organs (2) (3). They then severed the spine and pelvis (4), also the hind legs (5). Finally, the neck and skull were cut away for pemmican (6).

22 Southwestern Great Basin, looking northwest from the Greenwater Range, Inyo County, California: a landscape of mesas and basins. The distant Funeral Mountains are tilted blocks of Paleozoic rocks.

The most abundant food resources lay by major lakes and rivers, also in wetland areas and on estuaries and sea coasts, where shellfish flourished. As the climate warmed, so local environmental diversity intensified, triggering cultural variation from one group to another, even if basic toolkits and technology remained simple and highly portable, much of it cached at strategic locations for seasonal use. Mobility, flexibility, and detailed ecological knowledge – these were always the secrets of survival. The most vital artifacts in these arid landscapes were the wooden digging stick, the flat metate or grinding stone, the small stone muller, and coiled baskets, which appeared by 7000 BC. These simple objects enabled people to process an enormous range of seeds, plants, and tubers with minimal technology. One major innovation arrived in about AD 500 – the bow and arrow, reflected in much smaller stemmed points.

Most people lived in tiny family groups, moving intermittently, subsisting off seasonal foods at widely separated locations, their social organization revolving around "mapping" onto food resources. Plant foods were important everywhere, especially in more arid places, where people would harvest stands of grasses by knocking the seeds into baskets or gathering them by hand. Hardwood digging sticks assumed great value when harvesting root crops, especially in the northern Basin, where biscuit roots, yampa, and other tubers were abundant in spring. Berries, piñon nuts, and acorns were 23 significant crops wherever they were found, sometimes gathered by the women with special chest-mounted baskets. Piñon nuts contain between 10 and 24 percent protein, more than any other North American nut, while acorns have 16 percent protein and 45 percent fat. Both were also readily stored for long periods, which added to their value. Ethnographic accounts tell us that during the early fall, people used long poles to gather green cones by the thousand, carrying them to central processing stations in large baskets. The extracted seeds were parched, shelled, and ground, then eaten as gruel. People stored thousands of cones in open pits under piles of stones, in grass- or bark-lined pits, or skin bags. Stored in this way, cones could last four or five years. Agave, mesquite, and screwbean pods were gathered each spring.

River banks, marshes, and lakes acted as magnets for human settlement at certain times of year. Nearby caves like Danger and Hogup in Utah lie near 24 wetlands, but their dry layers preserve even delicate, perishable artifacts. People collecting pickleweed and other edible marsh plants visited them over thousands of years from about 6400 BC. The Hogup visitors hunted deer, pronghorn antelope, wild sheep, and bison. The cave deposits included thirty-two species of small animals and thirty-four of birds. Atlatls (spearthrowers), launching stone-tipped and wooden spears, sufficed to dispatch many larger animals. Judging from the fragments of nets and cordage in the deposits, the hunters also trapped rabbits and other small animals. They would stretch long nets across narrow defiles, then scare

23 Northern Great Basin peoples dug tubers such as bitterroot with wooden digging sticks, then roasted or dried them. They also stored them in underground pits and bags. Artwork by Eric Carlson.

24 Excavations at Hogup Cave, Utah.

25 Hogup Cave
preserved organic
material well in the
dry conditions, such
as these worn-out
moccasins.

dozens of rabbits into the broad traps with mass drives. Some simple loop snares came from Hogup, too, designed to catch the foot of a walking bird or one of the many rodents that lived in the cave. The people wore simple clothing, such as blankets fashioned from rabbit fur and transverse strands of plant fiber. Woven fiber sandals protected their feet.

25

Arid land adaptions in the west thrived on opportunism and flexibility. Much of the desert was a potentially edible landscape of extremes, where variations in elevation and rainfall allowed plants to germinate and ripen in different weeks and months. Survival required an intimate knowledge of one's surroundings and constant movement from one food area to another as the seasons unfolded. Lakes would dry up during severe drought cycles. The people would adapt by moving away from the dried-up basin and exploiting higher altitudes with apparently little effort or social change. When rainfall increased and lakes reappeared, they would congregate along the marshy shores, taking advantage of the new diversity of food resources. Great Basin peoples resisted "change through change" with subtle techno-logical innovations and intensive exploitation of a wide range of food resources. Had not European expansion disrupted and overwhelmed this ancient lifeway, it would have continued indefinitely. (For Fremont farming societies in the eastern Great Basin, see Chapter 5.)

The Eastern Woodlands   9000 to 4500 BC

Only a thin scatter of hunter-gatherers, descendants of earlier Clovis groups, dwelt across the better-watered Eastern Woodlands (a broad culture area that extends from the Atlantic Ocean to the Mississippi River and from the Great Lakes to the Gulf of Mexico) of North America in 9000 BC. The Paleoindians living on the northern tundra in areas like central Michigan relied heavily on spring and fall caribou migrations, when thousands of beasts would flow across strategic river crossings for days on end. The hunters arranged long alignments of low stone cairns or boulders to steer their stampeding prey toward waiting spearmen. Alignments used in caribou drives survive under the shallow waters of Lake Michigan. Groups living to the south exploited different foods – forest game such as deer and rabbits, and, more importantly, a wide range of plant foods. Large river valleys were especially important, for it was here that abundant fall nut harvests could sustain a band over the winter months. A combination of fishing and nut collecting allowed some groups to stay in one place for months at a time, but elsewhere population densities were much lower.

As far as we can tell, Paleoindian occupation began in large river valleys and other places close to good toolmaking stone. Some locations became important base camps, among them a group of sites in northern Virginia, where, as early as 8300 BC, the Flint Run quarry yielded jasper for toolmak-ing and people camped along the floodplain of the Shenandoah River.

During the summer, the bands would move to the floodplain to quarry stone, to trade, and to socialize, for the area was an anchor for large hunting territories. Away from food-rich areas, human populations fell away sharply. Over many centuries, the successors of the pioneers spread out, eventually forming discrete groupings, perhaps about 150 to 250 miles (250 to 400 km) apart. We can identify some of them from the many local projectile point forms of later times that reflect the increasing local diversity of Paleoindian society.

26   Dalton Culture   c. 8500 to 8000 BC

Between about 8500 and 8000 BC, a distinctive late Paleoindian and Early Archaic culture flourished in the Central Mississippi Valley, with a range that extended from the Carolinas deep into the Ozarks. Like every other Paleoindian society, Dalton has its distinctive lanceolate points, usually with a concave base, often sharpened with sawlike edges. These served as multipurpose tools and were sharpened again and again. Dalton people also developed a large biface, a thick and heavy tool that served as an adze for heavy woodworking tasks such as canoe building. Dugout canoes were essential to a people who tended to live along rivers, streams, and also in Mississippi bayous.

Dalton groups lived in a more crowded world, where mobility was more restricted than in earlier times. They obtained stone from local rather than exotic sources, as well as exploiting every form of food from small rodents, birds, and fish to deer. The Modoc Rockshelter in Illinois contains Dalton occupation levels where people ate muskrats, catfish, turtles, and mollusks as well as an extraordinary range of plant foods, including walnuts, hickories, and acorns. During late Paleoindian times, people evidently learned how to remove bitter tannins from acorns by leaching them in running water after crushing them into a fine meal – a laborious process. Why did Dalton people turn to such hard-to-process foods? More crowded landscapes meant broadening one's diet – and acorns have the advantage that they can be stored for long periods of time.

Restricted mobility also meant that people developed closer ties to their home territories, associations that passed from one generation to the next and lingered even after death. At the Sloan site, in an ancient sand dune in northeastern Arkansas, archaeologist Dan Morse recovered about thirty adult and child burials, also clusters of stone tools deposited in pits. The artifacts included both Dalton points and about a dozen so-called Sloan points, made from Burlington chert that occurs only at a small outcrop near St. Louis, roughly 185 miles (300 km) away.

26 A ceremonial Dalton point from Pettis County, Missouri.

With Dalton, we enter an era when the highly mobile hunter-gatherer societies of earlier times have given way to what are called "broad-based foragers," often loosely labeled as Archaic societies in archaeological parlance.

Icehouse Bottom   7000 BC and later
Thump, thump: the sound of repeated pounding echoes across the quiet valley from the small base camp, where modest conical dwellings stand well separated from one another in a sandy clearing close to the river bank. Each has its own red clay hearth from which white smoke wafts above the nearby treetops. Huge piles of hickory nuts lie on deerskins nearby. Women and girls pound the harvest in wooden mortars, then cast the pounded nuts into hardened clay boiling pits. The older women watch the bubbling water closely. At the right moment, they pour the oily mixture into fine strainers, carefully saving the rich, oily "hickory milk." Nothing is wasted. They knead the nut meat into small cakes, and dry them in the sun. The hickory shells serve as fuel for the fire.

When rains and floods formed sand bars, islands, and new bottomlands along the Little Tennessee River, generations of Archaic hunters used the same base camps there. Today, they form a kind of archaeological layer cake of human occupation that began in about 7000 BC. From this ideal location, they moved into the Upper Tennessee River drainage and into the southern Valley and Ridge Province of Virginia as well. Each mobile band had a base camp or series of repeatedly used settlements, of which Icehouse Bottom was one.

These camps lay close to stands of easily harvested hickories and acorns. Each fall also saw the upland forest floors covered with a rich mast, a carpet, as it were, of falling oil-rich nuts and other foods that were a magnet for white-tailed deer and other animals. The hunters used lighter spears in the forest, tipped with corner-notched points and propelled by weighted atlatls. After 7000 BC, these gave way to points with distinctive, bifurcated bases, perhaps a means to increase the lateral strength of the hafted point when cutting and scraping. Winter and early spring floods often inundated favorite seasonal camps near the rivers. In high flood years, people would move to higher ground, where game was to be found. As the water level fell, they would shift back onto the floodplain and spear fish in shallow pools left by the falling waters. As long as population densities remained relatively small, there was little incentive to exploit anything but a fairly narrow spectrum of animal, plant, and aquatic foods in favored locations.

Successful alliance formation may have been the key to the exploitation of river valleys such as the Little Tennessee. Close ties of kin and the reciprocal obligations that came with them were strong guarantees of long-term economic security that were far more powerful than any number of technological innovations. The production of elaborate and labor-intensive bannerstones (atlatl weights) and stone vessels makes little sense at a local

27 Paleoindian and Early Archaic projectile points from the Eastern Woodlands.

28 Artist's reconstruction of a camp at Icehouse Bottom, *c.* 6500 BC. The hut designs are conjectural.

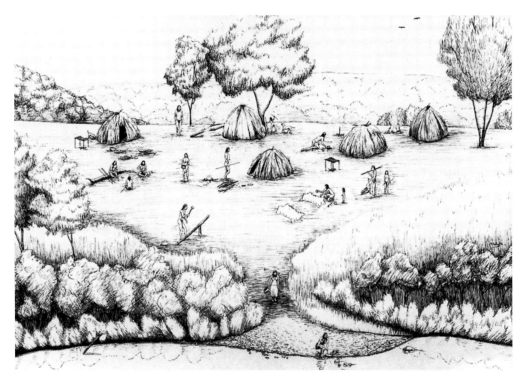

level, but when produced as objects used in broad exchange networks tied to cooperative alliances, such artifacts had considerable value.

The Windover site near Titusville, Florida, gives us a tantalizing look at the organic artifacts of Early Archaic groups in the Southeast that ranged from the St. John's River to the Atlantic coast. Windover was a burial area between about 6000 and 5000 BC, a place where human remains and artifacts were deposited in a pond. The remains of at least 160 individuals, ranging from newborns to people in their sixties and seventies, have come from the waterlogged archaeological levels, under 3 to 6 ft (1 to 2 m) of water. The bodies became submerged within forty-eight hours of death in peat and water deposits with a neutral chemistry that resulted in superb preservation. Brain tissue survived in at least ninety cases. The excellent preservation conditions also allowed the archaeologists to recover at least seven different textile weaves used for clothing made of the sabal palm and/or saw palmetto. Atlatls, consisting of wooden shaft, bone hook, and bannerstone, were found in the excavations, as were numerous bone artifacts, including awls and projectile points. The earliest known domesticated gourds, used to store water and perhaps to hold nuts or seeds, also come from this site.

Restricted mobility   *c.* 6500 BC onward

By 6500 BC, the Laurentide ice sheet had nearly imploded in the face of continued warming. Vast areas of eastern Canada opened up to human settlement for the first time. At the same time, rising sea levels and water temperatures along the Atlantic seaboard allowed a steady northward expansion of fish and shellfish habitats. River estuaries flooded too, creating more favorable conditions for anadromous fish (which spawn in fresh water and spend a portion of their lives in the ocean; they are harvested during the migrations up- and down-river) in spring or fall. Meanwhile, water levels in the Great Lakes climbed, reducing stream gradients and improving fishing conditions in the now warmer water. The Mississippi and other Midwestern and Southeastern rivers became more sluggish in the face of rising sea levels. Their swampy backwaters, low-lying levees, and lush floodplains became rich and diverse habitats for hunter-gatherers. Along the Gulf coastal plain, rising water tables established swamps and marshes over wide areas of Florida. Generally speaking, coastal resources were much richer than they had been for thousands of years. Rising temperatures also brought deciduous trees northward into parts of the once boreal-forest-covered Great Lakes region and into the Northeast, especially nut-bearing trees like oak, hickory, beech, and chestnut. This increased the amount of plant food available for human consumption over enormous areas.

At first, the Eastern Woodlands population had been very low, with the greatest concentrations in areas that offered the most diverse foods. Now people relied on food sources closer to seasonal base camps. The carrying capacities of many less-favored locations were reached. Slowly growing hunter-gatherer populations had few options except to lead more circumscribed lifeways.

The classic example of such a changing adaptation comes from the Koster site in the Midwest's Illinois River Valley, which attracted hunter-gatherer groups for thousands of years from as early as 8500 BC. By 5000 BC, the temporary encampments of Early Archaic times had given way to a settlement occupied from late spring through summer (see box p. 50). Koster is by no means unique, for stratified sites occupied for many centuries occur at other locations. One example is the Modoc Rockshelter near the Mississippi in Randolph County, Illinois, which lies in a hickory-rich riverine environment about 90 miles (145 km) southeast of Koster.

By about 2500 BC, sea levels in the Southeast were close to those of today. Extensive shell middens appeared close to Gulf estuaries, marshes, and brackish water sounds between 2200 and 1800 BC. Shell resources were probably exploited even earlier, but the resulting shell middens lie under modern sea levels. These environmental changes contributed to numerous adjustments in the catchment areas of each band's hunting and gathering territory. There was, however, one universal exception to local variability: a dramatic increase in the consumption of freshwater fish and mollusks, which eventually became a major component in the diet of nearly all Southeastern river-valley populations.

The issue of sedentism

Between about 4500 and 4000 BC, many Midwestern and Southeastern rivers stabilized and accumulated silt in their floodplains. Backwater swamps and oxbow lakes formed. Shallow-water and shoal habitats as well as active streams provided abundant, easily accessible fish and mollusks. Opportunism kicked in: people were quick to take advantage of newly plentiful river foods at a time when local populations were rising. Many groups settled down in favored locations and adopted more sedentary lifeways. Earthworks appear for the first time, many associated with funerary rites (we will discuss possible reasons for this below). At least sixty mound groups lie between Arkansas and Florida. The most spectacular is Watson Brake in northeastern Louisiana, built as early as 3900 BC. Eleven mounds and an oval enclosure cover 11 acres (4.5 ha) near the once swampy, lush Ouachita River Valley. For at least nine centuries, forager groups spent spring and early summer here, taking fish and exploiting stands of native plants.

Burial customs changed, too, as people were interred in concentrations that resemble cemeteries. Early Archaic settlements sometimes yield the

29 (*Opposite*) Excavations in the Modoc Rockshelter, Illinois.

Koster: Midwestern bounty

The Koster site in the Illinois River Valley, with its fourteen stratified occupation levels, provides an extraordinary chronicle of human exploitation of a bountiful Midwestern environment from about 8500 BC until AD 1200. The first people at Koster were transitory Paleoindian visitors. By 6500 BC, an Early Archaic group occupied a seasonal camp (Horizon 11) that covered about ¾ acre (0.3 ha). An extended family group of about twenty-five people returned over the centuries. They hunted white-tailed deer and small mammals, caught fish, ate freshwater mussels, and collected hickory and pecan nuts, a vital source of high-energy fat, by the tens of thousands.

Between 5600 and 5000 BC, a permanent Middle Archaic settlement (Horizon 8) flourished at Koster. At least four substantial settlements covering 1¾ acres (0.7 ha) or so followed on from one another, occupied on several occasions for a century or more. The houses measured 20–35 by 12–15 ft (6–10 by 3.5–4.5 m), their long walls formed by wooden posts up to 10 in (25 cm) in diameter set in trenches about 8–10 ft (2.5–3 m) apart. Perhaps they were covered with hides or mats. Apparently, there were no end walls. Evidence from the growth patterns of fish scales hints that people lived at Koster from late spring through the summer. In the fall, they gathered freshwater mussels and harvested hickory nuts. Perhaps they abandoned the site during the winter, relying on stored nuts and deer from the uplands for much of their diet.

30 Excavations in Horizon 8, Koster, Illinois.

bodies of individuals buried within the confines of the camp. In contrast, hundreds of burials can be found in later Middle Archaic sites. The Eva site in western Tennessee has yielded 118 burials dating to between 5000 and 3000 BC. The Black Earth site at Carrier Mills in southern Illinois is a rich Middle Archaic midden accumulated over a thousand-year period after about 4000 BC. The site is remarkable not only for its abundant food remains and many pits used for storing, processing, and cooking foods, but also for its 154 burials. Excavator Richard Jefferies estimates that as many as 400 to 500 Middle Archaic people may have been buried at this location over the centuries. One forty-three-year-old man lay with a bag or bundle of eagle talons, sections of bear's paw bones, projectile points, a miniature grooved axe, and other objects. Jefferies thinks he may have been a shaman, a man celebrated for his curing skills and ability to communicate with the ancestors.

Middle Archaic peoples in the central Mississippi drainage also buried the dead in formal cemeteries. These cemeteries usually consist of large, shallow pits that contain burials of up to forty or more people laid in randomly spaced graves. Sometimes a group raised a low, artificial mound

31 Artist's reconstruction of Middle Archaic life at the Black Earth site in southern Illinois. The hunters in the foreground are returning to camp with a deer killed with spears and atlatls, while the people in the background are collecting aquatic plants and fishing in the shallow lake.

32 Excavations in the Area A midden, Black Earth, Illinois.

over the cemetery to enhance its visibility. The artifacts or caches of offerings deposited in these cemeteries are usually associated with the gravesite as a whole rather than with specific individuals. These may represent the identity of the kin group that maintained the cemetery. Perhaps individual status was unimportant in what were still egalitarian societies. Age and experience were the key to leadership and authority, not material possessions.

Burials and the lands of the ancestors

The sudden appearance of cemeteries and artificial burial mounds near resource-rich river valleys may mark a dramatic change in Archaic life. When people start passing vital resources from one generation to the next through lineages and other kin organizations, they will tend to bury their dead in cemeteries. Mortuary rituals serve to affirm and legitimize the rights of kin groups to use and control vital food resources. A cemetery located on the land the group controls, the territory once owned by their ancestors, symbolized their ownership. Corporate bonding in human societies is actually a form of territorial behavior, a near universal among animals. The relationship between sedentary settlement, resources inherited through kin organizations, and cemeteries hinges on one reality – that the resources involved are fixed in space, predictable, and sufficiently abundant and diverse that a group can focus its activities around them. If a group wishes to claim rights of ownership and inheritance to these resources, one logical way to do so is through the maintenance of a corporate cemetery, the ritual home of one's ancestors.

With the emergence of fixed territories, perhaps during a warmer and drier period that tended to restrict denser human populations to river valleys, there may have been competition for resources and territories with fixed boundaries for the first time. This competition may have been reflected in sporadic tribal warfare. But it may also be reflected in a distinctive form of territorial marking: bluff-top cemeteries for the ancestors on knolls or under low mounds. Such locations remained in use for more than 5,000 years, until maize agriculture took hold throughout the Midwest during the late first millennium AD. Formal cemeteries, and the burial mounds, earthworks, or natural hills associated with them, were to remain a vital element in Eastern Woodlands life for thousands of years, to the end of pre-Columbian times.

Two processes were under way – increased utilization of floodplain aquatic species, and a long-term trend toward increasingly permanent settlement and carefully delineated group territories, sometimes reflected symbolically in conspicuous cemeteries used over many generations. These were the homes of the ancestors, the true owners of the land, a pervasive belief in ancient North America.

Chronological table of developments in the Far North

Dates	Alaska			Eastern Arctic	Sub-Arctic
	Aleutians	*Kodiak area*	*Bering Strait area*		
Modern Times	MODERN ALEUTS	MODERN ESKIMO GROUPS		MOD. INUIT	MODERN ATHABASCAN-SPEAKING GROUPS
		KONIAG	PUNUK BIRNIRK	THULE / POST-CLASSIC / CLASSIC	
AD 1100	Chaluka			THULE EXPANDS	
		KACHEMAK	NORTON / NORTON / IPIUTAK / THULE / OLD BERING SEA	DORSET	
AD 1					
			NORTON / CHORIS	SAQQAQ	
1300 BC	Chaluka	ALEUTIAN TRADITION / KODIAK TRADITION		ARCTIC SMALL TOOL TRAD.	NORTHERN ARCHAIC / SHIELD ARCHAIC / MARITIME ARCHAIC
			ARCTIC SMALL TOOL TRADITION	PRE-DORSET INDEP. 1	
2500 BC					
3800 BC			?		
		OCEAN BAY TRADITION			
4900 BC			?	No human settlement	
5900 BC					
7000 BC	Anangula		PALEOARCTIC TRADITION		No human settlement
8250 BC					

3 · The Far North: West to East

Just surviving in the unforgiving landscapes of the Far North was an achievement, the more so when you reflect that the handfuls of people who lived there 12,000 years ago relied on much simpler technologies than those of later millennia. Their ancestry lay in Siberia, but rising sea levels had submerged the Bering Land Bridge by about 7000 BC, inhibiting communication between Asia and the Americas for thousands of years. We know little of these groups, or of their legacy, for one of the great unresolved historical questions in the north remains the ancestry of the modern-day Aleuts and Eskimos. Who were their direct ancestors? When did these two northern peoples diverge biologically and culturally? Then there's perhaps the most intriguing question of all: why did tiny numbers of westerners move into the even harsher environments of the eastern Arctic much later, after 2500 BC? Against seemingly overwhelming odds, they and their successors thrived in a world of bitter cold and perennial ice. By the time Norse voyagers settled the southwestern coast of Greenland in the tenth century AD, hunter-gatherers flourished across the Far North from Attu Island at the extreme western end of the Aleutian Islands to the eastern shores of Greenland, more than 6,800 miles (11,000 km) by reasonably direct boat and sled routes. 33

The Paleoarctic tradition   ?8000 to *c.* 5500 BC

In 9000 BC, Alaska was still a cultural province of Siberia, as it had been in earlier times, occupied by peoples whose ultimate cultural roots lay to the west. Their microblades and other artifacts were part of a Stone Age tradition that extended east from the Lena Basin in Siberia throughout most of the unglaciated area of Alaska and the Yukon, south and east along the Pacific Coast, and perhaps as far south as British Columbia. The flooding of the Bering Strait reduced contacts between Alaska and Siberia, but a great variety of hunter-gatherer societies now flourished on the American side. They are known collectively as the Paleoarctic tradition and marked by both bifaces and microblades, most of them found in stone scatters, all that remains of temporary hunting camps.

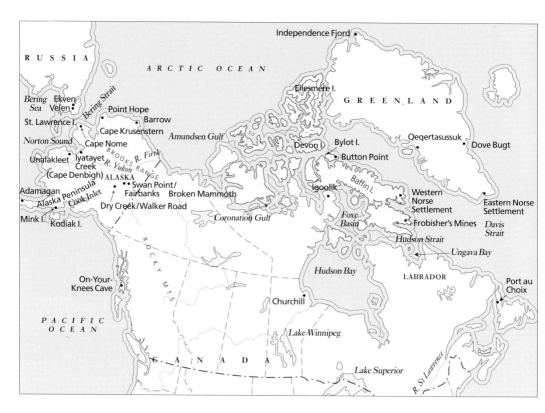

33 Map showing archaeological sites in Chapters 3 and 8.

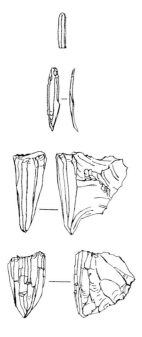

The Paleoarctic tradition occurs throughout Alaska and as far east as the west and southwest Yukon Territory. Paleoarctic populations were never large, but flourished along the coast and in much of the interior between roughly 8000 and 5500 BC, and in some areas even later. Unfortunately, we know little about their way of life, for almost all we have are their stone artifacts. Their microblades would have been set into the sides of bone points to create lethal weapons for taking caribou and other game. We can imagine hunters lying in wait along a river bank as a solid mass of migrating caribou cross a shallow fjord. They rise to their feet almost in the midst of the herd. Sharp spears rise and fall as the hunters leap from side to side to avoid slashing antlers. As the hunt ends, women

34 Paleoarctic tradition. (Top two rows) Two microblades from Ugashik Narrows, Alaska Peninsula. (Third and fourth rows) Two microblade cores from Onion Portage, Alaska. Height of largest core 1.69 in (4.3 cm).

and children arrive from the nearby camp with sharp knives. By evening, the caribou are butchered; their flesh dries on racks in the cold wind. We can also be certain that coastal people subsisted off marine foods, thanks to the discovery of the remains of a man in his twenties in On-Your-Knees Cave on Prince of Wales Island near Ketchikan, dating to before 7200 BC. The isotopic signature from his bones tells us that he lived almost entirely off marine foods. Even as early as the eighth millennium BC, many groups were living off fish, sea mammals, and waterfowl, especially among the islands at the foot of the Alaska Peninsula and in the Aleutians.

Coastal adaptations: Ocean Bay and Kachemak
5600 BC to *c.* AD 1000

By 4000 BC, the Pacific Ocean had stabilized at about its modern level, with ice-free coasts extending at least 15 degrees further north on the Alaskan coast than to the west in Siberia. Maritime cultures now flourished over a wide area. The densest populations lay near Kodiak Island and westward to Unimak Island, where sea mammals were abundant, especially whales. As early as 5600 BC, hunters visited Mink Island off the Alaska Peninsula to exploit Steller sea-lion rookeries, and they continued to do so for thousands of years. We can imagine skin boats landing quietly, the hunters setting

35

35 Mink Island, Alaska. A seal-hunting settlement contemporary with Ocean Bay flourished here as early as 5600 BC and remained in sporadic use for at least 2,000 years.

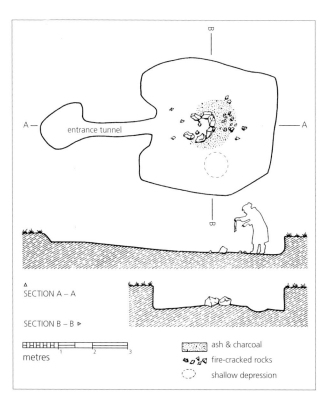

SECTION A – A

SECTION B – B ▷

metres

ash & charcoal

fire-cracked rocks

shallow depression

36 Kachemak tradition house, with sod walls and earthen interior benches. This particular house has an entrance tunnel and a central hearth, also earthen sleeping benches.

37 Ocean Bay slate lanceheads. The largest (left) is 7 in (17.8 cm) long.

38 Pecked and polished oval stone lamp with upper part of a human figure inside, from Knik River, Cook Inlet, Alaska. Drapery-like design on the outside in relief. Length 12.6 in (32 cm).

about the sea lions with wooden clubs, then butchering mothers and young for their hides, meat, and blubber.

By 5500 BC, a long-lived marine mammal hunting culture had appeared on Kodiak Island. This "Ocean Bay" tradition flourished on the island 37 and in nearby Cook Inlet and adjacent mainland coasts until 1500 BC. These masterly hunters used microblade-armed spears, then heavy thrusting spears with large stone blades against big sea mammals, weapons most likely coated with aconite poison from the monkshood plant, a practice that was commonplace in ancient times. During the summer months, most men spent almost more time afloat than ashore. To do this, they needed waterproof clothing for use in rough seas. Even this early, the women probably fabricated outer garments from seal gut, using delicate bone needles. It's worth going a long way to admire surviving examples of such clothing from more recent times preserved in museums.

The later Kachemak tradition developed in about 1800 BC, finally coming to an end in about AD 1000. This sea-mammal-hunting, salmon-fishing, and caribou-hunting culture appears to have originated in Ocean Bay, with the addition of techniques for working slate by grinding and sawing. The climate was now cooler and wetter, to which the people adapted ingeniously by moving partially underground into semi-subterranean winter houses 36 constructed with sod-covered wooden frames. Some had entrance tunnels and central hearths. A winter village was a series of low mounds, with few signs of life on cold days except for wood smoke drifting from roof holes, soon blown away by the strong winds.

By the time of Christ, the landscape was more crowded. Village competed with village; trade intensified in such exotics as labrets, ornamental plugs worn below the lower lip, which became marks of social status. Neighboring groups fought constantly and practiced elaborate mortuary rituals, dismem- 38 bering some of the dead, retaining some skulls as trophies, burying other people intact. These were the centuries, too, when the spiritual foundations of maritime life became ever more important, with their powerful shamanistic underpinnings, myths, and oral traditions. This was when the foundations of the elaborate Alutiiq culture of Kodiak Island in later centuries were laid, a culture that survives to this day.

The Aleutian tradition before 2500 BC to AD 1800

The baseline for Aleutian history is the Anangula site on a small island off Umnak Island in the central Aleutians. As early as 7000 BC, the inhabitants were taking fish and sea mammals and relying heavily on maritime foods of all kinds. They dwelt in at least semi-subterranean houses, which were like those used by later Aleutian communities. But does this long-occupied 39 Paleoarctic site represent ancestral Aleutian culture? If it does, then Aleut language and culture extends back over 8,000 years. Or did the Anangula

39 Historic Aleut winter house. This form of large semi-subterranean house was occupied by many related families, each with its own lamp and living space. Space was allocated on the basis of rank, the highest-rank occupant living on the eastern side. The inhabitants used notched logs as ladders to enter and leave through the roof.

community die out, to be replaced by a second occupation of the island chain by at least 2500 BC? Many argue that recent Aleut culture is a blend of later Eskimo influences from the Alaska Peninsula and the older Anangula tradition. The controversy is unresolved, but there is currently only scant evidence for cultural continuity between Anangula and later occupations, the earliest of which, on Unalaska Island, is said to date to about 3500 BC. What is universally called the Aleutian tradition began well before 2500 BC, with none of the microblade cores and other stone artifacts found at Anangula.

Until about 3000 BC, the people of the Bering Strait region and the Aleutians dwelt in small villages. Populations were small; each community subsisted off a broad range of birds, fish, mollusks, and sea mammals. Then, within the brief compass of about five centuries, dozens of new sites appear, at a time when marine productivity soared. After 2500 BC, the peoples of the Aleutian tradition enjoyed a culture that includes semi-subterranean dwellings and specialized toolkits that eventually led to historic Aleut peoples. Between about 2500 BC and AD 700, settlement patterns and subsistence remained virtually unchanged. However, there was great variation in living arrangements, varying from small kin-based settlements to what can only be called massive towns. Adamagan near the tip of the Alaska Peninsula, occupied from about 400 BC to AD 100, was a major settlement housing dozens of families (see box p. 61). But for all these shifts, and changes in symbolism and rank, the basic food supply remained the same. During these centuries, almost every village lay on open coasts, where maritime foods of all kinds abounded. The sea lion hide-covered

40

Adamagan: Aleut village

Adamagan was a huge Aleut village in Morzhovoi Bay, west of Cold Bay near the tip of the Alaska Peninsula, occupied between about 400 BC and AD 100. The site lay on a ridge that gave direct access to both the Bering Sea and the Pacific. Hundreds of families, at times as many as 1,000 people, lived there. The town, one of the largest hunter-gatherer settlements known from the ancient world, boasted over 250 semi-subterranean winter houses, as well as summer residences, storage areas, and numerous smaller structures. The winter houses were excavated 18 in (45 cm) into the ground, with a frame of driftwood and whalebone covered with a layer of sod or peat, which offered effective protection against savage winds. The inhabitants entered through a hole in the roof, with a ladder leading to the interior. The people lived off sea mammals hunted by the men from kayaks with atlatls and darts, burying offerings of walrus and sea-lion heads in pits under their houses.

Adamagan was abandoned in about AD 100, perhaps as a result of rising sea levels and changing coastal topography. Among other things, a spit cut off access to the Bering Sea, creating a lake where there was once a tidal channel.

40 The spectacular setting of the Adamagan site, an enormous Aleut village at the end of the Alaska Peninsula, occupied between about 400 BC and AD 100.

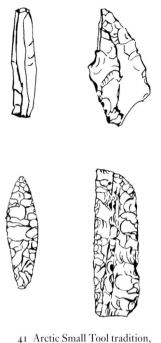

41 Arctic Small Tool tradition, upper Naknek Drainage, south-western Alaska (Top row). Microblade and burin (Bottom row). Projectile point and side blade. Length of side blade *c.* 1.3 in (3.3 cm).

baidarka kayak was a potent weapon for hunting and fishing, so much so that Aleut men spent most of their lives afloat from childhood.

After about AD 650–700, the settlement pattern changed completely. The large coastal villages disappeared, replaced by communities along the banks of salmon streams, where runs of sockeye and other species could be harvested. Defensive sites and refuges become commonplace, as if there was constant warfare. After approximately AD 1000, the salmon streams were abandoned and people returned to the coast, where at least three villages comprise large, multi-room houses that were probably households of fellow kin. No one knows why this change took place, but the corporate dwellings may have been an adaptation to intensified warfare and the need for defense.

Two centuries later, by 1250, the large communities had collapsed. People now lived in small extended families; villages comprised only a few dozen inhabitants. Judging from the small number of sites, the region was largely depopulated. Eskimo-related groups from the north began to move into the area. However, two centuries later, populations again rose rapidly and subsistence patterns returned to those of 2,000 years earlier, with sea mammal hunting reaching a peak. Massive villages rose across the Alaska Peninsula, reaching their maximum populations around AD 1600. Houses nearly tripled in size, with extended families of thirty to sixty people living within a single dwelling. Fifty years later, there were probably more people living on the western Alaska Peninsula than in all of the previous 4,000 years combined. Each village lay on the open coast, but always close to major sockeye rivers. The scale of the harvest must have been enormous. Today, the Nelson and Bear rivers run nearly a million salmon a year alone.

The Arctic Small Tool tradition   *c.* 2500 to 800 BC

41   Another broad cultural entity was land-based. By 2500 BC, the Arctic Small Tool tradition, with a distinctive, lightweight stone toolkit, appears along Alaskan shores. Why local technologies changed we do not know, but light weaponry was effective against caribou and other animals. The new artifacts were small, often diminutive blades or microblades, pointed at both ends, used as end or side barbs in antler or bone arrows or spearheads. Unfortunately, we know little of the organic components of the tradition, especially in the west.

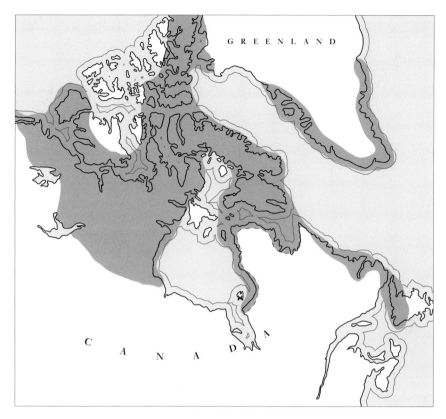

42 Probable distribution of the Arctic Small Tool tradition stone artifacts in the eastern Arctic.

The Arctic Small Tool tradition may have originated in contemporary reindeer hunting and river fishing cultures across the Bering Strait. In about 42 3000 BC, sea-level rises slowed, forming beaches around the Bering and Chukchi seas. This may have been the time when summer boat trips across the strait assumed importance in local life, bringing new contacts between Siberia and Alaska, even if fishing and sea-mammal hunting were apparently still unimportant. Arctic Small Tool groups may also have introduced the bow and arrow to North America, a weapon they used against caribou. Their greatest advantage came when hunting animals in open country, where stalking was difficult. A hunter crouched behind some rocks could take advantage of the terrain and inflict lethal wounds on caribou at much greater range than his ancestors. As early as 2300 BC, hunters in the south-western Yukon, perhaps using bows, took caribou at high elevations, where they grazed to escape summer mosquitoes. Bows spread south into Archaic societies in temperate zones as early as 2000 BC, but did not come into wide-spread use until as late as AD 700, having few major advantages in terms of range and effectiveness over atlatls and spears.

Arctic Small Tool-style implements occur in the Brooks Range and as far south as the Alaska Peninsula and Kachemak Bay. Some of these sites are little more than stone scatters, perhaps traces of hunting camps where a single tent was pitched. On the peninsula, Small Tool camps lie along rich salmon streams, presumably to take advantage of summer runs. Several locations have yielded evidence of more permanent structures. At the Brooks River site on the upper Naknek Drainage the inhabitants dug roughly square pits into the subsoil, about 13 ft (4 m) on each side, with a sloped entryway on one side and a central hearth.

First settlement of the eastern Arctic   *c.* 2500 BC

In about 2500 BC, Arctic Small Tool-using groups from the west appear along the shores of the Arctic Ocean, among the islands of the Canadian Archipelago, and in western Greenland. The causes of their remarkable, and still largely undocumented, migration remain a mystery. Given the simple toolkits and only rudimentary heat sources at their disposal, these little-known population movements are among the most remarkable in history. Three main Arctic Small Tool traditions developed: the ill-defined Independence I stage in the High Arctic, Pre-Dorset in the Low Arctic, and the Saqqaq complex in coastal Greenland.

Independence I Stage   2500 to 2000 BC
Independence Fjord is part of Pearyland, an enormous arctic desert in northeast Greenland. Small tent rings marked by circles of large boulders lie along the beaches of this, and neighboring, fjords, associated with scatters of stone tools, including implements for splitting and grooving bone and antler. The highest density of settlements is around Independence Fjord, but elsewhere they average 8½ miles (14 km) apart, a reflection of the scarcity of good sources of food or materials of any kind. Radiocarbon dates range between 2500 and 2000 BC. As many as twenty musk ox hide tents were erected at some locations, but most sites were no more than isolated dwellings. Covered with snow and equipped with a hearth and a passage-like storage area made of flagstones, they sufficed as winter homes.

The Independence people mainly subsisted off musk ox, which wandered over extensive, but restricted, ranges, unlike caribou, which migrated along predictable routes every year. Occasionally, the hunters took sea birds, ring seal, arctic char, and other fish. Everyone lived in tiny hunting bands, no more than four to six people, existing without oil lamps, which elsewhere provided light and limited heat. Their fuel was driftwood, occasional stunted willow branches, and the fat from musk ox bones. With such limited heating sources and a food supply that was constantly on the move, the people had to be nomads, perhaps coming together in slightly larger groups during the two-and-a-half months of darkness in midwinter. The houses

43

43 Remains of a 4,000-year-old Independence I camp at Port Refuge. The circular depression in the ground marks the place where a tent or perhaps a snowhouse once stood. The vegetation inside the circle is feeding off nutrients in the refuse left inside the house more than 3,500 years ago.

may have been unbearably smoky when fires were lit, so it is possible they were only kindled to cook or to thaw ice for water. As Canadian archaeologist Maxwell Moreau writes: "The bitter winter months might have been spent in a semi-somnolent state, the people lying under thick, warm musk ox skins, their bodies close together, and with food and fuel within easy reach."

Perhaps about 200 people lived in this area of northeastern Greenland, with an estimated population density of about one person per 112 sq. miles (290 sq. km). These Arctic Small Tool groups lived nearly 750 miles (1,200 km) further north, and in much more demanding landscapes than their distant relatives on the Bering Strait far to the west. The distribution of

Independence settlements extends south from Pearyland to Devon Island in the Canadian Archipelago. Independence sites also extend some 600 miles (950 km) south along Greenland's east coast as far as Dove Bugt, the easternmost ancient settlement in the Americas.

Pre-Dorset   *c.* 2500 to as late as 200 BC

Other sites with Arctic Small Tool-like artifacts occur far to the south, often grouped into the so-called Pre-Dorset culture. Whether these result from the same population movement that gave rise to the Independence I stage, or one some centuries later, is much debated. The artifact differences between them may simply reflect different seasonal activities on the coast and inland.

One focus of early Pre-Dorset culture lay in an area centered on the islands in the northern reaches of Hudson Bay, the northern and southern shores of Baffin Island, northern Labrador, and the west coast of the Foxe Basin. This region supported caribou and musk ox; walrus, seals, sea birds, and whales abounded. Unlike Independence, Pre-Dorset groups could rely on a diverse food supply throughout the year. This was an area where more permanent settlement was possible. As early as 2000 BC, the Igloolik site and other settlements literally followed descending sea levels down gravel beaches through the generations, from 200 ft (60 m) to 13 ft (4 m) above modern sea level.

The Pre-Dorset people relied heavily on seals for their subsistence, hunting them from the ice-edge and at their winter breathing holes. The latter requires great patience, endurance, and keen powers of observation. The hunter waits for hours for the moment when a seal comes up to breathe. A quick harpoon thrust snares the prey. Then the hunter rapidly widens the breathing hole with the chisel-like butt of his harpoon so he can drag the seal onto the ice before it carries the harpoon, and perhaps the hunter, into the water. This hunting method is most effective when there are enough hunters to keep watch on a number of breathing holes within a short distance. The thrusting harpoon used for ice-hole hunting was also useful for taking bearded and ring seals at the edge of ice floes, and for stalking walrus and seals basking on the ice. Pre-Dorset people also hunted sea mammals from skin kayaks. Perhaps as a result, harpoon designs became increasingly sophisticated through time. The arctic char was also an important food source, an anadromous species taken in weirs and traps, then dried for use in the lean fall months before the ocean froze over. The people used leisters, barbed fish spears with trident heads that speared the wriggling fish, and could then be sprung apart to release it on shore.

West of Hudson Bay, sizable populations appear not to have developed until after the late fourteenth century BC, and they were predominantly caribou hunters. The western region of Coronation and Amundsen gulfs may have been a dispersal area for hunting bands that pursued migrating caribou deep into the mainland interior. They were land hunters and fisher folk, only occasionally sealing on the coast. Some of these bands are thought

44

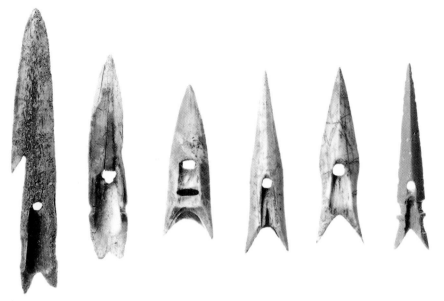

44 Pre-Dorset and Dorset harpoon heads. Their stylistic changes through time are useful chronological markers.

to have followed caribou herds far south during a period of increasing cold between 1200 and 900 BC and may have penetrated beyond the treeline, perhaps to Lake Athabasca by 900 BC. Sparse Pre-Dorset populations occur across the interior of the Barren Grounds, as far as the modern settlement of Churchill on the western shore of Hudson Bay. Judging from the major north and south shifts in the treeline in response to colder and warmer temperatures, these peoples' tundra hunting territories fluctuated constantly. To survive in such environments required both a near-encyclopedic knowledge of the environment at all seasons of the year, and the ability to respond instinctually to unexpected circumstances such as sudden temperature changes. Experience, and knowledge passed from one generation to the next, were all-important in a world where survival depended on careful preparation and assessment of dangers, and on persistence.

In the east, Pre-Dorset occupation occurs along the Labrador coast as far as the Strait of Belle Isle and western Newfoundland, the population concentrated in favorable areas. The first settlement was almost as early as Independence I and Foxe Basin Pre-Dorset, about 1880 BC, with a peak settlement about 1500 BC, thereafter declining, with only very sparse occupation, if any, until the mid-eighth century BC.

Greenland's Saqqaq complex   c. 2500 to c. 300 BC
Across the Davis Strait from Baffin Island, Pre-Dorset people, the so-called Saqqaq complex, occupied much of the west, south, and east coasts of Greenland. The earliest Saqqaq sites date to around 2500 BC, to about the time when Independence occupation began in the north. Some have argued

45 Overview of the Saqqaq Culture site, Qeqertasussuk, Disko Bay, Greenland. Excavations are in progress in the dwelling area and in the frozen midden deposits above the beach.

46 A section through the frozen midden layers at Qeqertasussuk. The culture layers consist of waste material from cleaning the dwelling floors and thousands of animal bones from the processing of game. Finds include fragments of artifacts of organic materials like wood, bone, baleen, and hide, which are preserved owing to the permafrost.

that Saqqaq was the result of southerly migrations from the bitterly cold Independence area.

The Qeqertasussuk site on an island in Disko Bay, occupied between 2400 and 1400 BC, reveals the great complexity of Saqqaq and Arctic Small Tool culture. The permanently frozen occupation deposits have yielded a wealth of organic finds, including wooden artifacts and fragmentary human bones. Intriguingly, mtDNA samples from a lump of hair came from a distinctive haplogroup shared with Aleuts and Siberians, as if there was an early migration from the west whose descendants died out. Controversy surrounds this finding, however. The Qeqertasussuk people used very light, toggle-headed harpoons that were thrown long distances with atlatls. They also carried light lances and bird spears as well as bows and arrows. All their artifacts were precisely manufactured and used with great effectiveness against seals and other sea mammals, also waterfowl. Saqqaq technology changed little over many centuries, with siliceous slate microblades, heavy bifaces, and end scrapers being skillfully hafted for domestic and hunting use. Qeqertasussuk was predominantly a summer camp, used during the harp seal migration season in June and July. The Saqqaq complex is also known from the Itivnera site, some 90 miles (150 km) inland from the coast. Itivnera, occupied between about 1250 and 340 BC, lies astride a migration route for caribou, the staple diet at the site.

Saqqaq was an Arctic Small Tool enclave for over 1,000 years, marked archaeologically by high percentages of ground and polished tools, and artifacts as small as arrow barbs manufactured mainly from siliceous slate. The relationship between Saqqaq, Pre-Dorset, and Arctic Small Tool is still somewhat uncertain, but they all form part of the same general Arctic cultural tradition, which ultimately derived from the Bering Strait region and endured for thousands of years until later settlers moved east from Alaskan shores.

45, 46

Chronological table of developments in western North America

Dates	West Coast		Great Basin	Southwest	Climatic stages
	Northwest	California			
Modern Times	MODERN GROUPS		MODERN GROUPS	MODERN GROUPS	LITTLE ICE AGE
	LATE PERIOD	AUGUSTINE / LATE / MIDDLE PERIOD / Many other variants	LATE ARCHAIC	HOHOKAM / MOGOLLON / ANASAZI	MEDIEVAL WARM PERIOD
AD 1100					
	MIDDLE PERIOD				LATE HOLOCENE
AD 1		BERKELEY	MIDDLE ARCHAIC		
1270 BC					
2500 BC	EARLY PERIOD	WINDMILLER / EARLY PERIOD		SOUTH WESTERN ARCHAIC	
3800 BC					MIDDLE HOLOCENE
4900 BC	?	?	EARLY DESERT ARCHAIC		
5900 BC					
7000 BC		? NORTH SOUTH			
8250 BC			PALEOINDIAN		EARLY HOLOCENE
10,000 BC and earlier	FIRST SETTLEMENT				YOUNGER DRYAS

4 · Foraging the West Coast

Coastal inlets teeming with sea lions and halibut, planked canoes paddling through calm southern California waters surrounded by hundreds of leaping porpoises, pods of gray whales swimming majestically close inshore: the Pacific Coast was a magnet for human settlement after the end of the Ice Age. What did the diverse environments of the West coast have to offer their descendants? What were the foundations of the rich Northwest Coast societies of later millennia? And how did more southern coastal peoples adapt to increasing aridity both inland and along the shore? What roles did maritime foods and edible plants play in the development of more complex societies in what is now California? The answers come from a still-incomplete patchwork of early archaeological sites scattered from southeast Alaska to the Mexican border.

A diverse coastal world

Great halibut, jostling salmon runs, sea mammals of every size – the Northwest Coast is the stuff of fishing legend and has supported maritime societies for thousands of years. During the Early and Middle Holocene, the Pacific Northwest Coast became a strip of green, forested landscape that stretched from the mouth of the Copper River in Alaska to the Klamath River in northern California. Here vast stands of spruce, cedar, hemlock, and Douglas fir mantled the coast and the great mountain ranges of the interior. The Pacific and the rivers that flowed into it provided whales, porpoises, seals, sea lions, and dozens of fish species, among them halibut, some of which weighed up to a quarter of a ton. Herring, smelt, and candle fish swarmed in coastal waters. No fewer than five salmon species appeared in inshore waters each year, jamming rivers as they crowded upstream to spawn. The rich and diverse coastal environment was highly productive, but the abundance varied from place to place and fluctuated through time.

Thanks to this fluctuating bounty, over many centuries the simple societies of earlier times became some of the most complex hunter–gatherer societies on earth. However, greater population densities meant that such groups were more vulnerable to variations in the food supply than small, mobile foraging bands. This, in turn, meant that some kin groups were more successful than others, with constant vying to acquire loyal followings among kin leaders. Thus, goes one argument, scarcities along the West Coast led to social opportunities that were not present in more abundant times.

In the Northwest, the damp, oceanic climate provided abundant natural resources to create an elaborate material culture, using straight-grained timber and only simple tools. One marvels at the thin, regular sides of large 47 Northwestern dugouts, hollowed out from great, straight-grained trees with fire and stone and shell adzes, and with high, flared ends that deflected rough water. Expert woodworkers made a magnificent array of artifacts, adorning many of them with a style that is among the most celebrated of American Indian art forms. Renowned ancestors, mythical birds, and humans appear on many boxes and small objects. The flowing lines and ripples reflect the gentle wavelets and fast-moving riffles of the dark waters where they lived. Commemorative posts, portal poles, and great totem poles recounted family PL. 2 genealogies and celebrated the deceased.

The Pacific Coast changes character beyond the Klamath River and stretches more than 1,250 miles (2,000 km) southward, backed by coastal mountain ranges from Oregon to central California. Strong winds and rough seas beset these exposed shores, making any form of offshore navigation a challenge, if not impossible, for low-sided dugout canoes, however large. A modern decked fishing boat might survive a breaking wave in open water; even a large dugout canoe would be swamped in short order. The diverse, but much drier, coastal environments of central and

47 Edward Curtis photograph of a Kwakiutl dugout canoe, with bird dancer in the bow. Northwest coastal peoples depended heavily on dugouts built of straight-grained cedar.

southern California were more benign and could provide a wide range of food resources in good years. However, drought cycles and changing ocean temperatures could devastate acorn crops and fisheries. As in the Northwest, abundance meant population growth, scarcity perhaps more social opportunities.

Three-quarters of inland California comprises the Great Central Valley, with flat lowlands drained by the Sacramento and San Joaquin rivers that merge into a great delta, pass through a gap in the coastal ranges, and ultimately flow into San Francisco Bay. The Lower Sacramento Valley region supported some of the highest population densities in ancient California. Relatively high concentrations also flourished in the Lower San Joaquin Valley, the San Francisco Bay area, and along the Santa Barbara Channel. In these areas, extensive sloughs and marshlands supported fish, mollusks, plant foods, and waterfowl, while natural upwelling from the sea bed in the Santa Barbara Channel brought an abundance of anchovies and other inshore fish.

Much of the coast supported only sparse hunter-gatherer populations, but in areas where aquatic foods abounded, much more complex societies developed, especially after 3000 BC. In the Northwest, salmon runs and increasingly focused maritime adaptations fostered sedentary settlement and greater complexity. Further south, too, it was groups settled near the coast or adjacent to estuaries and wetlands that enjoyed higher population densities, more diverse and reliable food supplies, and more elaborate social and cultural institutions.

Early settlement of the Northwest Coast
before 10,000 to *c.* 3500 BC

The earliest settlement of the Northwest Coast was a complex process. Both coastal and inland groups from the north took advantage of lower Early Holocene sea levels to move south and east along the Pacific. Some of the first settlers may have been caribou hunters, who followed herds from the Alaskan interior and the Yukon to the coastal steppe tundra exposed by retreating ice. Almost certainly the earliest coastal settlers combined caribou hunting with foraging for shellfish, fishing, and sea-mammal hunting. 48

No one knows when serious maritime exploitation began, but, by 6000 BC, some groups were relying heavily on salmon runs and herring fisheries, probably living at the same locations for prolonged periods of time. By 5500 BC, some coastal groups were using heavy woodworking tools, perhaps to make canoes. They were also hunting sea mammals with bone harpoons. A well-developed maritime tradition, whose roots went back much earlier into the past, was in full swing. The Canadian archaeologist Knud Fladmark argues that favorable environmental conditions at the time enhanced salmon productivity, making a combination of seasonal salmon-run exploitation,

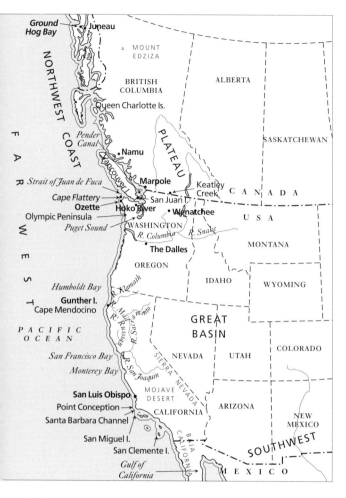

herring fishing, and intensive shellfish consumption a highly viable lifeway. Judging from ethnographic accounts, fishers in canoes would meet shoals of herring armed with wooden rakes, with which they impaled the crowded fish and harvested them in enormous numbers. Some of these early groups may have been ancestral to the historic Tlingit, Haida, and other Athabascan-speaking peoples living in the Northwest today.

As Northwest river waters warmed and lost their icy mantles, their up-river habitats became ideal salmon spawning grounds. Lake-spawning salmon began spreading up-river, and the ancient peoples who preyed on them also moved inland, into areas where they may have met expanding groups from the interior. From these complex movements emerged such historically known groups as the Salishan- and Wakashan-speaking peoples of the coast and interior today.

48 Map of sites in Chapters 4 and 9.

The Northwest: salmon, food surpluses, and exchange
c. 3500 BC to *c.* AD 500

Just how important were salmon, eulachon, halibut, and other fish along the Northwest Coast? The anadromous habits of salmon allowed them to be harvested in enormous numbers with traps and weirs, as well as with spears, the numbers only being limited by the ability of the fishers to gut and dry them before spoiling. But even in areas where they abounded, local salmon stocks varied dramatically over short and long periods of time and from one area to another, making it well-nigh impossible to assess salmon's importance in cultural change along the coast. However, between 3000 and 2000 BC, coastal groups began an increasingly intensive manipulation of their diverse environments to meet not only subsistence and other economic requirements, but to satisfy social and ideological needs. Shell middens are commonplace, testifying to the importance of mollusks; ground stone tools replace flaked artifacts. This progressively more efficient exploitation of marine and land resources was a key factor in the appearance of social complexity along the Northwest Coast and in the hinterland.

The food surpluses generated by the fisheries meant that careful attention had to be paid to the storage of smoked and dried catches. This may have become easier with the appearance of cedar forests, which are found in pollen records for the Northwest after 3000 BC. It was about this time that cedar-planked houses came into use, vital both for storage and as natural smoke houses. Coincidentally, woodworking tools came into more widespread use at about the same time.

Even as early as 3500 BC, one can recognize a nascent Northwest Coast cultural tradition that evolved continuously until European contact. By this time, maritime adaptations were in full swing. For example, halibut, often of enormous size, assumed great importance in coastal diet. We can imagine a canoe towing its huge catch to a nearby beach, men dragging the carcass ashore where the women cut it up, drying the flesh and carefully preserving the skin and bones. Carbon isotope analysis of a large sample of skeletons from coastal sites dating to the past 5,000 years reveals an almost total dependence on a maritime diet.

Many sites of this period are part of the so-called Charles Phase, centered on the Strait of Georgia area but representative of cultural developments

49 Excavations in the Rivermouth Trench at Namu, British Columbia, a site occupied as early as 7700 BC. By 6000 BC, the inhabitants relied heavily on salmon runs and herring fisheries, so semi-sedentary winter occupation was the norm.

over a much wider area, even as far north as the Alaska Peninsula. There are signs of a higher level of interaction between neighboring groups, too, reflected in widespread trade in toolmaking obsidian. Judging from X-ray fluorescence studies, much of the obsidian came from sources in eastern Oregon, reaching the Puget Sound region, Vancouver Island and the Gulf Islands, and mainland British Columbia. Mount Edziza in northwestern British Columbia, as well as local sources, provided supplies for communities at the headwaters of the Yukon, near Juneau, Alaska, and throughout much of coastal northern British Columbia. These exchange networks, and others handling different commodities, may have contributed to the spread of ideas and culture traits throughout the coastal regions. This was the time, also, when the basic characteristics of historic Northwest Coast culture appeared – an emphasis on status and wealth, and on elaborate ceremonial, reflected in new art traditions.

This long-term cultural development expresses itself archaeologically in many ways. By about 1500 BC, finely made polished chisels and adze blades and other specialized woodworking tools appear. A thousand years later, house builders and others used heavy mauls and pile drivers. By this time, too, women had long fashioned cedar-bark cloth into cloaks and other

50 Fishing for salmon with a plunge net on the Klamath River, California, before 1898.

51 A halibut hook in situ at the Hoko River site, Washington State. Note the bone barb, the Indian plumb wood shanks, and two-stranded spruce root leader attached. Experiments with modern replicas show such hooks were very effective.

garments; basketry had reached a high level of sophistication; and planked houses were in widespread use. Hunting and fishing technologies had reached new levels of elaboration, reflected in many forms of stone, bone, and wooden projectile points used against bear, beaver, elk, and waterfowl. Fishers in large dugouts now ventured further offshore. They used nets and a wide variety of bent wood and composite fishhooks, known from over 400 of them discovered at the Hoko River site on the Olympic Peninsula. Fish traps and weirs were critical artifacts for harvesting large catches, although the number in use fluctuated considerably over the centuries (see box p. 79). The earliest known weir dates to about 2000 BC, but they must have been in use much earlier.

We do not know how socially complex these societies were. Detecting changes in social status is challenging at the best of times, especially in the absence of burials, where wealthy individuals might lie accompanied by symbols of rank. Fortunately, there are a few examples. The Pender Canal site in the Gulf Islands of British Columbia was occupied between 2000 and 1500 BC, a location where burials show marked social differentiation, the wealthiest members of society being buried seated in stone slab cists with carved antler spoons or clam-shell dishes to help them satisfy their hunger.

Pender highlights the importance of prestigious ornaments, of which the labret, a conspicuous lip ornament, is the most significant, an emblem of rank worn by men and women. Labrets are, however, somewhat problematic social markers in that all women wore them, even if higher-status individuals possessed larger ones. Nephrite adze blades, used for canoe building and other activities, were also prestigious artifacts found throughout the Fraser River and Strait of Georgia regions. Graves with costly and exotic artifacts become more common after 500 BC. A social elite may have existed along the entire coast by this time, even if labrets were in widespread use at least 1,000 years earlier.

Prestige and wealth may have been the mechanisms that drove Northwest society by this time, as each group wrestled with the problems of managing increasingly large food surpluses and redistributing them throughout society. A few wealthy and powerful individuals may have controlled such redistribution as a way of acquiring personal prestige. One mechanism for doing this may have been ceremonial feasts, the ancestors of the potlatches (elaborate feasts accompanied by gift giving) of historic times. These would have been occasions for both gift exchange and more prosaic distributions of such commodities as furs and smoked fish. The participants would have donned their full regalia of rank – labrets, lip ornaments, and gorgets worn at the throat. Increasingly sophisticated art styles with animal motifs carved on bowls and spoons recall the prestigious crests that were commonplace in later times.

Widespread exchange, craft specialization, intensive exploitation of the Pacific, a preoccupation with wealth and prestige – all the basic elements of later Northwestern society were in place by AD 500. Soon, the trajectory of cultural change accelerated still further.

South of the Klamath River   before 10,000 to 1500 BC

Further south, the rocky and mountainous habitat of the northern California coast supported sparse Archaic populations for thousands of years. They survived comfortably with little contact with neighboring culture areas. Most groups subsisted off wild vegetable foods, mollusks, and some fish or sea mammals, moving seasonally from one concentration of edible foods to another. The size of local bands seems to have varied considerably, with little of the elaboration found in later coastal and Sacramento Delta cultures.

In San Francisco Bay, two great river systems converged – the Sacramento and San Joaquin. There had always been a large floodplain here, but as rising sea levels inundated the flat lands inside the Golden Gate, a huge shallow-water bay formed. For the first time, people living around the bay had reliable food sources at their doorstep. By 3000 BC, extensive marshes had formed around the margins of the bay, supporting a remarkable array of animal and plant life. As the marshlands grew, so human settlement in the bay lowlands became more long-term, much of it dependent on mussels and oysters.

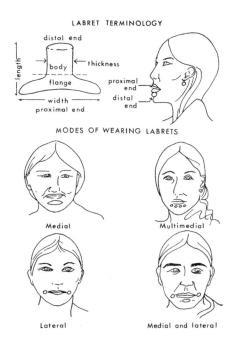

52 The variety of ways in which labrets could be worn.

Fish weirs and traps

Fish weirs were built in shallow estuaries, rivers, and streams, either to block the upward passage of salmon or to guide the fish into a trap or onto the spears of waiting fishers. Most weirs consisted of a lattice-work of branches, saplings, or vines lashed to stout posts set in the stream bed. The latticework was renewed each year; the posts permanent. Openings in the fence shepherded the fish into long, parallel-sided traps. Some more elaborate weirs had platforms where the fishers would catch trapped salmon with dip nets or spears.

Weirs were highly effective devices if properly maintained. So were basket traps used in conjunction with V-shaped weirs that funneled the fish into them.

Long, slender traps worked well in small streams, especially when combined with side weirs that steered the fish into them. Large, lattice-covered frames set below falls would trap jumping salmon after unsuccessful leaps.

Ethnographic accounts tell how communities downstream had an advantage when building weirs, but also an obligation to open them for other fishers upstream when they had caught enough fish. Large barriers across major salmon streams were often communally owned. Lesser weirs across smaller streams often belonged to wealthy or high-ranked individuals, who would permit others to fish from them in the off-peak periods of the run, especially during the day.

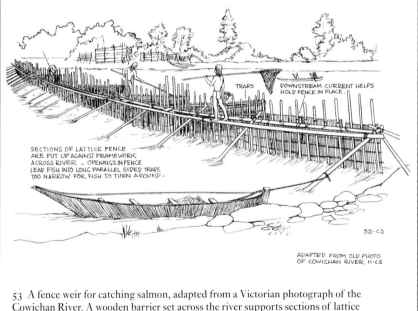

SECTIONS OF LATTICE FENCE ARE PUT UP AGAINST FRAMEWORK ACROSS RIVER — OPENINGS IN FENCE LEAD FISH INTO LONG PARALLEL SIDED TRAPS TOO NARROW FOR FISH TO TURN AROUND —

TRAPS

DOWNSTREAM CURRENT HELPS HOLD FENCE IN PLACE.

32·CS

ADAPTED FROM OLD PHOTO OF COWICHAN RIVER 11·CS

53 A fence weir for catching salmon, adapted from a Victorian photograph of the Cowichan River. A wooden barrier set across the river supports sections of lattice fence. Openings in the fence steer the fish into long, parallel-sided traps

For many bands, the bay was one stop on an annual round that extended far inland. People tended to live on mounds formed of discarded shells, mud, sand, and other debris, surrounded by muddy flats at low tide. In time, some mounds became large base camps, located near productive oyster beds, and places where clams could be taken or fish speared from canoes. Few of these early camps have survived the ravages of modern urban sprawl, so we know little of their occupants' lives. But one can imagine tule-reed canoes wending their way through narrow tidal channels laden with fresh oysters; and women and children with large baskets harvesting the mollusk beds at low tide, prying limpets off tidal rocks, and collecting seaweed for medicinal purposes.

Still further south, central and southern California also supported low populations for many thousands of years. During the Early Holocene, many groups may have exploited highly productive estuaries at the mouths of now submerged coastal canyons. Throughout this long period, shellfish formed part of the occupants' wider foraged diet, but exploitation of the shore was probably seasonal rather than permanent. From the very beginning, plant foods were of central importance, but this, and other aspects of the economy, are still little known. We do know, however, that some bands ventured offshore to the Channel Islands of the Santa Barbara Channel, probably using tule-reed canoes to cross what was then the 12 miles (20 km) of open water between the mainland and the nearest island. They must have traveled during the calm morning hours or on quiet winter days, paddling fast before their canoes became waterlogged. Visitors to the islands were eating shellfish there at least 10,000 years ago. It is submerged now, but there may have been a widespread Early Holocene maritime adaptation throughout the coast and offshore islands of the Santa Barbara Channel and perhaps elsewhere.

The origins of this early coastal tradition are still little understood, but the entire Archaic tradition of the shore seems to owe much to earlier Paleoindian cultures, with new artifacts for seed processing grafted onto an existing material culture. For thousands of years, archaeological sites throughout California yield little more than milling stones for processing small nuts and seeds. Such artifacts are nothing much to look at, crudely shaped rocks with a flat surface smoothed by hours of grinding. Nevertheless, they were vitally important, for they prepared the core of a plant-based diet. The soft scrape, scrape of milling stones would have greeted visitors to hunter-gatherer camps the length and breadth of the
54 California coast.

Archaeological finds are misleading, for life was probably a balance between seasonal hunting and foraging, especially at the time of fall acorn and seed harvests. However, shellfish, sea mammals, and fish of all kinds played an increasingly greater role over time, eventually allowing some groups to occupy base camps for long periods, despite unpredictable short-term climatic change. People used bone gorges and barbed, multi-part fish

I Two fine Clovis points from Washington State.

II Ipiutak stage ivory object,
perhaps a comb, *c.* AD 500.
Length *c.* 9.8 in (25 cm).

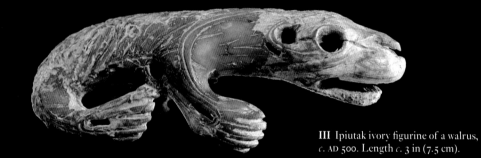

III Ipiutak ivory figurine of a walrus,
c. AD 500. Length *c.* 3 in (7.5 cm).

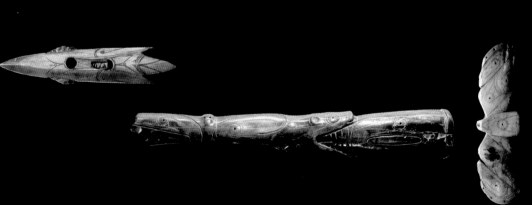

IV Old Bering Sea stage toggling harpoon components and reconstructed assembly. The weight of the ivory
harpoon head (left), foreshaft, and socket piece (center) were counterbalanced by an ivory winged object (right)
fixed to the butt of the harpoon.

V Dorset miniature mask in ivory, perhaps a shaman's device, from the Tyara site, Sugluk, Canada.

VI Inuit bowhead whale sculpture.

VII Eskimo in a skin boat approach a bowhead whale near Barrow, Alaska.

VIII Head-Smashed-In, in western Alberta, is among the oldest, largest, and best preserved of western Plains bison jump sites.

IX *Indians Hunting the Bison*, by the Swiss artist Karl Bodmer, painted during an exploratory journey through North America in 1832–34.

X *The Interior of the Hut of a Mandan Chief* (1833–34), by Karl Bodmer, published in the book *Travels in the Interior of North America, 1832–34*.

XI Tlingit ceremonial copper, dating to before 1876. These large beaten copper sheets of distinctive shape were important markers of prestige and status. Copper objects served such a purpose along the Northwest Coast for over 2,000 years.

XII Engraved and painted Haida storage box.

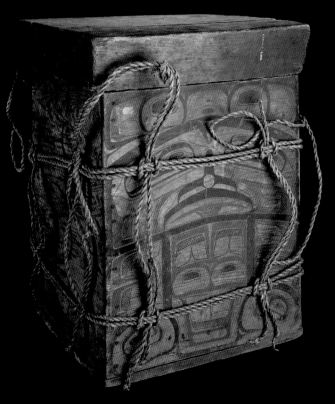

XIII Tlingit eagle helmet (*Ch'aak Shadaa*), dating to about AD 1800.

XIV Chumash rock art in a painted cave in Pleito Creek, Kern County, California.

hooks to catch both shallow- and deep-water fish. Mainland beaches were convenient places to net smaller species.

Judging from a rise in site numbers, admittedly a somewhat tenuous yardstick to use, Santa Barbara Channel populations may have first reached significant levels about 6000 BC, with a drop in coastal settlements in the Middle Holocene between about 5000 and 3500 BC, the lowest density occurring between 4000 and 3500 BC, perhaps during the dry and warmer-climatic optimum (Altithermal). Sea levels were rising, drowning the seed-rich coastal plain. The gradual reduction of these seed communities may have contributed to a shift to acorn harvesting in an environment of unpredictable rainfall and ocean temperatures, oaks having become more common than in the Early Holocene. Coastal populations then rose relatively rapidly, coinciding with the first use of pestles and mortars, perhaps with more intensive acorn exploitation, certainly with a greater emphasis on fishing and sea-mammal hunting. Similar patterns are thought to occur elsewhere in southern California. The population growth after 3500 BC may have also coincided with an increase in the productivity of the inshore marine habitat as kelp beds reappeared, even if climate conditions were as unpredictable as they are today.

Why did the people of the coast take advantage of this increased productivity? As populations grew, the overall energy cost of providing food for everyone would also increase, especially in drought cycles. More effort would have been needed to obtain food, perhaps triggering a shift to new food sources that may have required a greater time and energy investment to catch or process. There are some obvious signs of change. Both large sea mammals and deer were favored resources as long as they were fairly easy to obtain. As population densities rose, these same resources probably became scarcer, requiring more energy to collect. For example, seals and sea lions that frequented convenient beaches were an easily hunted resource. But once

54 Seed-gathering technology: a California Pomo woman collects seeds with a beater and basket.

An abundance of acorns

In the past, fifteen oak species grew from southern California to Oregon. In a good year, they produced enough acorns to feed both animals and humans. Yields of 1,750 lb per 2½ acres (800 kg per ha) were not uncommon. A reliable food supply, one would have thought, but harvests varied sharply from year to year. Acorns have excellent nutritional value, higher than that of maize or wheat, and can be stored for several years.

Acorns are a labor-intensive and time-consuming crop to process. Shelling and pounding takes hours, far longer than milling grass seeds. The meal is inedible, for acorns contain bitter-tasting tannic acid, which has to be leached away before they are eaten. Reducing acorns to meal requires pestles and mortars, whose presence in archaeological sites in large numbers is a sure barometer of acorn processing. Many mortars were little more than pecked out depressions on rocky outcrops near the oak groves. The women would shell the acorns with a hammer stone, then winnow them in a basket to remove the rust-colored skin. Then they pounded them with pestles of different weights, crushing the nuts, not grinding them, until they formed a fine powder. The best way to leach acorns is to pour the meal into a depression, then flush it with water repeatedly for two to four hours. In one experiment, the anthropologist Walter Goldschmidt obtained 5⅓ lb (2.4 kg) of meal from 6 lb (2.7 kg) of pounded acorns. Leaching alone took four hours. The equivalent processing time and yield from wheat would be about the same.

55 Woman pounding acorns, a drawing from the late nineteenth century.

the hunters had to mount special expeditions to remoter areas, the hunting cost rose rapidly.

Fishing, too, has varied costs. Catching inshore fish by hook and line in tide pools or from outlying rocks is a cheap way of getting food, but the yield is usually low. Canoes would be needed to exploit the rich kelp beds close offshore, but the yields would be much higher. However, building and maintaining boats requires considerable effort, as does sewing and repairing seine nets to be used from shore or canoe. Sea craft more substantial than a reed raft could have been used for the catching of larger fish like halibut or sharks as well, species with a high meat yield per specimen landed.

Acorns are the most obvious example of a higher-cost food resource, for the elaborate processing procedure required has been documented from ethnographic observations (see box p. 90). Both seeds and acorns have a major advantage over other foods: they are easily stored for long-term use, to be drawn upon in lean winter months. Both require considerable collecting and processing effort, but acorns came into more widespread use as rising sea levels reduced seed harvests. Acorn harvesting required exquisite timing, for the harvesters had to reach the tree before the ripe corns fell off into the mouths of waiting deer. Come fall, each band would camp near the oak groves that were traditionally theirs to harvest. The harvest itself was a lengthy process, for the yield from a single large tree could be as high as 55 lb (25 kg) and take a full day to collect. But the labor of gathering the acorns paled beside the work of carrying them back to camp, then processing and storing them dry and safe from rodents. Many historic groups erected bark granaries raised off the ground. Others kept them in baskets mixed with bay leaves, which gave off a pungent aroma and discouraged insects.

The Middle Holocene also saw an increase in long-distance exchange, especially of exotic materials and ceremonial objects such as pipes. Interestingly, rare but distinctive shell beads known as "Olivella Grooved Rectangles" appear at many sites on the southern Channel Islands, in coastal and inland California, Nevada, and central Oregon dating to about 4000 to 2500 BC, evidence for cultural interaction over an enormous area of the west.

The broadly distributed Archaic lifeway of the California coast survived into later millennia, adapting to changing climatic conditions, and devising far more diverse subsistence strategies. Notable among these was a much greater focus on acorn harvesting, fishing, sea-mammal hunting, and shell-fish collecting. Here, as in the Northwest, we now witness the emergence of more complex hunter-gatherer societies, described in Chapter 8.

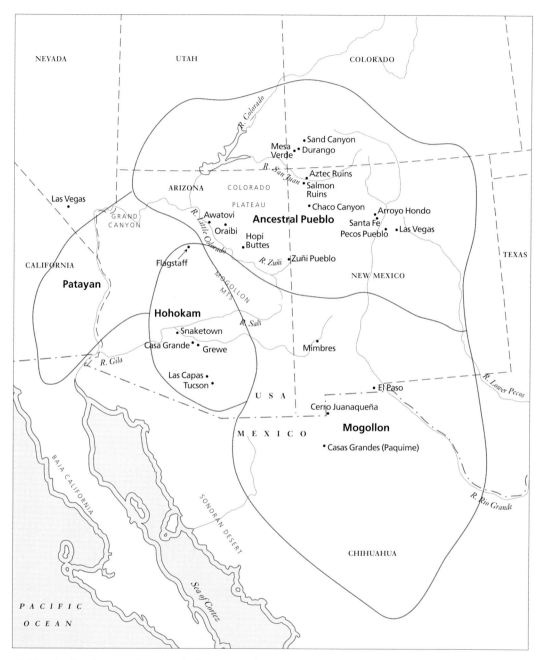

56 Map showing sites and culture areas in Chapters 5 and 10.

5 · Before the Pueblos

The area known as the "American Southwest" extends from Las Vegas, Nevada, in the west to Las Vegas, New Mexico, in the east, and from Durango, Mexico, in the south to Durango, Colorado, in the north. This is a region of dramatic environmental contrasts, between deserts and forested mountain ranges, areas of low and moderate rainfall. Desert and semi-arid terrain extended southward through the Southwest to what is now the Mexican border and beyond. For thousands of years, the hunter-gatherers in this slightly better-watered region adapted to their harsh surroundings in the same ways as other desert peoples. Then, in about 2100 BC, they made a seemingly inconspicuous change to their food quest: they began to cultivate maize. Why did they add horticulture to their foraging? Was it a response to environmental stress, a logical way of preserving their traditional lifeway? Centuries passed before maize, and much later beans, dominated local diets, but the story of the ancient Pueblo peoples of the Southwest begins among much earlier Archaic societies.

Archaic societies   *c.* 6000 BC to *c.* AD 200

The beginning of the Archaic coincided with drier conditions in some areas of the Southwest and further south. Early Holocene forest cover gave way to desert scrub and more grassland around 6000 BC. A complex mosaic of Archaic hunter-gatherer societies settled the Southwest and adjacent areas. These diverse groups maintained the same general technological traditions for many thousands of years over wide areas, but there was great local, and often short-term, variation. Projectile point styles may offer one potential way of distinguishing between different groups. The same designs extended over enormous areas during Paleoindian and Early Archaic times, just as they did in other parts of North America. But this standardization gave way to a proliferation of point styles used over smaller areas during later centuries, at a time when each group made increasing use of purely local sources of toolmaking stone. This may reflect higher population densities, less mobility, and more restricted territories where plants were exploited more intensively.

Archaic traditions in the Southwest

Many years ago, archaeologist Cynthia Irwin-Williams identified four interacting Southwestern Archaic traditions, a terminology still widely used, if poorly defined:
San-Dieguito-Pinto (Western) Tradition (*c.* 6500 BC to *c.* AD 200 or later)
This is the westernmost Archaic manifestation, extending from southern California in the west deep into southern Arizona. It is found within the Great Basin as far north as southern Nevada. Pinto apparently evolved from Paleoindian roots and is identified by "Pinto Basin" points with straight stems and concave bases, especially in the eastern Great Basin (*c.* 6300 to 4300 BC).
Oshara (Northern) Tradition (*c.* 5500 BC to *c.* AD 600)
This tradition is centered in north-central New Mexico, the San Juan Basin, the Rio Grande Valley, southern Colorado and southeastern Utah. The Oshara may have roots in earlier Paleoindian traditions, but these postulated connections are much disputed and the debate is unresolved. Oshara may have been the earliest manifestation of the later Ancestral Pueblo tradition (see Chapter 10).
The Cochise Tradition (?before 5000 to *c.* 200 BC)
This southern Southwestern tradition lasted for a very long time, with its earliest manifestations, known as Sulphur Spring, perhaps before 5000 BC. Its two later phases, the Chiricahua (before 1500 BC) and San Pedro (1500 to 200 BC), are much better known. Cochise may have been the ancestor of the later Hohokam and Mogollon traditions (see Chapter 10).
Chihuahua (Southeastern) Tradition (?6000 BC to *c.* AD 250)
This tradition of south-central New Mexico and Chihuahua, Mexico, is still poorly defined and probably includes several local adaptations that evolved over long periods of time.

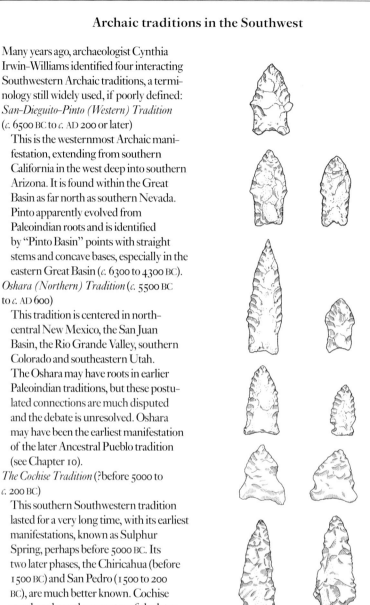

57 Southwestern Archaic projectile points. (Top) Pinto Basin point. Length of Pinto Basin point 1.4 in (3.7 cm). (Second, third, and fourth rows) Bajada, San Jose, and Armijo points respectively. (Fifth row) Chiricahua Cochise points. (Bottom row) San Pedro Cochise points.

Except in highly favored locations, Southwestern Archaic peoples lived in generally arid environments, where food supplies were widely dispersed and where survival depended on constant mobility. Many Archaic settlements were highly transitory, occupied for a few days or weeks at a time, as groups passed through large territories. Possessions, known to us mainly from stone tools, were portable and easily replaced. Only a few caves and rockshelters preserve a wider range of artifacts, including such perishable items as basketry, fiber sandals, and fur blankets.

The expansions, contractions, and shifts in Archaic settlement were never conscious migrations. Each band exploited animal and plant foods that changed from year to year. Movements were short-term reactions to abrupt changes in the availability of game and edible plants. Much depended on intelligence that passed from one band to another by word of mouth. One can imagine a band camping at a temporary water hole. A fellow kinsman visits from a nearby group and tells of newly ripened seeds near a marsh in a small valley. The next morning, the band shifts camp several miles to harvest the wild crop.

Rainfall patterns changed fairly drastically in about 1000 BC, as conditions became drier throughout the Southwest. Many groups overcame food-shortage stress as they always had, by covering large distances and by possessing knowledge of diverse food sources over wide areas. In the Southwest, as elsewhere, Archaic bands fell back on less-preferred plant foods like agave in times of hunger. Some Southwestern Archaic groups also began planting maize as a logical response to prolonged drought conditions. They did so for generations only as a supplement to their ancient diet, as a way of preserving their traditional way of life.

Maize comes to the Southwest   *c.* 2100 BC to AD 200

Maize was the staff of life for many Native American societies at European contact. A tropical grass, *Balsas teosinte,* is its ancestor and was growing in Oaxaca, Mexico, by 8000 to 6000 BC and the Balsas Basin of central Mexico by 7200 BC. By 5000 BC, small-scale maize cultivation by mobile foragers was widespread in Central America, also in adjacent areas of South America and southern Mexico. A sudden and mysterious expansion in the range of maize cultivation in about 2500 BC brought corn cultivation into a broad array of environments in both the Southwest and South America. In the Southwest, maize arrived at a time of cooler and moister climate, with fairly predictable rainfall and filling river drainages. Many hunter-gatherer groups slowly adopted maize as an opportunistic, additional food, planting small plots on regularly flooded river banks, then leaving them alone to grow while they foraged elsewhere. Such sporadic horticulture had taken hold over a wide area by 2100 BC. In time, the nascent farmers recognized its superior productivity, excellent storage qualities, and perhaps its supernatural associations, which assumed great importance in later times.

Archaic societies in the Lower Pecos Valley

Long-lived arid landscape adaptations thrived for thousands of years in areas like the Lower Pecos Valley in extreme south-western Texas. Here, dry caves provide an unusual portrait of the more perishable material culture of Archaic groups. Like their contemporaries in the Southwest and Great Basin, Lower Pecos people made extensive use of plant fibers, especially from desert succulents, to make twined, plaited, and coiled baskets, also sandals, mats, and bags. They wove cane partitions to separate living quarters in the caves. Bags, blankets, and pouches from bison, deer, and rabbit hide come from many sites, as do fragments of rabbit-fur robes ingeniously made from long strips twisted to bring fur upward on both sides of the garment. People used wooden digging sticks to forage for plants and curved boomerang-like sticks for clubbing rabbits.

58 Baker Cave, Val Verde County, Texas. This site yielded evidence of Early, Middle, and Late Archaic occupation, the earliest settlement dating to about 7000 BC.

How and why did maize cultivation spread into the Southwest? What incentives were there for undertaking the laborious processes of planting and harvesting corn? Maize farming is an economic activity that may require sedentary living for much of the year, but we can assume that there were at least some sporadic contacts between cultivators in Mexico and nomadic hunter–gatherers living in desert regions to the north. Thus, it would have been easy for knowledge of plants, even gifts of seeds or seedlings, to pass from south to north. We shall probably never know what specific mechanisms diffused farming to the Southwest. The opportunity for adopting the crops was probably there long before anyone thought it worth doing so. But domesticated plants had one major advantage: they

The Lower Pecos region is best known for its rock art, both pictographs (drawn or painted on the rock) and petroglyphs (pecked out in the rock surface). The earliest, so-called Pecos River Style, dating to about 2000 BC, includes abstract representations of humanoid figures in various mineral colors, some painted almost life-size. Deer, fish, animal forms, weapons such as atlatls and darts, shaman figures, and shaman's paraphernalia accompany the large polychrome figures. Other Pecos River Style artists depicted miniature human figures in red engaged in group activities, including deer roundups and processions in which headdresses identify individuals with special status. Bison and deer are sometimes shown being driven into netlike barriers or into jump areas. Much of the art may represent spiritual visions seen during trances.

At European contact, the descendants of some 11,000 years of a continuous hunter-gatherer tradition lived in central and south Texas. Dozens, perhaps hundreds, of small hunter-gatherer groups shared similar lifeways, divisible linguistically into at least seven main groups. Everyone dwelt in small, round brush- or mat-covered huts and wore blankets or capes fabricated from deer and rabbit skins.

59 Lower Pecos rock art: white shaman from Val Verde County, Texas.

60 "Curly tail panther" frieze from Devil's River, Lower Pecos, Texas.

might not be highly productive, but they were predictable. Cultivators of the new crops could control their location, and their availability at different seasons through storage. Uncertainties about the productivity of the natural environment would have been one of the conditions favoring adoption of cultigens by Archaic groups.

The Southwestern climate made hunting and gathering high-risk lifeways, mainly because of variable rainfall distributions. Despite generally low population densities, local populations may have occasionally reached saturation point, resulting in food shortages. Many Late Archaic populations grew steadily as the distribution of piñon, desert succulents, and other valuable supplementary foods expanded during the arid Middle Holocene.

The scattered hunter-gatherer groups lived mainly in stream drainages. However, as contrasts between vegetational zones became more pronounced when the climate became more arid, many groups changed strategies. They exploited lowland foods during the winter and early summer, then moved to the cooler uplands to harvest piñons and other foods during midsummer and fall. More predictable food supplies like maize would have been an invaluable addition to Archaic diet.

Hunter-gatherers tend to accept crops as a survival strategy to preserve their lifeway, not because they want to become farmers. Thus, lowland desert groups may have planted maize to offset seasonal shortages in spring, for they could store the resulting grain. Upland groups might have adopted maize to allow them greater effective control over upland areas. Whatever the precise cause, the origins of horticulture in the Southwest appear to have resulted from an imbalance between population and available natural resources. In a sense, Archaic culture in the Southwest, as elsewhere in North America, with its elaborate seed-processing equipment, hand stones, and grinders, was pre-adapted to agriculture. Had Southwestern peoples wanted to adopt agriculture as an opportunistic venture perceived to be of advantage, they would have done so much earlier, cultivating maize soon after it appeared far to the south. Ultimately, however, they adopted a low-yielding form of maize in the late third millennium BC, a long time after it came into use in Mexico. The addition of farming to the economy, even as a part-time activity, placed immediate boundaries on seasonal movement, for people had to return to the locations where they had planted crops, both to tend and to harvest them.

Maize is not a cereal that one can rely on to provide all one's food if one plants it casually and simply returns to harvest the resulting stand later, as one can many native plants like goosefoot. Maize also lacks two of the vital amino acids needed to make protein, lysine and tryptophan, and is only an effective staple when grown in combination with other crops like beans (lysine-rich) or squash (tryptophan-rich) that together provide the necessary protein ingredients for a fully rounded diet (meat in fact provides valuable protein and the people ate sufficient flesh for the purpose). Since most Southwestern groups continued to enjoy a highly mobile way of life for at least a millennium after maize first appeared north of the present international border with Mexico, there is good reason to believe that it first served as a casual supplement to wild plant resources, especially in favorable areas where corn could be planted and then left largely untended, the process of cultivating it not being allowed to interfere with other subsistence activities. One should remember, too, that the Southwest was a high-risk environment for any form of cultivation, so a logical strategy would involve diversification of options rather than placing all one's dietary eggs in one metaphorical basket.

61   The hardy, low-yielding maize that first entered the Southwest was the highly varied Chapalote form, a small-cob popcorn of great genetic

diversity, which was in use by at least 2200 BC. It was not Chapalote but flour corn which is thought to have been the key development in Southwestern life. This type of maize may have resulted from a selection for a large-kerneled corn, which was easier to grind, also for earlier flowering. This last attribute was vital in the hot and arid Southwest, where growing seasons are often restricted by irregular timing and distribution of rainfall, leaving little time for large kernels to fill out.

61 Drought-resistant Hopi maize.

The spread of maize across the Southwest was not a linear process and happened gradually, beginning with a pattern of reduced mobility and floodplain horticulture that involved seasonal base camps in the uplands and near rivers. This was an ideal adaptation for Late Archaic people, who simply added maize to their existing wild plant exploitation, thereby expanding available food supplies. As maize dependence increased, so technological innovations came into play, among them pottery for storage and cooking, new food preparation methods, and specialized equipment for processing maize. There was a cultural continuum between the Late Archaic Cochise and a later food-producing culture. This, in general terms, formed a "basal society" throughout much of the Southwest, from which the later Ancestral Pueblo, Hohokam, and Mogollon cultural traditions may have developed (see Chapter 10). The same general process of increasing dependence also took hold in northwestern Mexico, where archaeologists Robert Hard and John Roney excavated the Cerro Juanaqueña Archaic settlement with its 5 miles (8 km) of stone house foundations and found a few maize cobs dating to about 1150 BC.

The earliest known Southwestern maize, from the Old Corn site near Fence Lake south of Zuni, New Mexico, dates to about 2250 BC. A century later, people in the Arizona deserts, the Mogollon Highlands, and the Colorado Plateau cultivated maize as a dietary supplement. All Southwestern cultivation involved careful water management, using methods appropriate for specific landforms and topography. Canal systems, dams, and terraces first came into use as ways of controlling seasonal water flows and also for fertilizing the soil. The Las Capas site (1200 to 800 BC) lies where two tributaries join the Santa Cruz River near Tucson in southern Arizona. Here impeded groundwater flow raised the water table. Large oval houses and smaller circular dwellings stood along slight rises in the floodplain, surrounded by storage and roasting pits. They overlooked closely packed fields watered by canals, where the excavators uncovered thousands of small individual planting holes for the crops. Maize was only

62

63

a small part of the diet; wild plant foods were still very important. By 800 BC, some communities lived in rings of houses around shared courtyards, perhaps an indication of more extended households, which are advantageous when land is abundant and labor is in short supply.

Maize is at the northern limits of its range in the Southwest, intolerant of too short growing seasons and such hazards as crop disease and strong winds. The most important factors of all were soil moisture and water supplies. By careful seed selection, the farmers developed higher-elevation varieties with distinctive structures whose seeds could be planted at considerable depth, to be nourished by retained ground moisture. They became experts at selecting the right soils for cultivation, those with good moisture-retaining properties on north- and east-facing slopes that receive somewhat less direct sunlight. The farmers favored floodplains and arroyo mouths where the soil was naturally irrigated. They would divert water from

63 Las Capas excavation, Arizona, showing small pithouses, post holes for the roofs and storage pits on many house floors.

62 (*Opposite*) Aerial view of Cerro Juanaqueña, northwestern Mexico.

streams, springs, or rainfall runoff to irrigate their crops. The cultivators dispersed their gardens widely to minimize the dangers of local drought or flood. Over the centuries, a great diversity of highly effective dry-climate agricultural techniques developed throughout the Southwest.

Common beans probably appeared in the Southwest by 500 BC, and became a widespread staple throughout the region. Beans were a very important crop in the Southwest especially when grown with maize, for the two complement each other. Being legumes, they can return vital nitrogen to fields depleted by maize. Thus, by growing maize and beans in the same garden, Southwestern farmers could maintain the fertility of the soil for longer periods of time.

The dispersal of domesticated plants into the Southwest was not just a matter of them being available for cultivation. Their adoption involved a conscious decision by individual Archaic hunter-gatherer groups to utilize these more storable foods. This decision perhaps involved deliberate efforts by stressed groups living at low elevations to enhance winter and springtime food supplies.

The beginnings of village life   AD 200 to 900

The first appearance of corn did not trigger a dramatic revolution in Southwestern life. As the Southwestern specialist Linda Cordell points out, a plot of corn tended and harvested in a small garden would require less caloric energy to grow than collecting wild seeds scattered in isolated locales over a wide area. This is not a problem when people hunt and forage over large territories. If mobility is restricted, however, then the advantage of stands of even low-yielding corn is considerable. Maize doesn't have as much food value as some wild foods, especially piñons and walnuts. But piñon harvests in particular are subject to variations, making them a less reliable food source than cultivated crops.

Serious maize agriculture in an arid region like the Southwest requires a great investment of time and energy, strong incentives for adopting more sedentary lifeways. As people settled down near their maize fields, they still relied on wild plant foods exploited in far smaller territories restricted in size by their sedentary lifeway. Once agriculture took hold in the Southwest, exclusive reliance on hunting and gathering was no longer a viable adaptation. Nevertheless, agriculture may not have been an enduring pattern everywhere for many centuries.

64   It was not until AD 500 to 700 that permanent villages appear in any numbers. This sedentary way of life developed over many centuries, partly because agriculture was a high-risk activity in contrasting environments where rainfall varied constantly from year to year. Everyone now relied on efficient storage and large storage pits to guard against shortages. At the same time, people built more substantial permanent dwellings. The new,

64 Backhoe trenches reveal the locations of pithouses and the village plan at the Valencia Vieja site, Arizona, in foreground.

fixed communities varied greatly in size, but were made up of individual oval-to-circular houses occupied over some length of time.

These early village communities, grouped under the loose term "Basketmaker" over much of the northern Southwest, owed much to their Archaic predecessors. At first, the people used simple, small hand stones and basinlike nether stones to grind both wild and domesticated seeds. In time they developed more elaborate grinders – large troughs worked with *manos* needing two hands to operate, presumably for grinding larger amounts of maize more efficiently. Field hunting was very important, involving snares, nets, and traps to catch birds and rabbits. Flaked stone technology remained much the same as in earlier millennia, except for the introduction of the bow and arrow for hunting solitary game like deer. This may have coincided with the rising importance of agriculture. One important innovation appears in the Southwest in about AD 200: pottery. We tend to think of pottery as a revolutionary invention: it was not, for anyone sitting by an open fire knows that wet clay bakes hard. Indeed, baked clay objects like figurines were in use much earlier and occur at Las Capas, for example. However, clay containers made a significant dependence on agriculture possible, because they enabled households to store seed in jars, and also to boil stored maize and beans, a process that maximized their nutritional value. They allowed food to be cooked unattended, and were useful for other types of storage, were strong and easily manufactured, and lasted for a long time. 65

65 A Hopi woman making pottery in an Oraibi village. She is using a coiling technique to build up the walls of the vessel.

In the north and in the mountains, the earliest villagers lived in pithouses, dwellings where part or all of the walls are formed from the sides of an excavated pit. Pithouses are thermally efficient, for the heat loss from underground structures is less than for above-ground pueblos. They required less manpower and fuel to heat in winter, which made them adaptive at higher altitudes. Most pithouses were round or oval, up to 16 ft 6 in. (5 m) across, their floors dug to varying depths, but often about 1 ft 6 in. (0.5 m) below ground surface. Pithouses often contained storage pits or fire hollows. Like Eskimo dwellings, they must have been smoky and the inhabitants prone to lung diseases. As far as is known, the superstructures were usually made of poles and mud, the roof supported on four posts. Pithouse forms evolved into more-or-less standardized designs as the generations passed. Ventilators and air deflectors were common features, as were roof hatches accessed by a wooden ladder.

Lower Sonoran desert houses, in what is now southern Arizona, were quite different, not pithouses as such, but rectangular or square houses built in pits. The floor was excavated up to 8 in (20 cm) below the ground, the roof and walls being formed of poles, reeds, grass, and mud. Small hearths lay just inside the entrances.

Early villages in the north varied greatly in size, from hamlets of merely two or three pithouses to large settlements that contained as many as twenty-five to thirty-five houses, perhaps occasionally many more. Everywhere, the houses were arranged without apparent order, associated with storage pits and cooking ovens. At all but the smallest villages, one or more structures appear to have had special functions. These are usually pithouses, but ones that display unusual architectural features or greater dimensions than residential structures. Shabik'eschee village in Chaco Canyon, New Mexico, comprised at least sixty pithouses and forty-five well-built storage bins. One structure stood out, a pithouse with a difference: a low bench encircled the interior and the floor area was more than five times the size of the average dwelling in the settlement. The excavators believe the structure was only partially roofed. Perhaps this is one of the earliest examples of a "Great Kiva," a ceremonial building commonplace in later centuries.

By AD 700 to 900, such kiva-like structures were a regular feature of northern and central Southwestern villages, which, by now, placed great importance on rituals that commemorated the endless cycle of passing seasons, reinforced the close kin ties that were central to farming in a high-risk environment, and provided a context for redistribution of food supplies, as well as reducing the potential for conflict.

Were these villages independent entities, or were some of them linked by alliances or other political ties? Do early farming settlements large and small, with a great diversity of pottery styles and material culture from village to village, represent differences in social organization? Despite occasional large centers, most settlements were little more than family households. Not that these were completely self-sufficient settlements: anyone farming in the Southwestern highlands had to maintain regular contacts with the lowlands, which were often only a short distance away. To argue that early Southwestern farming villages were autonomous, egalitarian, and self-sufficient appears to go against the environmental realities of the area. Any form of long-distance exchange of essentials and luxuries by farming cultures usually results in some form of ranked society. Modern Pueblo groups are far less egalitarian than often thought, a phenomenon that can also be observed in early Spanish records. Whether earlier Archaic, or even Paleoindian, societies were ranked is a matter of ongoing debate.

66

66 Reconstruction of a Mogollon pithouse village from the Pine Lawn phase by the Chicago Natural History Museum.

Trade relationships probably played an important role in village social organization. Many essential commodities like obsidian, chert, and other raw materials were exchanged over considerable distances, sometimes even hundreds of miles. Utilitarian artifacts like pots passed through many hands. Luxuries like sea shells passed from individual to individual over enormous distances. The trade was apparently highly organized and conducted by local leaders. Judging from historical records of inter-community exchange in the Southwest, it involved a complex series of economic and social processes. It was conditioned by the great environmental diversity and the differences in productivity from one area to the next. With unpredictable rainfall, survival depended on gift exchanges between trading partners and friends, and on the social ties between them. Exchange equalized resources and allowed the acquisition of valuable surpluses of luxury goods that might be traded later for food and other necessities. Every Southwestern group was dependent on others for ritual paraphernalia, items such as red ocher, tropical bird feathers, sea shells, even coiled baskets used in naming ceremonies. The exchange could be between neighboring communities, or along long, well-established trails that were in use for thousands of years, between friends or complete strangers.

At first, exchange may have resulted from regular informal contacts, but in time these became more formalized. One set of rules and conventions applied to fellow villagers, normally based on notions of continuous sharing and mutual assistance, seasonal gambling, ceremonial redistribution, and trading parties. Everyone had access to local commodities and goods from afar. Neighboring communities carried out exchange with relatives or non-strangers, with visitors bringing gifts in the expectation that they would be reciprocated in the future. Long-distance trade was normally in the hands of men and conducted along a myriad trails, some possibly marked by petroglyphs and shrines. One ancient trail brought Pacific sea shells from near Los Angeles across the desert to Needles, along the Gila River, and then along various branches to many villages and pueblos. A complex trail network linked the Plains, Great Basin, Sonora, the Southwest, and California at European contact, most of them maintained by chains of exchange and gift friendship that handled different exotica. Exchange was an integral part of social relations, one that corrected economic differences, forged alliances, and served as a basis for resolving disputes before warfare erupted.

Fremont farmers in the Great Basin

Farming also thrived in the Great Basin, in areas north of the Four Corners region, from about 2,000 years ago, in seemingly unpromising environments. The first cultivators moved northward from the Southwest as early as 200 BC. A new farming culture developed out of interactions between indigenous foragers and immigrants. The main Fremont home-land extended along the mountains that form the eastern rim of the Great Basin, with small pithouse hamlets located in places where mountain streams flow onto flatter terrain forming alluvial fans (pioneering Mormon farmers occupied the same locations). The Wasatch Front between Bear and Utah lakes, to the west of the Great Salt Lake, enjoyed the densest farming population. It was a relatively well-watered environment with a longer growing season and numerous wetlands. Fremont cultivators also pushed westward, almost as far as Ely, Nevada. Their rock art – anthro-pomorphic figures, animals, lines and spirals, and other symbols – extends over a vast area. But by AD 1350, most Fremont communities were empty, as climate change and other factors caused profound changes in traditional life at a time of considerable upheaval over the wide area of the Great Basin and Southwest. Over time, Southwestern society became more complex, but never to the higher degree of stratification that developed to the south in highland and lowland Mexico. Alliances waxed and waned, but wherever they developed, they were associated with dramatic

67,
68

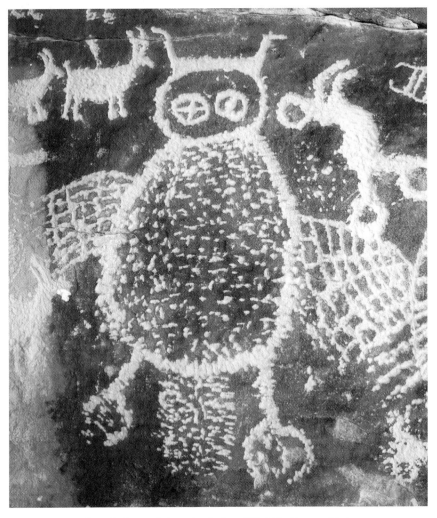

68 Fremont art. An owl, about 3 ft (0.9 m) tall, from Nile Mile Canyon, Utah.

population increases. The closing centuries of pre-Columbian times saw a dramatic efflorescence and elaboration of Southwestern culture as population densities increased rapidly in the central and northern Southwest during the eleventh century AD, described in Chapter 10.

67 (*Opposite*) Fremont art. Temple Mountain Wash panel, Utah.
An anthropomorph grasps a snake in its hand.

Chronological table of developments on the Plains

Dates	The Plains			Climatic Changes
	Hunter Gatherers	*Farmers*	*Developments*	
Modern Times				LITTLE ICE AGE
		Hidatsa, Mandan, Arikara, Pawnee	Horses introduced to Plains (after 1640) Onate expedition (1598) Coronado expedition (1541)	
AD 1541	PROTOHISTORIC PERIOD LATE PREHISTORIC PERIOD	PLAINS VILLAGE (Central Plains & Middle Missouri)		MEDIEVAL WARM PERIOD
			Communal bison hunting reaches greatest intensity after AD 550 Bow and arrow introduced to the Plains	
AD 15	LATE PLAINS ARCHAIC	PLAINS WOODLAND	Pottery appears (c. AD 500) Maize appears (c. AD 300)	LATE HOLOCENE
1267 BC				
2477 BC	MIDDLE PLAINS ARCHAIC			
3795 BC			McKean Complex on Northwestern Plains Head-Smashed-In site first in use	
	EARLY PLAINS ARCHAIC			MIDDLE HOLOCENE
4935 BC				
5876 BC				
7056 BC			Olsen-Chubbock site Bison hunting assumes predominant importance	EARLY HOLOCENE
8247 BC	PALEOINDIANS			
9368 BC			Extinction of Ice Age megafauna	
11,400 BC			CLOVIS	YOUNGER DRYAS

6 · People of the Plains

Thundering buffalo herds, hunters with bows and arrows driving stampeding beasts over precipitous cliffs: during the early nineteenth century twenty-seven tribes of horse-mounted Indians dominated the Great Plains. All of them were either nomadic buffalo (bison) hunters subsisting almost entirely off Plains game herds, or semi-nomadic hunters who relied on crops for a substantial part of their diet. Such colorful societies were the stuff of which legends were made, with stereotypes of "feathered braves" and spectacular raids perpetuated in the circus ring and later in movies. Today, the stereotypes are gone, for the assumption that Plains Indian culture was static over long periods of time is long discredited. We now know that the cultural roots of the twenty-seven Plains tribes lie in much earlier Paleoindian societies, described briefly in Chapter 2, and that their diversity arose through many centuries of constant change. What innovations led to more refined hunting methods and the greater elaboration of Plains hunting societies? Why did many groups to the east take up at least part-time agriculture? What were the consequences of the introduction of the horse to the Plains? These questions have fascinated generations of researchers.

The Great Plains cover an enormous area of North America's heartland, from the Rockies in the west to the Eastern Woodlands near the Mississippi. They are a grass sea that extends across about a half-billion acres (200 million ha) from Canada in the north to Mexico's Rio Grande in the south. They were, and still are, a harsh place to live, with often brutally hot summers and long, bitterly cold winters. The actual boundaries between the Plains and neighboring environments are often blurred. In places, long mountain ridges finger into the open country, forming intermontane basins. The eastern frontiers of the Plains pass imperceptibly into the Eastern Woodlands as annual rainfall rises and short grass prairie gives way to tall, lusher grasses, then woodland. The Plains were, above all, the world of *Bison bison*, a smaller beast than the larger *antiquus* hunted by Paleoindians.

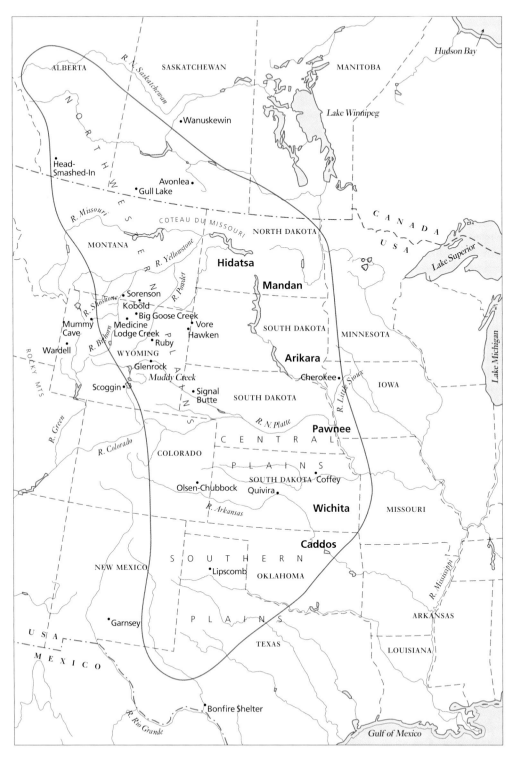

69 Map of Plains sites.

The Plains Archaic   *c.* 5500 to *c.* 500 BC

Abrupt changes in projectile-point forms from lanceolate Paleoindian types to side-notched points mark the beginning of the Archaic. Side notches allowed a much tighter and stronger binding of the point to foreshaft or spear handle. By all indications, Early Archaic hunter-gatherers lived in much the same way as their predecessors, even if they relied on a wider variety of game and vegetable foods. The Hawken site in Wyoming, dating to about 4400 BC, records an Early Archaic hunt where bison were driven up a narrow arroyo until they reached a perpendicular cliff that impeded further progress up the gully. Hawken was used at least three times. Judging from the bison teeth, the hunts occurred in early or midwinter. The hunters were taking both mature beasts and driving nursery herds, but the killing was tough work. At least 300 projectile points lay among the bones, many of them broken by the brutal impact against struggling animals. Many points had been reworked again and again, with carefully ground bases and needle-sharp tips that penetrated hides and muscles very effectively.

The Plains Archaic flourished during the Mid-Holocene climatic optimum. Warmer and drier conditions may have meant focusing more intensively on plant foods. In about 3250 BC, Archaic groups occupied the Coffey site on the edge of an oxbow lake alongside the Big Blue River, north of Manhattan, Kansas. Here, people took not only bison and other game, but also pursued waterfowl and collected goosefoot and other plants. They caught large numbers of catfish, indicating the site was occupied during the late summer, when fish crowded into small shallow pools at the edge of the drying oxbow.

Between 2900 and 1000 BC, both hunting toolkits and bison-hunting methods became more refined. People now mainly hunted them in the fall, often at favored locations that were used again and again. Much of the meat from the carcasses became pemmican (dried, pulverized, then mixed with

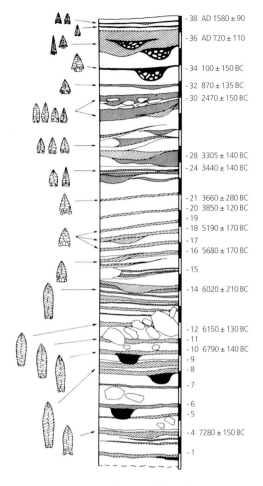

70 Mummy Cave, northwestern Wyoming: stratigraphic profile showing periods of human occupation separated by silt layers. Projectile point forms illustrated at left show the change from Paleoindian lanceheads to side-notched and then stemmed forms, starting about 5600 BC.

71 The jump-off point at the Kobold site, southern Montana.

fat), easily stored food for the winter. Hunters trapped their prey in arroyos, also in stone and wood corrals, and used bison jumps: witness the Kobold site in southern Montana that remained in use right into later times. Kobold is a 25-ft (7.5-m) high sandstone bluff close to well-watered grazing land. The arroyo below the cliff is wide and spacious, which was ideal for butchering large numbers of animals. The terrain is favorable for game drives, allowing but one approach to the bluff. Judging from the many broken bones among the bison remains, many animals died in the precipitous fall.

During the 3rd century BC, a highly sophisticated bison hunting culture emerged on the Northwestern Plains, known by side-notched "Besant" projectile points and clay vessels. These people used much more complicated bison corrals built of logs set in deep post holes, well documented at the Ruby and Muddy Creek sites in Wyoming (see box p. 115). The Muddy Creek site corral was built on sloping ground, a structure about 40 ft (12 m) in diameter. It lay upslope from extensive, fertile grazing tracts, hidden from view by a low ridge until the very last moments of a drive. Both this, and the Ruby corral, were designed to handle relatively small numbers of bison, perhaps a nursery herd of about twenty-five beasts. On the Central Plains, some groups were semi-sedentary and consumed a wide range of foods. Woodland-style burial mounds appeared along the Missouri River and into central Nebraska and Kansas after AD 1.

Bison jumps

Some time around AD 1, large-scale bison hunting on the northern and Northwestern Plains intensified. This intensification reflects the initial stages of a large-scale trade in meat and hides from the Plains, exchanged for plant foods with people living at the margins of the grasslands. Bows and arrows came into use by at least AD 1, marked by the appearance of slender "Avonlea" stone points. The bow was adopted quite quickly, but still did not

The Ruby site

The Ruby site in Wyoming, dating to after AD 100, features a corral placed on a low-lying stream bed so that the stampeding animals did not see it until the last minute. The hunters also used natural features like ridges and arroyo banks to funnel their quarry toward the pen. They erected the corral using pairs of stout posts separated by the diameter of the horizontal timbers wedged between them. The corral was built on a slope, so the lowest wall was subjected to the most stress. It was rebuilt several times, strengthened perhaps, as this was where the animals could be crowded for slaughter purposes. Excavator George Frison estimates twenty hunters would have taken between ten and fourteen days to build the Ruby corral, final drive lane, and wing walls.

Bison bones filled the downslope area of the corral to a depth of over a foot (30 cm). A processing area covering at least 10,000 sq. ft (900 sq. m) lies about 1,000 ft (300 m) up the arroyo. Nearby lies a possible ceremonial structure formed by the intersection of two arcs of circles each about 33.5 ft (10.2 m) in radius. Five post holes across the 15-ft (4.5-m) widest axis separated the structure into two enclosures, at least one of which was roofed. Eight male bison skulls lay at the southern end. Frison believes the stout building was a form of shaman's structure, where the priest who supervised corral construction sang and smoked to invoke his spirit helpers.

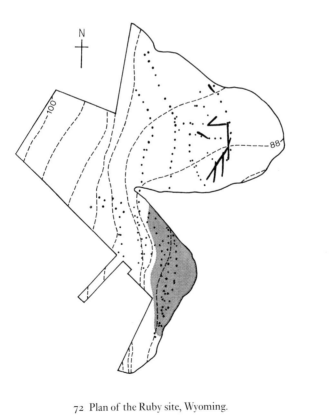

72 Plan of the Ruby site, Wyoming.

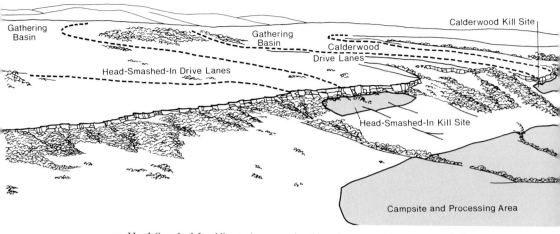

Gathering Basin

Gathering Basin

Calderwood Kill Site

Calderwood Drive Lanes

Head-Smashed-In Drive Lanes

Head-Smashed-In Kill Site

Campsite and Processing Area

73 Head-Smashed-In, Alberta, is among the oldest, largest, and best-preserved of western Plains buffalo jump sites. Plan shows the major features of the site and the neighboring Calderwood site, including gathering areas where the hunters maneuvered the herds into position, drive lanes, and processing areas.

solve the problem of driving and controlling the movement of the quarry. Communal bison hunting on foot reached its greatest intensity after AD 550. As time went on, the hunters made increasing use of bison jumps, high bluffs approached by long lines of stone piles, over which they could stampede large herds.

Bison jumps lay at strategic locations, such as precipitous cliffs, sink holes, and other natural features. Unlike a corral, a successful jump hunt, a rare event, depended on a large number of stampeding animals. With a large group, the leaders would be prevented from turning aside, as would happen with a small herd. Locations such as Glenrock, Big Goose Creek, and Vore, Wyoming, document how the hunters moved herds over distances of several miles to their deaths.

The Head-Smashed-In buffalo jump in western Alberta was used for more than 7,000 years, a remarkable length of time. Six streams feed into a shallow basin in the plains surrounded by higher ground. A large creek forms the only entrance. More than 500 stone cairns up to a foot (30 cm) high mark drive lines as much as 5 miles (8 km) long leading to the sandstone cliff that formed the jump. Deep deposits of bison bones lie below the cliff, dating back to as early as about 5400 BC.

This type of bison drive was still in use when Hudson Bay Company trader Peter Fidler spent six weeks among the Piegan Indians in 1797. He witnessed many bison drives as he camped among them at one of their drive pounds. At one, the hunters killed more than 250 beasts and would have taken more. But "when the wind happened to blow from the pound in the direction of the tents, there was an intolerable stench of the large numbers of petrified [sic] carcasses, etc. on which account the reason of our leaving it."

John Speth's excavations at Garnsey, New Mexico, reveal that ancient Plains hunters were expert observers of their prey. About AD 1550, a group of hunters visited a small gully where they knew bison would congregate in late March or early April. Instead of just killing every animal, they tended to concentrate on the male beasts, for females perpetuated the herd. Speth believes this was also because males are in better condition in the spring, and their bone marrow has a higher fat content. Hunters everywhere prefer fattier meat, for it is an important source of energy and essential fatty acids. In spring, such flesh was hard to come by, for the herds would be recovering from the lean winter months.

Without horses, ancient bison hunters depended on ever-changing herd densities for successful communal hunts. Individual or small-group hunting would be far more adaptive with lower densities, for bison drives have a high failure rate and a herd could move out of foot range if allowed to escape unless herd densities were unusually high. While the most spectacular finds come from the Northwestern Plains, there is abundant evidence for widespread, specialized bison hunting in later times, from the northern limit of the Plains at Wanuskewin near Saskatoon, Saskatchewan, to the Southern Plains.

Protohistoric times   sixteenth century AD to modern times

In AD 1541, Spanish conquistador Francisco de Coronado ventured eastward from Pecos in the Southwest onto the Plains, in search of rumored Indian gold. Coronado journeyed east on horseback for thirty-seven days, over featureless plains without landmarks except occasional lakes and buffalo wallows. Coronado, riding on geldings, returned without gold, but later horse-riding Spanish settlers introduced full breeding stock.

About 150 years later, some time during the eighteenth century, horses – "mystery dogs," as the Indians called them – reached the northern Plains. Horses were commonplace long before firearms appeared, a reflection of strict Spanish policies that forbade the trading of muskets to the Indians. The Plains people obtained horses through barter and through theft. In contrast, the French fur traders in Canada and along the Mississippi had few horses but plenty of firearms and ammunition that they traded for furs.

74 Reconstruction of a bison jump at the Head-Smashed-In site.

Horses gave their riders the ability to locate dispersed bison populations effectively inaccessible to hunters on foot and to carry large quantities of meat. Plains groups were now less dependent on the year-by-year, season-by-season fluctuations of bison herds, for they could cover enormous distances. Horses put the nomadic groups of the Plains in a strong position. They could either live off their farming neighbors, or trade bison meat and hides for grain when it suited them. Some formerly sedentary groups like the Dakota and Cheyenne even became nomads, joining others like the Blackfeet and Comanche, who had been hunting for centuries. The Bison Belt became an economic battleground, as war parties raided each others' camps, to seize horses and loot food stores.

Military advantage was obviously important, the ability to defend oneself the key to survival. This ability depended on numerical strength – concentrating large numbers of people in the largest camps possible, even if many raids were on a small scale. To do this, one had to have the ability to support oneself in the Plains environment. The communal hunt was a time when large numbers of people came together at one location, providing not only more food, labor and hunting skills, but also information on the whereabouts of bison herds. The hunters could even work several corrals or jumps at the same time. Larger concentrations of population meant more marriage partners, also access to trade goods obtained from a wide geographical area. The number of a leader's followers depended on his skills in war and in the chase. Ambitious individuals could manipulate the communal hunt to their benefit, to obtain power and prestige, and thus more followers, and eventually their groups would obtain long-term military advantage.

The advent of the horse, and to a certain extent of the rifle when it was introduced during the nineteenth century – a weapon that made people dependent on European traders – led to a chronically imbalanced and unstable way of life. The millennia-old communal values that stressed cooperation in large groups for survival gave way to highly individualistic doctrines and smaller bands that pitted family against family, with little concern for the common welfare. The wealth obtained in battle could be used to promote family status. Hunter vied with hunter for the allegiance of followers and fellow warriors. A flamboyant, almost frenzied era of Plains life dawned, one where most nomadic groups believed old age was evil, that it was better for a man to die in battle.

The Blackfeet of the northern Plains rose to prominence as European fur traders and settlers pressed on to the Plains hunting grounds. Fur traders were among the first to sow the seeds of wholesale bison slaughter, for they gladly exchanged firearms for beaver pelts. Soon white hunters with their repeating rifles joined the fray, leaving thousands of wasted carcasses rotting on the Plains. Like the beaver, the bison began to dwindle, affected also by exotic cattle diseases. Then the railroads spread over the prairies. During the 1860s and 1870s, special excursion trains took hunters into a sea of bison. The great herds of thundering animals, with their seemingly inexhaustible

75 *Indians Hunting the Bison*, painted by Karl Bodmer (1843).

supplies of meat and hides, disappeared almost overnight. The last vestiges of the primeval North American hunting life vanished in an orgy of nine-teenth-century musketry. Only a handful of buffalo survived, to form the nucleus of the managed herds that graze on the Plains today.

Village farmers on the Plains

To many people, the Plains mean nothing more than vast herds of bison pursued by small bands of nomadic hunters. Such a portrait is misleading, for semi-sedentary farming groups flourished on the eastern Plains after AD 1000. For the most part, agriculture was confined to major river valleys and their tributaries, such as the Middle Missouri Valley, the Republican River Valley, and the Arkansas and Red rivers to the south.

The Middle Missouri was a world of its own, a deep incised trench that flowed through North and South Dakota. The river cut into the surround-ing plains as it flowed toward much lower and distant seas. In places the

76 Plains Indians at a rendezvous, their tipis stretching away into the distance.
A detail from a nineteenth-century painting by A. J. Miller.

valley drops 200 to 400 ft (60 to 120 m) below the adjoining higher ground.
The so-called "breaks," which delineate the edge of the valley, are steep and
heavily eroded, the trench itself being between a half-mile and 4 miles
(0.8 and 6.5 km) wide. Long, grass-covered terraces line much of the valley,
dropping sharply onto the river floodplain itself. Most human settlement
was on the terraces, escaping even the highest spring and summer floods.
West and south of the valley lie open, drier plains, where bison once roamed
in large numbers. These plains were a vital part of village life along the river,
which depended not only on maize and bean agriculture, but also on bison
hunting. The Middle Missouri Valley and other such sheltered locales were
places where two worlds met, that of the nomadic Plains bison hunter and
the more settled existence of the village farmer.

Two realities affected agriculture in the valley. The first was irregular and
often highly localized rainfall, the second the risk of early or late frosts.
Anyone farming maize in the Missouri trench was planting a tropical crop
at the northern limits of its range, with a growing season which averaged
about 160 days in the southern portions of the valley to a mere 130 days in
the Knife-Heart Rivers area of North Dakota. The frost-free growing
season was considerably longer in the valley than on the surrounding plains.
For all its harsh conditions, the Middle Missouri Valley was a remarkably
diverse environment, especially for people who relied on a combination

of agriculture, hunting, and foraging. The valley itself provided not only winter game and many edible plant foods, but fish in abundance. The Missouri Valley was also a major flyway for migrating waterfowl in spring and fall. Those who lived on the western bank enjoyed ready access to bison-hunting grounds on the plains and to trade routes which crossed open country to the Rocky Mountains and far to the north and west. The Plains hunters and settled valley farmers each produced commodities the other lacked. The hunters brought hides and blankets, pemmican, and toolmaking stone. The farmers bartered grain and other agricultural products. For centuries, two ways of life, one very ancient, the other more recent, interacted across the eastern boundaries of the Plains.

Plains Woodland tradition   500 BC to AD 1000

The Central Plains and Middle Missouri Valley were open to cultural influences from the east, which passed up rivers and along inter-village trails. It comes as no surprise to find Hopewell-like settlements and burial mounds in the valley during the early first millennium AD (for Hopewell, see Chapter 11), marked by the characteristic plain, or cord-roughened pottery similar to that found over a wide area of the Eastern Woodlands. This "Plains Woodland" tradition is remarkable for four major innovations: the bow and arrow came into use; maize was cultivated for the first time, even if infrequently; many groups now manufactured pottery; and burial mounds, which appeared over much of the northeastern periphery of the Plains.

These earthworks date to between 500 BC and AD 1000, and usually lie on bluffs overlooking river valleys, lakes, or creeks. Most often, up to forty circular mounds cluster in groups. Linear earthworks are much rarer and consist of simple platforms or low embankments running in straight lines for hundreds of feet, occasionally connecting one mound with others. One or more circular-to-oblong burial pits, containing a single or several skeletons, lie under many of the mounds. Most were roofed with poles or logs, while bison carcasses and skulls were sometimes placed with the dead.

The artifacts found in Plains mounds are personal ornaments such as stone pipes and items made from exotic materials like Great Lakes copper. They symbolize an individual's subordinate status in nature: the ability to kill large animals like bison but powerlessness in the face of drought and other natural phenomena. Humans reconciled themselves with the forces of nature by subordinating themselves to the animals they killed, an ideology which may have originated among Archaic societies. The family band was still the focus of most subsistence activity, in contrast with many contemporary Eastern Woodland societies, where individual status and prestige were coming to the fore. But, as exploitation of game and plant foods intensified in later times and semi-sedentary communities became more common, so rankings of different families and kin groups emerged, to reach a high degree of development in later village communities.

Plains Village Indians   *c.* AD 1000 to 1500

By the tenth century AD, perhaps one or two centuries earlier, the Woodland cultures of the eastern Plains had developed into more sedentary societies dependent on maize agriculture in fertile valley bottoms and on some hunting and gathering. Maize and beans became staples in the Central Plains between AD 900 and 1100, during four centuries of warmer, moister conditions, which fostered western expansion of the tall-grass prairie. Good climatic conditions sometimes allowed the spread of cultivation well into the High Plains, even to the foothills of the Rockies, along drainages such as the Arkansas River. These agricultural societies, often called "Plains Village Indians," subdivided archaeologically into several traditions; they developed a way of life that dominated the eastern Plains from the Dakotas to Texas for nearly 1,000 years. For example, the Upper Republican Culture of the Republican River Basin thrived along flood-free tributaries in hamlets of fifty to seventy-five people. They were small-scale farmers, who also hunted bison, and are believed to be Caddoan-speaking ancestors of the Pawnees in Nebraska and Kansas and the Arikaras in South Dakota. The Middle Missouri tradition people were Siouan and ancestral to the Mandans.

By AD 1500, Plains Village Indian cultures all shared some general characteristics. Every society used substantial lodge houses. All developed effectively permanent bases used for most of the year, sometimes fortified with ditches and stockades. Every village contained underground storage pits, which were of great importance in environments with short growing seasons and unpredictable rains. Every group used small, triangular arrowheads and bone hoes, manufactured from bison scapulae (shoulder blades) set at an acute or right angle to a wooden handle. And all made and used round-bottomed or globular pottery.

There was great diversity among peoples farming along the Missouri and other river drainages, which need not detain us here. In drought cycles, the people tended to rely more heavily on bison hunting and plant foods rather than agriculture, adapting their settlement patterns and toolkits accordingly. Agriculture came to the fore during wetter years. The riverine village remained a distinct, resilient unit. The members of each village community shared common traditions and customs. They had their own social hierarchy, their own ways of organizing communal labor, of distributing wealth and measuring prestige. Their relationships with other communities depended on territorial proximity, on common language, and sometimes on kin ties or religion. Most villagers abandoned their settlements for much of the year, moving out onto the plains for spring and summer bison hunts to acquire meat surpluses for the winter and for the harvest ceremonies that lay ahead. Come winter, they shifted to smaller encampments on sheltered terraces where game could be found and firewood was abundant. But the agricultural months of mid- and late summer were at the center of village life. Farming was the enterprise that integrated all other activities in the community.

A well-defined social hierarchy was fundamental to village farming life: there were men and families of rank – the leaders – and commoners. These leaders belonged to families whose prominence came from spiritual powers and monopoly over wealth. For most high-ranking families, rank had to be validated by lavish gifts and by personal achievement. These rankings, stable over long periods, were far from the stratified classes so characteristic of pre-industrial civilizations.

Caddoans and Siouans

At European contact, three village farming groups lived along the Middle Missouri Valley. The Arikara, a Caddoan-speaking culture, were dominant along the Missouri, living in thirty or forty earth-lodge villages along the lower portions of the river. The Siouan-speaking Mandan lived upstream, in as many as thirteen communities, while a small number of Hidatsa flourished further north, near the confluence of the Heart, and later the Knife rivers. Conservative estimates place at least 45,000 farmers along the river valleys at European contact. The origins of these historic groups lie deep in the remote past. The Caddos were in the south, people whose cultural affiliations lay closer to the Mississippi Valley and the Eastern Woodlands than the Pawnee, Wichita, Arikara, and other groups to the north. Caddoan farming culture achieved some complexity as maize agriculture took hold in the fertile river bottomlands from eastern Texas and Oklahoma into Kansas and to the north. Over the centuries, the Caddoan-speakers showed a tendency to coalesce into larger political units than merely single villages, often into ephemeral chiefdoms, which linked larger regions into more complex polities. In the

77 Dance-drama: detail of a Mandan *okipa* (or buffalo dance) in the 1830s, depicted by Karl Bodmer.

south, such developments culminated in the cultural traditions found at Spiro, Oklahoma, and other major ceremonial centers (see Chapter 12).

The late archaeologist Preston Holder described how the organizational and spiritual rationale of Caddoan farming villages centered around the sacred village bundle, "a physical device which contains, and reminds the owner, and outsiders, of the supernatural powers controlled by its individual possessor." The bundle also had group affiliations, to the point that Holder describes it as a "sort of portable ceremonial center." Among the Arikara and the Pawnee, the village bundle was a skin envelope which

Historic villages

Large, circular or oblong eighteenth-century Plains villages had as many as 100 or more houses, closely packed together, often with only narrow walkways between them. A deep ditch, up to 10 ft (3 m) deep when freshly dug, surrounded each settlement, backed on the inner side with a massive log-and-brush palisade. The earth lodges were between 30 and 50 ft (9 and 15 m) in diameter, the outer walls closely set circles of poles covered with earth, grass, and willow saplings. So crowded were fortified Mandan villages that refuse was piled up against the palisades or thrown in the surrounding ditches.

Historic Mandan villages lay on terraces above the river. A number of nuclear families occupied several dozen earth lodges in each settlement, clustered around a central open space for games and public ceremonies. The lodges had four massive uprights and an open smoke hole at the peak of the earth-covered roof. A short, timber entrance way led into the house, the central hearth placed in the square formed by the four roof posts. Curtained beds lined the walls, while deep storage pits in the floor contained corn and other food supplies. A favorite horse might be corralled near the entrance, while a small shrine lay behind the fire opposite the entrance. These permanent settlements were almost deserted during summer bison hunts, and also for much of the winter, when the people camped in sheltered woodlands in the valley, where game and firewood were plentiful.

78 Big Hidatsa village site, occupied between 1600 and 1845, at the confluence of the Knife and Missouri rivers, North Dakota. The aerial view shows circular earthlodge depressions and trails. In 1845, the occupants moved upstream to found a new village, joined by Arikaras and Mandans. Today, the three groups are known as the Three Affiliated Tribes.

contained objects that symbolized complex ideologies and rituals. The cosmic powers within the bundle assured the continuity of the village. A bundle also controlled all production and social relations within the village. Hereditary chiefs considered themselves stars living on earth, "earthly reservoirs," as Holder put it, of power that made them protectors of their people. They were the life forces of the village through the power given them by the bundle. If the bundle was lost or destroyed, then the people would die.

PL. III

Chiefs and priests were men of knowledge, patience, and complete understanding, serene individuals with a reputation for generosity and largesse. They presided over the great seasonal ceremonies: the winter bison hunt when meat was obtained for planting ceremonies, spring gatherings which focused on the bundle – their contents handled by priests, their magical forces renewed by the spring sun so the world would be born again for the harvest. These, and other rituals, were occasions when individuals and the people as a whole came in contact with the powers of the world through private mystic experiences and communal feasts.

North from Pierre, South Dakota, the Mandan dwelt in six or seven well-fortified villages in 1742, said by French visitors to contain between 100 and 200 houses each. These populous communities were the climax of Plains Village Indian culture on the Middle Missouri. The productive maize, beans, and squash agriculture yielded dependable food supplies, easily supplemented by hunting bison on horseback. The farmers had always been middlemen. Now their role became crucial in an emerging, and ever more complex, trading environment. The villages acquired horses and firearms from the south and west and soon became important trading centers, which attracted English, French, and Spanish traders. As the late archaeologist Waldo Wedel wrote: "They participated deeply in the main currents of Plains cultural development; and like other middlemen before and since, rose to pre-eminence and prosperity. There was a price on this pre-eminence, however, and part of it is reflected in the defensive works with which the communities found it necessary to surround themselves" (see box p. 124).

However, by 1804, when the celebrated explorers Meriwether Lewis and William Clark traveled up the Missouri, the Hidatsa, Mandan, and Arikara, devastated by exotic diseases, were a shadow of their former selves, with many villages abandoned and survivors clustered in poorly fortified settlements.

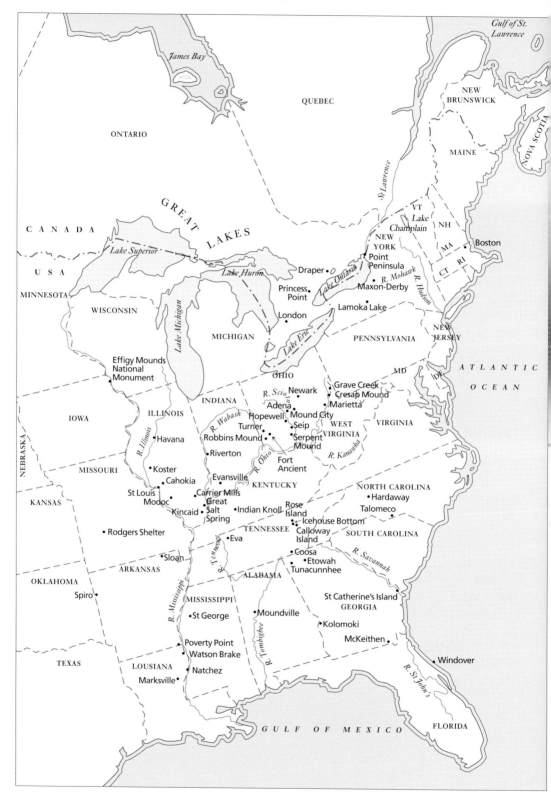

79 Map showing sites in Chapters 8, 11, and 12.

7 · The Eastern Woodlands:
Nuts, Native Plants, and Earthworks

Rising populations and foraging territories that were increasingly confined by neighbors and the carrying capacity of the environment: Eastern Woodlands society, extending from the Atlantic Ocean to the Mississippi River and from the Great Lakes to the Gulf of Mexico, changed in response to a more circumscribed world after 4000 BC. What were the social and technological innovations that defined this slowly changing situation? With larger, more permanent base camps and increasingly complex social and political relationships came a new concern with defining one's relationships with the natural and supernatural realms. These relationships often revolved around the ancestors – those who had gone before. A new emphasis on commemorating the dead and on earthworks and burial mounds appeared during the Late Archaic (see chronological table on p. 202).

The densest Late Archaic populations thrived in areas like river valley bottoms where fish, plant foods, and game provided a reliable diet for most of the year. Subterranean storage pits full of nuts created larger food surpluses and allowed more people to live at one location year-round. Baskets, pits, and perhaps special storage bins formed a new technology of storage, enhanced by another innovation: waterproof clay vessels that first appeared along the South Carolina coastal plain by 2500 BC.

A container revolution

Pottery-making spread widely, apparently hand-in-hand with an extensive trade in steatite for weights, large containers, and ornaments throughout the Southeast. Thick-walled pottery came into use in some parts of the Southeast as early as about 2000 BC, and became widespread after 500 BC from the Mississippi to New England, and from the Ohio to the St. Lawrence Valley. Many Early Woodland pots were like crude flowerpots, heavy containers that were difficult to carry around. In time, much better-made ceramics developed into a highly effective way of storing not only grain and other foods, but also water and valuables. Clay pots and bowls could also hold boiling water, enabling people to process foods like acorns and seeds much more readily than they could with fire-heated stones and other simple devices.

Archaeologist Bruce Smith has aptly described the introduction of pottery, and a widespread trade in gourds, as a "container revolution" in the Eastern Woodlands. Pots must have played an important part in the more intensive exploitation of wild seeds, especially in the midcontinent from Middle Woodland times onward. For instance, experiments have shown that pottery allows more efficient processing of hickory nuts, and probably other species. Crushing and boiling increases the amount of nutmeats processed in one hour at least tenfold, in large part by separating nutritious oil from inedible nutshell. The greater demand for waterproof containers may be associated with highly efficient seed collecting and the deliberate manipulation of native plants, followed by the domestication of several indigenous plant species.

Cultivating native plants   after *c.* 2000 BC

Early hunter-gatherers probably overcame food shortages by covering large distances, by possessing knowledge of potential food sources over wide areas. But what happens if population growth or social conflict restrict people's ability to feed themselves by expanding their territories in times of need? They could forage for less-preferred food plants, increase the energy expended collecting food and processing it, and exploit alternative food sources like, say, acorns, that required a great deal more effort to prepare – or they could cultivate certain native annuals that flourished in disturbed habitats maintained by deliberate human intervention.

After 2000 BC, some groups in the Eastern Woodlands deliberately cleared small plots where they could cultivate familiar wild plants, including native squash, on a small scale. To what extent stress actually played a role in spurring such cultivation is unknown. In many places, people created and sustained environments that transported seeds of a wide variety of plants from their natural floodplain and upland niches into disturbed habitats. These were casual activities, which linked humans, plants, and animals in opportunistic adaptations to changes in the structure and composition of those ecosystems. New variables such as human base camps produced significant changes in floodplain ecosystems, allowing some plants to occupy, and evolve within, newly disturbed habitats. A number of ongoing selective pressures may have increased seed production in sumpweed, gourds, and squash, and other native plants, by reducing dormancy periods and enhancing the ability of species to occupy disturbed ground. All humans would have done to achieve this was to sustain a disturbed habitat and to tolerate species with economic value.

Eventually people categorized some plants as useful, others as weeds. All botanical knowledge passed from father to son, mother to daughter, in a form of verbal plant dictionary and pharmacopeia refined and memorized by each generation. A family may have casually watered and weeded as time and opportunity permitted, discouraging weeds in favor of economically useful plants, thereby managing natural stands of the latter. This simple process of encouraging, intervening, and deliberately planting harvested seeds, even on a small scale, marked the beginnings of deliberate cultivation. At this point, automatic selection within the affected plant population begins, with minimal effort by human beings. Human land clearance and genetic changes in plants may have been a major factor in the emergence of horticulture in eastern North America independently of elsewhere – making the region one of the few independent areas of plant domestication in the world.

Some Eastern Woodlands groups relied heavily on a variety of native plants for as much as 1,000 years before they turned to non-indigenous maize. In fact, a few of these native plants show signs of domestication, such as larger seed size, as much as 2,000 years before they became major components of diets. Gourds were among the earliest domesticates. The bottle gourd (*Lagenaria siceraria*) made excellent containers. This African native appears to have floated across the Atlantic to the Caribbean, then spread northward, perhaps as a weed following human populations. But when gourds were domesticated and arrived in the north is unknown – it was perhaps as early as 5000 BC. Thinner-walled, North American forms provided edible seeds, not containers.

The wild sunflower (*Helianthus annuus*) was widespread in the west, became a favorite food source valued for its nutritious oil, and was apparently domesticated as early as 2250 BC. Sumpweed or marsh elder (*Iva annua*) was a common domesticate, a lake- and river-side oily-seeded plant that flourished in river valley bottoms. Wild sumpweed was commonplace in Koster 6 in the Illinois Valley by 3800 BC; domestication was well under way by 2000 BC. Goosefoot (*Chenopodium berlandieri*) with its small, starchy seeds, knotweed, maygrass, and perhaps Jerusalem artichokes (*Helianthus tuberosus*) were also heavily used by about the same time. Lastly, tobacco (*Nicotiana* sp.) seeds arrived from Mexico at an unknown

80

80 Native plants. (Left) Bottle gourd *Lagenaria siceraria* with immature fruit. (Center) Goosefoot, *Chenopodium berlandieri*. (Right) Knotweed, *Polygonum erectum*.

date and became widely cultivated throughout the east in later times. Many clay-stone pipes occur in eastern sites, but they do not necessarily document tobacco smoking. People smoked kinnikinnick (an Algonquian word for a variety of plant substances including bearberry leaves) and other plants as well.

Until about AD 800, agriculture was a way of producing valuable supplemental foods, of amplifying food supplies by enhancing wild plant yields, of helping feed locally dense hunter-gatherer populations. It was only with the introduction of maize during the first millennium AD that agriculture became the dietary staple of most eastern societies.

Late Archaic societies   after 4000 BC

Deciphering the multitude of later Archaic societies that developed in North America after about 4000 BC and over at least 3,000 years challenges even experts. At least five major groupings are known, with numerous local variations (see box). In general, they reflect different environmental settings. Sparse descendants of Paleoindian groups moved into the deglaciated lands north of the Great Lakes; maritime adaptations flourished along northeastern coasts and into the St. Lawrence Valley. Forest environments

---

Collecting and studying plant remains

Studying ancient crops and plant foods is among the most challenging tasks for fieldworkers, unless exceptionally dry or wet preservation conditions allow collection of large samples, which are the only reliable way of assessing the importance of plant foods in ancient diets. Some useful approaches:

• Carbonized and unburnt seeds occasionally survive in hearths and middens, while large samples have been recovered from dry caves in the Great Basin and Southwest.

• Human feces, again preserved in dry caves, can be a mine of information about ancient diets, not only about seeds, but also small animals, even insects.

• Flotation techniques, which pass earth or occupation residue through water or chemicals, can produce large collections of plant remains – the

vegetal remains float and settle on very fine screens; the residue sinks to the bottom of the container. Some excavators use quite elaborate devices for capturing large samples. No fewer than 36,000 hickory fragments came from the Apple Creek site in the lower Illinois Valley alone.

• Minute pollens from wild grasses, cereal crops, and even cultivation weeds can provide an impression of human impacts on the surrounding environment, especially of forest clearance.

• Plant phytoliths, minute particles of silica from plant cells, are produced from hydrated silica dissolved in groundwater absorbed through a plant's roots and carried through its vascular system. They are studied like pollens and have been valuable for tracing the origins of maize.

supported relatively small populations from the Great Lakes to New England, and as far south as the Carolinas. The densest Late Archaic societies thrived in the deciduous forests and river floodplains of the Midwest and into the Southeast, as well as on the South Atlantic and Gulf coasts, where more complex societies were to develop in coming centuries.

Koster, already described in Chapter 2, became an even more permanent settlement. Horizon 6, dating to between 3900 and 2800 BC, was now a year-round, 5-acre (2-ha) settlement of temporary houses large enough for nuclear families. The people exploited nearby shallow backwater lakes and swamps. They speared and netted vast numbers of shallow-water fish that could be eaten fresh or dried or smoked for winter, and collected mollusks by the thousand. Large catches of fish came from poisoning the water with the chemicals in powdered hickory nut husks, or by driving fish into oxygen-starved pools, to be scooped up with baskets. One Illinois fisheries biologist has estimated that the people of Koster 6 could have taken between 300 and 600 lb (135 and 270 kg) of fish flesh per acre (0.4 ha) every year from backwater lakes that once covered huge areas, this apart from rich mollusk beds.

Like their predecessors, the Koster 6 people relied on the fall hickory and acorn harvests, as well as black walnuts, pecans, and hazelnuts. But they now exploited many more seed plants, including sumpweed, grinding the seeds with stone pestles and mortars. They also exploited another a seasonal food: waterfowl that paused to feed and rest on the shallow lakes of the Illinois Valley during spring and fall migrations. The Illinois is on the Mississippi flyway, the migration route used by millions of waterfowl flying to and from their Canadian breeding grounds each year. The Koster people could take hundreds of ducks, geese, and other migrants with bows, and by throwing light, weighted nets over sleeping birds. Smoked and dried waterfowl could sustain families during the lean months – the flesh is delicious.

Here and elsewhere, Late Archaic groups exploited a far wider range of 85 animal, aquatic, and plant foods, probably because they needed larger food surpluses to feed more people in much more crowded landscapes. To the east, on the Green River, a tributary of the Ohio River, between about 3000 and 2000 BC, large, stable Indian communities flourished on the food-rich floodplain. They remained at, or near, the same locations for centuries, accumulating huge shell middens. The most famous, Indian Knoll in Kentucky, yielded over 1,000 burials. Indian Knoll and other large Green River sites lie in highly favored locations. The richness of the local environment was remarkable, especially in its variety of plant foods, with easily stored hickory nuts a clear favorite.

Judging from the Indian Knoll graves, the Green River people lived in a fairly egalitarian society, where everyone owned much the same material possessions. At least seventy male graves contained handles, weights, and atlatl hooks, still lying in place with the wooden shaft decayed away. Women owned nutcracking stones. Some men and women carried turtle-shell rattles, bone flutes, and shamans' bones with them at death.

Late Archaic variants in the Eastern Woodlands

Shield Archaic (*c.* 6000 BC to modern times)

Shield Archaic groups settled over an enormous area from the north shores of the Great Lakes to the headwaters of rivers flowing into James and Hudson bays, and eastward into Quebec and the Maritimes. Most of their diet came from caribou and fish. The Shield Archaic thrived for centuries with little change, its people the ancestors of the Algonquian-speaking hunters of the Canadian Shield at European contact.

Maritime Archaic (*c.* 6000 to *c.* 1000 BC)

Caribou and sea mammal hunters, also fishers, were part of a maritime adaptation along the coasts and rivers of New Brunswick and Maine, also through the Maritimes. Further south, maritime groups enjoyed sophisticated coastal adaptations, based not only on the exploitation of inshore fish and harbor seal hunting, but also on offshore cod and swordfish fishing.

Lake Forest Archaic (*c.* 3200 to *c.* 1000 BC)

This predominantly inland adaptation flourished in pine and hardwood forests from the Great Lakes into New York State and the St. Lawrence Valley. Population densities were generally low and subsistence based on game, plants, and aquatic foods. Lake Forest groups living close to copper outcrops in the Lake Superior

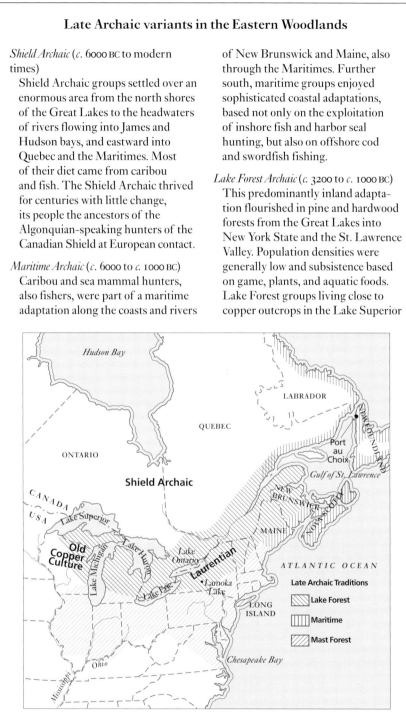

81 Map of Late Archaic traditions of the northeast. The boundaries distinctions between these traditions are still ill-defined.

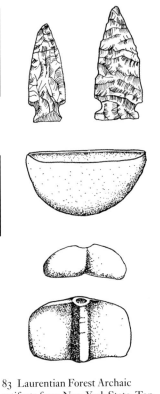

82 Artifacts from Port aux Choix, Newfoundland. (Above) Bone comb in the shape of a waterbird. (Below) Bayonetlike dagger.

Basin traded this prized metal over wide areas through increasingly complex trading networks.

Mast Forest Archaic (*c*. 2700 to 1200 BC)
The Mast Forest Archaic (named after the mast layer in oak forests) extends from the Merrimack drainage of southern New England through coastal drainages as far south as North Carolina and west across Ohio River tributaries to the southern shores of Lake Erie and into southern Michigan. Population densities were generally low, except in favored areas such as Lake Lamoka in New York State.

83 Laurentian Forest Archaic artifacts from New York State. Top to bottom: two side-notched Otter Creek points, a groundstone *ulu*, and two perforated bannerstones. Length of longest point *c*. 4.9 in (12.5 cm).

Central Riverine Archaic
(*c*. 4000 to 1000 BC)
The Central Riverine Archaic flourished in or near the Mississippi, Ohio, Cumberland, and Tennessee valleys. Rich deciduous forests and bountiful floodplains provided a superabundance of aquatic, animal, and plant foods – also unlimited potential for human interaction, an important factor in fostering more complex societies. Year-round settlements became more common in such areas.

84 Spearheads hammered from Lake Superior copper.

Five Indian Knoll burials included metal ornaments of Lake Superior copper. Conches and shell ornaments such as beads and gorgets, also cups, accompanied forty-two skeletons. Shells were from the *marginella* and *olivella* species, found in the Gulf of Mexico and the southern Atlantic seaboard hundreds of miles away. Both adult men and women owned valuable copper and conch objects, as did infants and children. Some 18,378 disk-shell beads of imported shell came from 143 graves. The distribution of shell beads is such that it appears certain people held in high esteem for their special abilities maintained broad contacts with other individuals, including members of neighboring groups. These beads ended up being interred with them or members of their family, including children.

Exchange and interaction

By 2000 BC, Eastern Woodlands societies lived under more closed social conditions, with more rigidly defined territories. Much greater regional variation in artifacts and stylistic traditions reflects this greater degree of closure. Now relationships with neighbors assumed greater importance. Such relationships would take many forms: informal bartering of fine-grained rocks, occasional communal hunts and ceremonies, more formal gift exchanges, and ever-shifting political and social alliances based on obligations of kin and reciprocity between individuals. As time went on, the manipulation of social alliances, and the barter and exchange that went with them, led to enhanced concerns with prestige and social distinction, and to more complex social orders. Not that social change was rapid, for there was a profound, inherent conservatism reflected not only in artifacts and choice of base camps, but in burial customs, subsistence patterns, and inter-community relationships as well. Few eastern societies of 1000 BC were much larger than a few hundred souls, and even those were still predominantly egalitarian in their social organization.

Long-distance exchange of prized materials such as marine shells and   85
copper appeared for the first time between about 5000 and 4000 BC and esca-
lated gradually over the next 3,000 years. Exotic materials of all kinds passed
from band to band, occasionally over enormous distances – Lake Superior
native copper and hematite, Atlantic and Gulf coast sea shells, cherts, horn-
stones, and other exotic rocks for ornaments and tool-making from all over
the Midwest and east. All these materials passed between individuals and
groups, "down the line" from settlement to settlement, valley to valley,

85 Eastern Woodlands peoples exchanged prized materials over vast distances. Marine shells,
one such material, are seen here in use for a luxury drink at a council meeting of Florida Indians
in this fanciful engraving by Theodore de Bry (1591).

through informal exchange networks that evolved and maintained an essential continuity over many centuries. The Green River burials show that not everyone had the same access to these prestige goods, presumably because some people were more charismatic than others, or had some other widely recognized and essential skill that translated into greater contacts with members of neighboring groups. Some transactions were likely sealed by gifts such as beads.

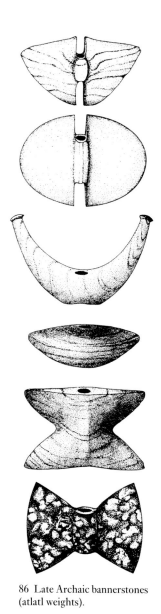

From the Middle Archaic onward, people invested more labor in fashioning socially valued artifacts and ornaments like finely ground bannerstones, delicate slate ornaments and weapons, and steatite gorgets and bowls. These precious objects may have played an important role in alliance building. Some groups living in areas where different trade networks intersected may well have exploited their strategic locations and become middlemen in long-distance trade. It is possible, for example, that the Green River people exploited the opportunities of both the copper trade from the northwest and the shell exchange from the south and southeast.

Within this context of regular social gatherings and exchanges, a modest degree of social differentiation based on reciprocity may have emerged in Late Archaic society. This may have been nothing more than a degree of ranking between younger and older members of society, or perhaps the emergence of one kin group as the "ranking" lineage, the one from whom social and ritual leaders traditionally came. Judging from increasingly elaborate mortuary customs, both kin-based and individual social ranking took place within a context of increasing ritual elaboration, in which exotic objects and fine ornaments worn by ceremonial office holders played a major part. Cemeteries themselves assumed a special significance, often placed on elevated ground, sometimes beneath low, artificial mounds.

How did social differentiation develop? One possible scenario might go something like this: some individuals, perhaps respected shamans or elders, leaders of a particular lineage, might assume roles as ritual and social mediators in newly sedentary societies. They were the people who arbitrated disputes and controlled relations with neighboring, and sometimes perhaps competing, groups. It was they who gave gifts to influential neighbors and participated in formal gift exchanges, who became points of contact with people, including other kin leaders, living near and far. It was they, too, who were responsible for redistributing food, essential raw materials, and luxury goods through the community. Some of these people were better at trading, at dealing with

86 Late Archaic bannerstones (atlatl weights).

allies and enemies, at attracting the loyalty of kinspeople and followers. They had the quality of being able to persuade people to work for them, hunting, fishing, and gathering, perhaps digging out chert and blocking it into preforms. Social and ritual arbitrators, skilled diplomats and acquisitors, these individuals became prominent in the ever more complex human societies of the Eastern Woodlands after 1000 BC.

Cemeteries and burial mounds   before and after 1500 BC

As ancestors became more important in ritual life, so mortuary rites assumed increasing complexity and importance during the Late Archaic, when the first small burial mounds came into use. Many communities had buried their dead in low, natural ridges overlooking river valleys and at other strategic locations for generations. Late Archaic groups living between southern Ontario and Indiana around 1500 to 1000 BC interred the departed in the summits of low hills of glacial gravel. From using such ridges and hills, it was but a short step to erect small artificial mounds in strategic places, which served the same symbolic purposes – perhaps to mark territory and commemorate kin affiliations.

During these centuries, hunting, foraging, and cultivation were family activities, but exchanges of goods and commodities between neighbors involved more complex relationships. Such exchanges may have helped foster elaborate communal burial cults involving the interment of kin group members and perhaps the commemoration of lineages and ancestors. These cults sometimes involved constructing burial mounds and earthworks. Such tasks required communal labor to dig and pile up basketfuls of earth, perhaps gatherings of close kin or several neighboring communities. We can imagine a man and woman lying in a fresh graves on the ridge top overlooking the valley. Their resting place looks out over the river and the woodland that presses upon its banks. Burial rituals are complete, but people from several nearby settlements are still hard at work. They've already scraped away the topsoil around the graves, piling stones from clearings among the trees to form the nucleus of a low mound. Meanwhile, men and women gather loose soil into baskets, then dump the loads onto what is soon a growing oval tumulus. A few dozen fellow kin work together for several days, hefting baskets, filling in hollows, smoothing out the surface. They leave a low burial mound behind them, a sacred place that is soon overgrown and virtually indistinguishable from a natural ridge, symbolic of the return of ancestors to the supernatural realm.

The earthworks became ever more elaborate. Middle and Late Archaic people constructed some mound complexes of impressive size, especially in the Lower Mississippi Valley and along the Gulf Coast. One of the earliest is Watson Brake, Louisiana, eleven mounds connected to a low ridge forming an oval about 920 ft (280 m) in diameter. Mound construction began here as

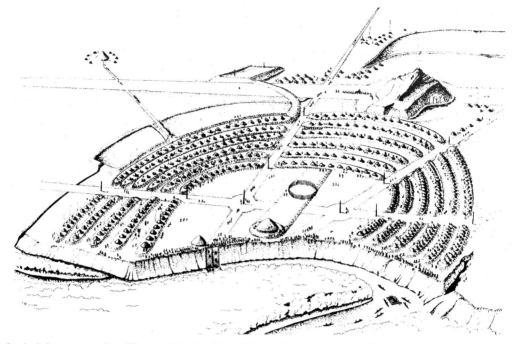

87 Artist's reconstruction of Poverty Point, Louisiana. The earthworks cover 1 sq. mile.

early as 3400 BC, the people exploiting the surrounding resource-rich swamps near the Ouachita River.

Poverty Point   *c.* 2200 to 700 BC

After 2200 BC, more than 100 Late Archaic sites in the Lower Mississippi Valley and adjacent Gulf Coast form ten discrete clusters within natural geographical boundaries, each apparently grouped around a regional center that belongs within what is known as the Poverty Point culture, which flourished for some 1,500 years. Poverty Point itself, occupied between about 1000 and 700 BC, lies on the Macon Ridge in the Mississippi floodplain, near the confluences of six rivers. This was a strategic point for trading up and downstream, also for receiving exotic materials, not only along the Mississippi, but the Arkansas, Red, Ohio, and Tennessee rivers as well.

88

Poverty Point's great horseshoe earthworks and several mounds are a remarkable contrast to the humble base camps typical of the Eastern Woodlands at the time. Six concentric semi-circular, but not entirely symmetrical, earthen ridges divided into segments average about 80 ft (25 m) wide and 10 ft (3 m) high. They are set about 130 ft (40 m) apart, each capped with midden deposits in places over 3 ft (1 m) deep. Perhaps they elevated houses above the surrounding, low-lying terrain. To the west lies a huge artificial mound more than 65 ft (20 m) high and 660 ft (200 m) long. Poverty

87

Point took more than 1,235,000 cu. ft (35,000 cu. m) of basket-hefted soil to complete, an organized building effort the like of which would not be undertaken again in North America for another millennium. One authority has calculated that 1,350 adults laboring seventy days a year would have taken three years to complete the earthworks.

Why build such complex earthworks? How many people lived there, or was Poverty Point a place where hundreds of visitors congregated for major ceremonies, perhaps on important occasions such as the solstices? A person standing on this mound can sight the vernal and autumnal equinoxes directly across the center of the earthworks to the east. This is the point where the sun rises on the first days of spring and fall, but whether this had ritual significance to the inhabitants is a mystery. It could have been a measure of the passing seasons.

For a short period, the Poverty Point site and nearby lesser centers were the nexus of a vast exchange network that handled enormous quantities of exotic rocks and minerals such as galena from more than ten sources in the Midwest and Southeast, some of them from as far as 620 miles

88 Aerial photograph of Poverty Point looking toward the northeast.

(1000 km) away. But this brief flowering endured little more than two to three centuries before the exchange system collapsed.

Poverty Point people enjoyed the same general adaptation as other Late Archaic riverine societies, collecting plants and fishing in nearby oxbow lakes, as well as cultivating native species such as sunflowers, bottle gourds, and squashes. The major centers lie near natural escarpments, close to floodplain swamps, oxbow lakes, and upland hunting grounds. However, many questions about Poverty Point remain unanswered. Did people from throughout Poverty Point territory contribute labor to the great earthworks, or were they merely the work of the actual inhabitants? What were the social and political relationships within the Poverty Point culture? Who were the leaders who organized the communal efforts needed to build earthworks, organize trade, and handle the local exchange of goods throughout the Poverty Point area? How did they secure the loyalties of the people who erected and used the great earthworks? At present, Poverty Point stands as a prophetic symbol of cultural developments that were to emerge in later centuries.

Considerable variability in projectile-point styles in northern parts of the Eastern Woodlands after 1000 BC may reflect a trend toward better-defined local territories, and toward more formal exchange mechanisms that structured the bartering of essentials and prestigious luxuries from area to area in a web of reciprocal obligations and formal gift-giving that connected powerful kin leaders and other prominent individuals. Perhaps inevitably, these interactions became reflected in elaborate commemorations of revered ancestors.

Part II

Apogee

Beyond the sky lies another world,
a world of everlasting life,
and this is where people go
when they have used up the days
allotted to them on the earth.

And thus we understand:
whoever follows the way of our creator
will remain in happiness
in that world forever.

From a Cayuga Iroquois Thanksgiving Address
Swann, Brian (ed.), *Coming to Light*
(New York, 1994, p. 487).

8 · The Far North: Norton, Dorset, and Thule

Most people associate the Far North with sophisticated maritime hunting societies, a stereotype that is only partially correct. The great elaboration of maritime adaptations and specialized hunting and fishing technologies took place over the past 3,000 years, but many northern societies still relied heavily on caribou and other game, also summer plant foods. What caused this gradual elaboration, this concentration on sea mammals and whales? The answers are still being deciphered, but revolve at least in part both around contacts between different groups in Alaska and Siberia and on changing climate conditions.

Between 1500 and 1000 BC, the long-lived Arctic Small Tool tradition gradually disappeared along the shores of the Bering Strait. No one knows quite what happened, for few sites in the region date to this time period, but, toward the end of these five centuries, contacts between the Siberian and Alaskan sides intensified, ushering in a new chapter in far northern history (see chronological table on p. 54 and map on p. 56).

The Norton tradition   *c.* 1000 BC to AD 800

PL. II,
PL. III
The Norton tradition, named after an Alaskan sound, is a poorly defined cultural tradition that was probably a network of different groups linked by constant interactions and exchanges. Norton appeared in the Chukchi and Bering Sea region during the first millennium BC, its origins in the Arctic Small Tool tradition and other societies, probably on the Siberian side. It developed at a time of somewhat warmer Arctic temperatures, sporadic long-distance trading, and considerable cultural diversity. Then temperatures cooled in around 700 BC, a cold cycle that endured for about five centuries; Norton people moved south of the Bering Strait. By the time of Christ they had colonized the base of the Alaska Peninsula and were exploiting the rich waters of the northern Pacific from Takli Island and other locations, overwhelming the indigenous Kodiak tradition there (see box pp. 144–45).

Norton groups settled near fish-rich Arctic Ocean river estuaries, and, in the south, by major salmon streams. These people were consummate

open-water sea-mammal hunters. Part of their success came from toggle-   PL. IV
headed harpoons, whose heads detached in their prey. The hunters used
such harpoons from kayaks and other small craft, relying on the float and   89
detachable head to track their prey, even animals as large as whales.

Unlike their predecessors, many Norton groups occupied more-or-less
permanent settlements, marked by great concentrations of substantial,
year-round dwellings. The Safety Sound site near Cape Nome has yielded
almost 400 house depressions, Unalakleet on Norton Sound itself almost
200. Not all the houses were occupied at once, of course, but they reflect
dense, long-term occupation. At both these locations, people lived in square
dwellings excavated about 20 in. (50 cm) into the ground, with short,
sloping entryways, central hearths, and pole-and-sod roofs. During the
summer months, many groups used temporary hunting and fishing camps.

The Thule tradition in the west   *c.* 700 BC to modern times

In about 700 BC, the Norton inhabitants of St. Lawrence Island and coastal
Chukotka developed an even more specialized culture, based entirely on the
ocean. Here, local narrows determined the direction of summer sea-
mammal migrations and natural current upwellings maintained areas of
open water even in midwinter. The new sea-mammal hunting equipment
with its efficient toggling harpoons and other ingenious devices was to
revolutionize coastal life throughout the Arctic. This technology was the

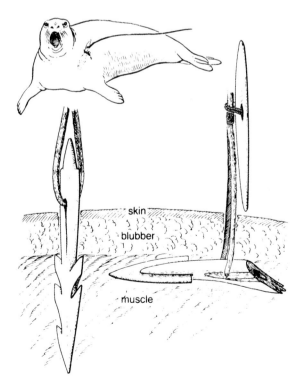

89 Harpoon technology.
The non-toggling or
"male" harpoon point
holds an animal in its barbs
(left). The toggling harpoon,
a more complex design,
was developed later for
sea-mammal hunting. The
head toggles beneath the
skin and blubber where it
cannot be dislodged by ice,
and is effective with heavier
prey like walrus and whales.

Norton tradition stages

The Norton tradition is still ill-defined, but three stages are commonly identified:

Choris stage (*c.* 1000 to 500 BC) Coastal sites north of the Bering Strait, found on the Seward Peninsula and perhaps in the Brooks Range. Characterized by fiber-tempered pottery with linear stamping. Mostly isolated communities, so the relationship with Norton is poorly defined.

Norton stage (*c.* 500 BC to AD 800) Probably derived from Choris and subsumes several local cultures in the Bering Strait area and Alaska Peninsula. Terrestrial and sea-mammal hunters, also fishers. More refined pottery, slate artifacts, and stone seal-oil lamps.

90 Ipiutak stage engraved ivory "mask" found in a burial at Point Hope, probably once with a wooden backing.

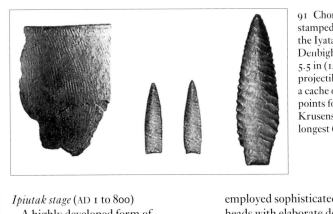

91 Choris stage linear-stamped potsherd from the Iyatayet site, Cape Denbigh, Alaska, height 5.5 in (14 cm); Choris projectile points, from a cache of about 60 points found at Cape Krusenstern, length of longest 6.9 in (17.5 cm).

Ipiutak stage (AD 1 to 800)
A highly developed form of Norton culture centered on the Cape Krusenstern and Point Hope areas of the Chukchi Sea, also the Brooks Range. Summer and winter sea-mammal hunting employed sophisticated harpoon heads with elaborate decoration. The Ipiutak art tradition was lavished on ivory artifacts – animal carvings, human figures, some of which recall Siberian motifs.

foundation of the Thule tradition (pronounced the Danish way – Tuleh), in which whaling played an important role.

Old Bering Sea stage   *c.* 200 BC to AD 800
The earliest Thule tradition sites, subsumed under the Old Bering Sea stage, come from St. Lawrence and Okvik islands, also from the Chukotka coast of the Bering Strait. Both kayaks and *umiaks* (large skin boats) appear in archaeological sites for the first time, as do more durable polished-slate points and knives, which replace many of the flaked stone artifacts of earlier times (all these artifacts were in fact in use much earlier). Antler, bone, and ivory provided implements of all kinds, including harpoon parts, snow goggles, and needles. Iron objects first appear, also delicate carvings made with iron tools. Whale hunting generated enormous food surpluses, but seal oil was probably the mainstay of the Strait economy.

At Uelen and Ekven on the Siberian shore, Russian investigators have uncovered richly decorated Old Bering Sea graves lined with whalebone and sometimes with wooden floors, and furnished with fine ivory artifacts, including harpoon parts and mattocks. Conceivably, these were the sepulchers of important individuals, perhaps whaleboat captains, men of prestige who were owners of whale-hunting *umiaks*. Such social distinctions are known to have been important in later centuries. These sepulchers may be the first signs of social differentiation in the north.

Punuk and Birnirk stages   *c.* AD 500 to 1400 and later

92   Harpoon styles and art motifs distinguish the Punuk stage, a development of Old Bering Sea on the major Strait islands and along the shores of much of the Chukchi Peninsula. Large Punuk communities lived in semi-subterranean, square, or rectangular dwellings with wooden floors, sleeping platforms along the walls, and driftwood or whale-jaw sides, the sod roofs held up with whalebone rafters.

The Birnirk variant on the Old Bering Sea tradition developed between AD 500 and 600, along the shores of the Chukchi Sea from Cape Nome northward, also on the Siberian coast west from East Cape to at least as far as the mouth of the Kolyma River. Birnirk people were not artists. They did, however, use sleds, of the same basic designs as were later hauled by dog teams. Some Birnirk sites, like those near Barrow and Point Hope, are situated close to whale-rich locales.

Alaskan archaeologist Owen Mason believes that the intensification of long-distance trade, warfare, and whaling in the Bering Strait region between AD 600 and 1000 led to intense competition between Old Bering Sea and Birnirk groups, also with the Ipiutak people on the Alaskan shore. The main center of political power lay at East Cape in Siberia, at the twin sites of Uelen and Ekven. Ekven was contemporary with chiefdoms on St. Lawrence Island and at Point Hope on the Alaskan side. Mason argues that the East Cape people were the powerbrokers in the region, while Ipiutak, ruled by powerful shamans, with its elaborate art tradition and burials, was a place where spiritual capital was more highly valued. But the similarities in artifacts to East Cape sites may hint at some form of political alliance with the western side of the Strait. There were connections with caribou-hunting groups in the Siberian and Alaskan interiors as well.

Old Bering Sea held sway over most of the southern Bering Strait coast on the Siberian side, while Ipiutak's shamans controlled much of the Alaskan shore. Mason is probably right when he describes the reality as "a welter of small villages with divided and shifting loyalties, multiple

92 The evolution of Punuk art, as exemplified by winged objects (harpoon butts) from St. Lawrence Island. (Left) Early Punuk stage winged object in "butterfly" shape, width 6.3 in (16 cm). (Center) Middle Punuk stage trident-like winged object, width 3.9 in (10 cm). (Right) Late Punuk winged object with hardly any wings, resembling a coronet, width 2.75 in (7 cm).

origins, and limited spans of occupation." There was some fighting, but the threat of war may have been more prevalent than war itself. Mason argues for still-undocumented links with climatic conditions as well. The success of the Bering Strait/Chukchi Sea polities depended on the persistence of southerly wind conditions that prevailed during the stormy months of fall. Such conditions may have endured through the late first and early second millennium AD, during the Medieval Warm Period.

Thule artifacts occur at Cape Denbigh on Norton Sound by AD 900, and in the Naknek Drainage of the Alaska Peninsula by AD 1100. This spread was not necessarily a population movement, but more likely a diffusion of new artifact styles, more efficient house designs, and sophisticated hunting methods to southern coastlines and river estuaries, much of it connected with seasonal sea-mammal migrations. Throughout the Bering Strait and along the Alaskan coast from Barrow to the Alaska Peninsula, and far offshore to the islands and Siberian coast, communities of Thule sea-mammal hunters were in constant, and regular, contact for many centuries. The Eskimo peoples of what is now Alaska, who came into contact with Europeans during the eighteenth century, all formed part of this powerful and long-lived cultural tradition.

The Dorset tradition of the eastern Arctic
200 BC to AD 1200 or later

Far east of the Bering Strait, the Pre-Dorset culture of the eastern Arctic developed into the Dorset tradition in about 200 BC, at a time when climatic conditions became colder after some centuries of warmer temperatures. Why the transition occurred remains a mystery. Was it the result of an Arctic Small Tool population decline in the eastern Arctic about 3,000 years ago, followed by an expansion of Dorset peoples? Or did dwindling caribou herds in Quebec cause major adjustments in both population distribution and hunting methods? Perhaps the people developed new ice-hunting techniques that were successful in intensely cold winters, leading to the emergence of the Dorset tradition.

93, 94

The Dorset culture is defined, above all, by a remarkable art tradition with powerful magical and symbolic undertones that stand in sharp contrast to its simple technology (see box p. 148). This was a utilitarian society that dwelt in rectangular, semi-subterranean buildings, used triangular projectile points for sealing, and manufactured prosaic ground-slate tools. Dorset people possessed no dog sleds, so their land-travel range was restricted to the limits of human pulling and walking ability. They had no bows and arrows or throwing sticks, just simple lances and harpoons. The Dorset people had only small oil lamps and far-from-sophisticated winter houses. In some ways they were even less prepared for arctic conditions than their predecessors, yet they thrived for centuries.

Dorset art

Dorset is famous for its art, especially for its life-like portraits of what were once living individuals. Dorset carvers worked with antler, bone, ivory, soapstone, and wood to make tiny figures, depicting almost every arctic animal. More than half their carvings were of human beings or polar bears, sometimes highly naturalistic, sometimes merely stylistic impressions. The attention to detail is astonishing – complete polar-bear skulls, tiny seals modeled complete with whiskers and miniature eyes. Unlike later Thule and Inuit artists, Dorset carvers and engravers usually ignored utilitarian objects and created work that had a strong ideological undertone. Masks, figurines, and plaques probably played important roles in funeral rites, and in shamanistic and magical ceremonies.

Human beings sometimes appear in distinctive portraits, in carvings that display rectangular or round eyes, outward facing nostrils, and a pug nose. One portrait may represent a living person, perhaps a famous shaman, who suffered from an infantile skull condition that made him stand out from his fellow priests. The Late Dorset site at Button Point on Bylot Island yielded wooden masks, one with simulated tattooing and at one time pegged-in hair and a mustache. There are smaller masks, too, no more than 2.8 inches (6 cm) long, many with X incisions across the

93 Dorset wooden doll from Button Point, Bylot Island.

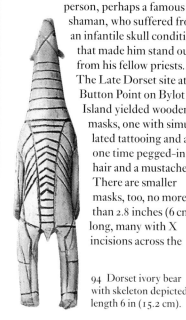

94 Dorset ivory bear with skeleton depicted, length 6 in (15.2 cm).

face, even dolls with detachable arms and legs. Small animal amulets to provide good fortune during the chase are common, often suspended on thongs or sewn to clothing. The carvers also made small ivory teeth plaques, with ridges on the back, that may have been worn over the mouth during shamanistic rituals.

The Dorset art tradition was a unique efflorescence over an enormous area of the eastern Arctic, a reflection of basic ideologies that were to survive for many centuries. Without question, some of the fundamental spiritual beliefs of modern Inuit groups have their roots in the complex spiritual life of the Dorset people.

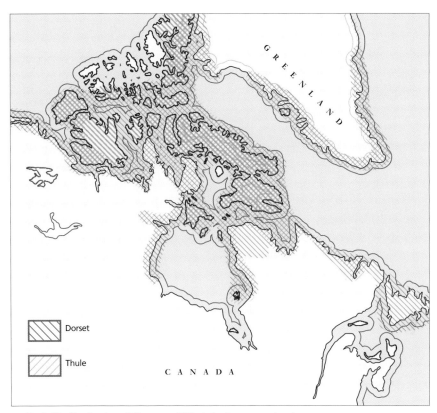

95 Probable distribution of Dorset and Thule in the eastern Arctic.

Like all eastern Arctic groups, the Dorset people were predominantly hunters, although they undoubtedly consumed berries and other plant foods in season. They pursued caribou, musk ox, smaller land mammals, and some nesting birds, perhaps snared with nets on long poles. Seals were an important staple. So were such formidable animals as the walrus, narwhal, and even the occasional beluga whale or polar bear. Dorset hunters usually employed simple thrusting harpoon designs, the heads bound to the fore-shaft so that the shaft slid backward and the head came off attached to a line wedged in a split in the harpoon shaft. This design works much better at close quarters, when the hunter thrusts the head into the animal. Such weapons were probably effective for ice hunting. The staple fish was the arctic char, a species that is easily filleted and speared during seasonal runs. We can imagine fishers standing on rocks by a fast-moving stream, thrusting light spears tipped with delicate ivory barbed heads at the fast-running fish crowding upstream along the rocky bottom. They would haul in fish after wriggling fish, quickly killing them with clubs.

Early Dorset culture may have developed in one core area and then spread rapidly over a much wider region. The most logical origin is the northern Foxe Basin, where earlier Pre-Dorset traditions flourished. There was such

96 *Aleutians striking humpback whales off Akootan Island, Bering Sea*, undated. Henry William Elliot's considerably romanticized painting gives a sense of the hazards of whale hunting from kayaks.

97 *Handlining and clubbing a halibut from kayaks*, 1872. Another painting of kayak hunting by Henry William Elliot.

98 Use of floats enabled hunters to recover sea mammals such as these belugas, line and inflated float still attached. Photographed in 1865.

regular communication with other communities in the general area that cultural change must have been more or less simultaneous over a wide area. The same basic lifeway flourished throughout Dorset times, but with constant adjustments in response to ever-changing cold and warm cycles. About 2,000 years ago, the climate became progressively colder, so parts of the High Arctic and northern Labrador may have been abandoned. By AD 100, people relinquished favorite locations in the Foxe Basin. The populations of Newfoundland and the Labrador coast now increased as people retreated from the north. Many Middle Dorset settlements in these areas were small villages, some of them, like Port aux Choix, Newfoundland, semi-permanent loca- tions where people fished and hunted for most of the year. Port aux Choix was also a base for hunting pupping harp seals in late winter, a place favored earlier by Maritime Archaic groups (see Chapter 6). Up to between thirty and thirty-five people lived at Port aux Choix, using a toolkit that has clear ties to northern Dorset, but with a strongly local flavor.

Around AD 500, temperatures warmed somewhat at the onset of Late Dorset times. The five or six centuries that followed saw a population increase, with an explosion in artistic skills, resulting in the incredible Dorset art tradition. The Late Dorset saw an expansion of relatively standardized Arctic culture not only over the Foxe Basin area and into northern Labrador north of Nain, but also into the High Arctic again.

Many widespread communities participated in a vast cultural network in which shamans may have played a leading role. Some sites, like Button Point on Bylot Island, may have been ceremonial centers. Button Point is rich in carved wooden figures, including life-sized ceremonial masks and wooden dolls of humans and stylized animals. There are fragments of drums, too. "It is easy to imagine nighttime ceremonies where rhythmic chants and drumbeats restored the sacred balance of nature," writes Canadian archaeologist Moreau Maxwell. "In the dimly lit houses, shamans, frighteningly masked, would manipulate little figures for magical protection from the only predators dangerous to humans – the giant polar bear and humans who were not part of the kinship web."

99 Inuit hunters hunting seal at a breathing hole in the ice.

There is also evidence that there were sporadic contacts with Greenland Norse in the form of smelted copper from a twelfth- or thirteenth-century Dorset site on the eastern shore of Hudson Bay and from another on the coast of Ungava Bay. Encounters between Dorset groups and Norse occurred over several centuries over a wide area of Baffin Bay and on Davis Strait coasts from Labrador to the High Arctic. Many of these contacts must have been indirect, but a find of spun arctic hare and domestic Norse goat yarn from Nunguvik in northern Baffin Land may hint at least at some more direct meetings, although the dating of this, and other, sites remains uncertain.

Thule expansion in the eastern Arctic   mid-thirteenth century AD

Some time during the mid-thirteenth century AD, Thule people, perhaps speaking an archaic form of Inupiat language, migrated to the eastern Arctic. Judging from their artifact styles, they came not from whaling communities on the Bering Strait but from somewhere on the western or northwestern Alaskan coast. Groups in this area had a long-standing involvement in the iron ore trade between Siberia and Alaska, probably controlled by people around the Strait. Perhaps rumors of other metal sources filtered westward from groups in the east who were using meteoric iron and had made contact with Norse, prompting an expedition or expeditions across the north. The movement eastward was apparently a rapid one, perhaps taking about half a century, or even much less, with dog sleds making the journey possible in just a few years. This was, in many senses, a commercial venture, a form of mercantile exploration. These were entrepreneurial people, who moved eastward in search of metal and to trade with Europeans.

With their superior hunting technology, more elaborate social organization, and vastly enhanced mobility by sled and boat, Thule groups apparently took over Dorset hunting territories, assimilating the original inhabitants or driving them out to starve in marginal areas. What actually happened? There is no archaeological evidence for sustained contact between Dorset and Thule, even if the newcomers borrowed some artifacts like ivory sled shoes and knives for building snow houses, and took the use of iron and soapstone from Dorset groups. Perhaps the explanation lies in different hunting strategies. The Dorset people tended to hunt prey that was within walking distance of home, concentrating on the more easily taken, most abundant animals. Thule hunters ranged over much larger territories in their boats and with sleds. They exploited a wider range of food resources, were better organized, and had the ability to move in and take over, say, a seal migration route through a narrow defile miles from their base, thereby depriving the local people of the resource at a critical time of year. Nevertheless, deeply conservative Dorset and innovative Thule groups existed alongside one another in the Arctic for two or three centuries.

The Thule migrations took place during the Medieval Warm Period, an era of warmer temperatures throughout the Northern Hemisphere, which lasted from about AD 800 to 1250. This was a time when the southern boundary of Arctic pack ice retreated northward in the Atlantic, allowing Norse seamen to expand to Iceland, onward to Greenland, and as far south as Newfoundland. The warming was probably never sufficient to melt the ice that blocked the central parts of the Arctic archipelago between Amundsen Gulf and Lancaster Sound, a distance of about 600 miles (1,000 km), but some reduction of ice may have allowed bowhead and Greenland whale populations to mingle, distributing abundant populations of these great mammals right across the north. Whales migrate east along the Alaskan coast in spring, and west in fall, keeping to narrow ice leads close to shore. At the same time, reduced ice between the Canadian Arctic islands may have opened up the normal summering grounds of the bowhead whale to open-water hunting. So people could pursue whales for many months, not just for short periods in spring and fall.

96, 97, 100

Thule settlements were smaller (there are only a few as large as twenty-five to thirty-five houses) and more widely separated than those in the far west, for kayak and *umiak* teams from five or six families were powerful hunting combinations. In both east and west, the *umiak* was the stable platform used for harpooning whales, which were consistently in the 26 to 28 ft (8 to 8.5 m) range.

Better whaling conditions may have been another reason for the population movement. Another may have been a search for new sealing grounds, for there are signs of overhunting of ring seals in the Point Barrow region at the time. Perhaps population pressure and warring factions in the west caused some groups to move eastward, bringing their whale hunting expertise with them. Most early Thule sites seem to have ancestry in Birnirk communities along the northern Alaskan coast near Barrow, villages influenced by new whale-hunting techniques and innovative technologies developed by local Punuk people. Later, more people, this time with Punuk and Birnirk artifacts, followed in their footsteps, settling along the southern shores of the Canadian Arctic. Exactly when the migrations took place is also a matter of controversy, but there is universal agreement that they unfolded between AD 1000 and 1300, many authorities favoring the later date.

100 An *umiak* and crew, Cape Prince of Wales, Northwest territories, 1927. These tough skin boats were the work horses of Arctic life and extensively used for sea-mammal and whale hunting.

Classic Thule   ?AD 1250 to 1500

Classic Thule culture is remarkable not only for its hunting skills, but for the extraordinary range of ingenious gadgets that the hunters developed for the chase. The Thule people were ardent technologists, as clever with their low-tech life as we are with computers today. Like Birnirk in the west, however, Thule artistic endeavors were relatively modest, confined in the main to simple engravings on utilitarian artifacts such as combs, often Y motifs and straight lines. Sometimes, the engraver depicted humans and animals, even scenes of the chase. Three-dimensional figures in wood and ivory depict women without arms or legs, often with topknot hairstyles. Tiny ivory carvings of loons and other birds are relatively commonplace, and are perhaps game pieces, or important ideological symbols, links between the people and the supernatural world.

Thule whale hunters concentrated on bowheads, *Balaena mysticetus*,   PL. VII
relatively placid creatures which swim near the surface. Their thick blubber means that the carcass floats even when dead, a major advantage for hunters with skin boats. The average baleen whale from Thule sites weighed between 13,250 and 26,450 lb (6,000 and 12,000 kg). As little as 20,000 lb (9,000 kg) of blubber would have provided heating, lighting, and cooking oil for months. The bones were invaluable for rafters and house walls.

The whalers used slate-tipped toggling harpoons attached to large foreshafts and wooden shafts. Inflated sealskins formed the floats attached to the harpoon line that helped tire the harpooned whale. Judging from contemporary engravings, between four and seven people manned the sealskin and driftwood *umiaks*. The helmsman would approach the whale from the rear as it came up to breathe. The harpooner in the bow would cast at a vital spot, the man behind him throwing out the floats. Several casts and a long fight might ensue, until the dead whale could be towed tail-first to a convenient beach or into shallow water, where butchering could proceed.

While Thule communities also consumed other foods, the sheer mass of whale meat and blubber probably overshadowed other supplies. Outside the whaling zones, the other classic arctic resources formed the diet: caribou, walrus, seals, and fish. Thule hunters with their more efficient technology and transportation took a wider range of prey than their Dorset predecessors, not only musk ox and smaller mammals like fox, but birds, clams, even bird eggs. However, predictable caribou migrations and seal harvests, especially of ring seal, often helped determine where winter settlements were located. The hunters would drive caribou into shallow lakes where waiting men in kayaks would kill the frightened animals. On land, they drove small herds through converging lines of stones piled up to resemble human beings, killing the stampeding beasts with recurved bows and arrows at a range of about 33 ft (10 m). They took birds with multibarbed spears or a small whalebone bolas, or snared them with gorges and hooks embedded in blubber.

101 Classic Thule technology made use of many materials. Clockwise from left, an antler adze handle with polished stone blade; a flensing knife with ground slate blade; an *ulu* with iron blade; a whalebone snow knife, used to cut blocks for snow houses; an ivory engraving tool with small iron point; and a drill bit with groundstone point.

Many Thule groups lived in large semi–subterranean winter houses constructed of stone, sod, and whalebones. Four to six houses holding some twenty to twenty-five people appears to have been a widespread norm, an adaptive size for efficient hunting of available resources in many areas. In summer, Thule groups moved into skin tents, the edges held down by circles of stones, the most ubiquitous archaeological sites in the eastern

101 Arctic today. Sometimes they would move only a short distance, perhaps to get away from the stench of rotting sea-mammal carcasses that had been deep frozen through the winter.

This sophisticated Arctic society maintained at least sporadic contacts between dozens of scattered communities. Exotic materials including copper and iron passed from group to group over enormous distances. Old Bering Sea, Punuk, and Birnirk groups all used iron for knife blades and other tools, most of it from the Amur-Okhotsk Sea region of Siberia. By AD 1000 some Siberian iron was moving across the Bering Strait. Groups in the central and eastern Arctic relied on native copper, also meteoric iron, the latter from a large shower at Cape York in northwest Greenland, used by Dorset peoples as early as the eleventh century. Metal was part of the Thule adaptation to the Canadian Arctic and the trade in this precious commodity was a unique aspect of their culture. It allowed them to reduce large bones, antlers, and wood fragments to finished tools, boat frames, and other artifacts. Perhaps *umialiks*, family heads and owners of whaling boats, controlled, managed, and distributed resources like metal obtained from afar.

Post-Classic Thule   AD 1400 to European contact

By the thirteenth century, Thule sites appear in areas where whales were scarcer. The caribou, seal, and fish bones from these settlements argue for a more gradual settlement of less whale-rich areas, using the familiar subsistence strategies of the west. Thule settlements now occur as far north as northern Greenland, possibly reflecting growing population pressure in the classic areas.

The onset of the Little Ice Age brought cooler conditions after 1400 and very cold temperatures between 1600 and 1850, a time when glaciers advanced on Greenland and Baffin Island. Summer pack ice may have been so heavy that boat work was severely restricted, shortening the seasons for open-water whale hunting. Many Thule sites show that baleen whale hunting declined after AD 1400. By the late sixteenth century, *umiak* and kayak whaling had ceased in the High Arctic and in the central Arctic channels. The people probably turned to fishing, musk-ox hunting, and fox trapping for much of their sustenance. These may have been hard times. Moreau Maxwell excavated an isolated Post-Classic dwelling at Ruggles Outlet, on Lake Hazen in the interior of Ellesmere Island. A hunter took several foxes and a musk ox before he died. His widow buried him under some rocks outside the house. She was left alone and ate three sled dogs, then died on the sleeping platform inside the house. Climatic conditions became so severe that by AD 1600 much of the High Arctic was abandoned.

As early as AD 1000, Norse ships based on Greenland were probably irregular, but familiar, sights to Dorset groups living on the western shores of the Davis Strait. The foreigners traded iron, copper, cloth, and other trade goods for furs, walrus ivory, and gyr-falcons. The sporadic exchanges persisted until about 1480, when the Norse settlements in Greenland were abandoned. Their inhabitants were cattle herders; they used European methods and lacked the hunting expertise of the Inuit, who had adapted to extreme cold over a long period of time. The intensifying cold of the Little Ice Age may have caused the demise of the Norse communities. A century later, English voyager Martin Frobisher arrived in search of the Northwest Passage, the first of occasional contacts with European explorers, interactions which persisted until modern times.

9 · The West Coast:
Not a Garden of Eden

As we have seen, the Pacific Coast was never an ancient Garden of Eden, but an unpredictable world at the mercy of short-term climate change. The west coast's complex history after 1000 BC raises important questions. Why did coastal societies in some locations develop significant complexity and boast of large settlements? Why were such elaborations so volatile? The answers appear to lie in the complex relationships between climate change, food supplies, sea-water temperatures, and that most important of short term climatic events – El Niño (see pp. 165–67).

The Late Period Northwest Coast   *c.* 1000 BC to modern times

By AD 500 the Northwest Coast cultural pattern was well established everywhere, marked by an increasing emphasis on salmon fishing (see chronological table on p. 70 and map on p. 74). Both artifacts and art styles reflect historically known cultures. Along the northern coast, from southeast Alaska to northern and central British Columbia, the Late Period saw the development of large, permanent villages inhabited by people living in sizable houses, in groups of twenty to sixty individuals. At the same time, many settlements became fortified redoubts on bluffs and cliff tops. In Tebenkof Bay, southeast Alaska, congregations of formerly independent villages lay not near the best food resources, but along straight coastlines, at easily defended locations where one could see for long distances. Perhaps the bow and arrow was now a strategic weapon, so that people were forced to live in fortified villages, where they could protect themselves against enemies, living cheek-by-jowl with families from other kin groups. On the basis of his Tebenkof data, archaeologist Herbert Maschner theorizes that from being small, independent kin-group-based hamlets, northern Northwest Coast settlements became large, multi-kin-group villages, circumscribed by the realities of locally dense populations, regular conflict, and the need to redistribute food resources, many of which came from some distance away.

The development of political complexity along the northern Northwest Coast resulted from several closely linked circumstances. First, population density reached a critical level in an environment where food resources were distributed unevenly or within well-defined areas. Such realities caused individual groups to organize their lives around the areas where food was most abundant, and to take advantage of periods when they were most plentiful. Simultaneously, the coastal population rose to the point where groups in competition or conflict could not simply move away to another area with plentiful food supplies. Under such circumstances, social complexity is likely to develop; the natural striving among humans to achieve status and political advantage came into play. A few individuals assumed control over the redistribution of food supplies and over political relationships between neighbors. Politically and socially more complex societies were the result of volatile and rapidly changing conditions.

The southern Northwest Coast, from northern Vancouver Island to north of Cape Mendocino, witnessed a similar trend toward more complex societies, with locally high population densities, heavy reliance on storage, and intense manipulation of the environment. Here, also, local populations rose rapidly after 1000 BC, then fluctuated considerably in the centuries of climatic change after AD 500. As time went on, semi-subterranean dwellings gave way to large, planked houses occupied for several centuries, a clear sign of greater sedentism.

Coastal plank houses (and long houses built of thatch and matting in the interior) now increased in size, housing large domestic groups. The archaeologist Ken Ames believes they reflect societies where domestic tasks such as harvesting salmon runs or catching and drying herring were highly organized and closely supervised, as part of a strategy for intense manipulation of the environment and for creating large stocks of food. This manipulation was locally focused, but had much broader regional implications. We can be certain that large-scale social networks, marked by different art styles, tattooing, and ornaments, connected widely separated parts of the Northwest Coast.

Social complexity did not appear once and for all by about AD 500, then remain constant until European contact. Rather, complexity developed in many forms along the Northwest Coast, probably in different places at various times and, on more than one occasion, manifested by sophisticated division of labor, specialized production, and very intricate patterns of regional exchange.

Links to historic peoples

At European contact in the late eighteenth century, the northern Northwest Coast supported some of the most socially complex hunter-gatherers along the Pacific Coast. At least 43,500 Tlingit, Tsimshian, and Haida lived along this indented coastline of deep inlets and offshore islands, from southeast Alaska to the Queen Charlotte Islands and the Prince Rupert area of the British Columbia mainland. There is abundant evidence for volatile cultural

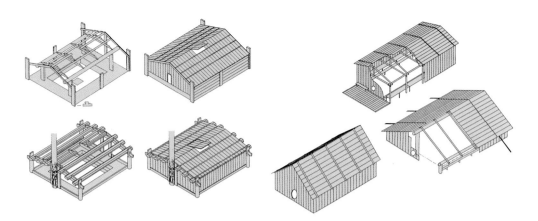

102 House styles typical of the Northwest Coast. Type 1 houses are northern-style houses; Type 2 houses are found on the southern coast.

103 Village at Nootka Sound, Vancouver Island, showing the roof style of planked houses in central coast villages. Drawing by John Webber, Cook Expedition, 1778.

change and elaboration over the past 3,000 years, processes at first accelerated, then drastically interrupted, by European contact – by Russians in
1741, by Spaniards in 1774, and by Captain James Cook four years later.   103

Some archaeological sites along the central and southern Northwest Coast
document historic cultures during earlier times. For example, the Marpole
culture of southern Vancouver Island, and also the San Juan and Gulf
Islands, developed from earlier roots in about 400 BC and flourished until
roughly AD 400. By this time there are clear signs of differing social status,
both in the value and amount of grave goods and in the presence of skull
deformation, a characteristic of socially prominent birth on the Northwest
Coast. Marpole art traditions and antler and bone artifacts are quite distinct
from those of the Salish, the people living in the area at European contact.
Salish culture can be traced back to at least AD 1200. Despite the major differences between Marpole and Salish, most authorities believe that the former
developed into the latter during the first millennium AD.

Nootka-speaking peoples flourished along the shores of the Strait of Juan
de Fuca, and on the west coast of Vancouver Island. Basketry types from
Hoko River reflect 3,000 years of Nootkan style. Whaling became more
important during the Late Period, epitomized by the Ozette site on the
Pacific Coast south of Cape Flattery, perhaps the most important
sea-mammal hunting location for thousands of miles along the West coast
(see box pp. 162–63).

104 Haida village photographed in the late nineteenth century, with totem poles,
large plank houses, and canoes.

An ancient Makah village at Ozette

For many centuries, the ancestors of modern-day, Nootka-speaking Makah Indians lived in a cluster of cedar-wood houses at Ozette, on the Pacific Coast of the Olympic Peninsula. In about AD 1750, a huge mudslide buried at least four planked dwellings without warning. During the 1960s, Richard Daugherty of Washington State University excavated the still-water-logged remains of the collapsed houses. He used high pressure and small garden hoses to expose a rich treasure trove of well-preserved wooden artifacts that proclaim the great richness of Makah culture before European contact.

Hundreds of small household items lay jumbled among the collapsed walls – animal bones, storage boxes, baskets, and cooking hearths. Dozens of cod and halibut fishhooks and pieces of harpoons and whaling kit also came from the Ozette houses. Bark cloth, hide, and netting survived in perfect condition. There were carved wooden bowls that once held seal and whale oil. Heavy wooden clubs bore carvings of humans, seals, and owl heads. Ozette

105 Ozette, Washington: carved panel depicting Thunderbird and Wolf found in a broken state on a house floor.

The interior plateau 8500 BC to modern times

Before traveling south along the California coast, we must describe the hunter-gatherer societies of the northwestern interior, which interacted intensively with coastal communities. The interior Plateau lies between the Pacific Coast and the Great Basin and is bisected by two major rivers: the Columbia in the sagebrush grasslands of the southern Plateau and the Fraser in the more wooded north. During early Holocene times, the climate was cooler and moister than today, with warmer and drier conditions after 6000 BC. Warmer temperatures reduced pine forest cover; grassland and

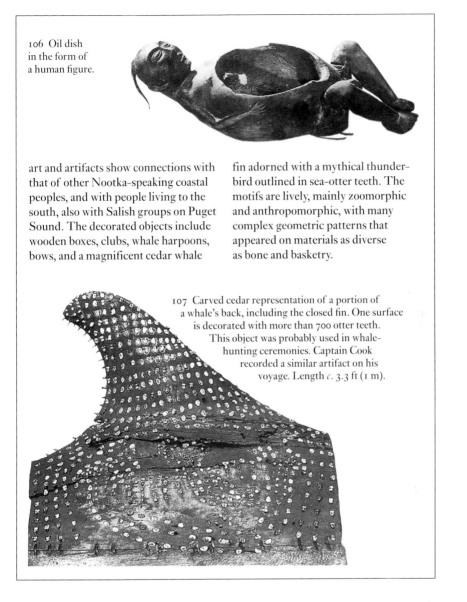

106 Oil dish in the form of a human figure.

art and artifacts show connections with that of other Nootka-speaking coastal peoples, and with people living to the south, also with Salish groups on Puget Sound. The decorated objects include wooden boxes, clubs, whale harpoons, bows, and a magnificent cedar whale fin adorned with a mythical thunderbird outlined in sea-otter teeth. The motifs are lively, mainly zoomorphic and anthropomorphic, with many complex geometric patterns that appeared on materials as diverse as bone and basketry.

107 Carved cedar representation of a portion of a whale's back, including the closed fin. One surface is decorated with more than 700 otter teeth. This object was probably used in whale-hunting ceremonies. Captain Cook recorded a similar artifact on his voyage. Length c. 3.3 ft (1 m).

shrub-steppe now covered much of the semi-arid landscape. For thousands of years, a sparse hunter-gatherer population occupied the Plateau, with the densest settlement near rivers and other permanent water sources. There they harvested salmon runs, often living in small pithouse communities.

Fishing has a long history on the Plateau. The Dalles of the Columbia River are long, rapids-choked narrows at a natural boundary between the Plateau and the coast, an extremely productive salmon fishery in historic times and perhaps as early as 8000 BC. Along the Fraser River in British Columbia, hunter-gatherer groups were catching salmon at the Drynoch site as early as 5100 BC. In about 2500 BC, winter pithouses appeared.

These were substantial, well-insulated circular houses dug about 5 ft (1.5 m) into the ground, with a diameter of 30 ft (9 m) or more. Some of the larger structures may have been dwellings for higher-status families.

108

Some locations remained in use for long periods. The Keatley Creek site on the Fraser River near Liloot, British Columbia, has yielded a long sequence of human occupation, starting as early as 9000 BC and ending in historic times. From about 5000 to 1500 BC, the location occasionally served as a base camp for salmon fishers. Between 1500 and 400 BC, major winter pithouses rose at Keatley Creek, occupied by residential corporate groups with rights over productive fishing locations. After 400 BC, isotopic analyses of human skeletons reveal that the inhabitants were obtaining as much as 60 percent of their food from fish. Much of the remainder of the diet came from mountain roots.

The best British Columbia fisheries lay along short stretches of narrows, near rapids, and in canyons, where the people took thousands of salmon in summer and fall. While the men speared and netted, the women gutted and dried the catch, storing dried fish in bark-lined pits as much as 6 ft (2 m) deep. The fishers developed more specialized barbed fish spears and composite toggling harpoons, also ingenious nets and weirs. Other foods were not neglected. Many interior groups used pits to roast enormous quantities of wild onions, balsam roots, and other tubers.

During the Late Period, complex trade networks linked coast and interior; they brought sea shells far inland, and turquoise from the Great Basin and Southwestern areas. Art objects like wooden masks used to proclaim

108 Reconstruction of a typical Columbia Plateau village. Four sloping rafters supported a roof of logs, poles, and bark, covered with earth and sod, with a smoke hole that also served as the entrance.

rank and status moved from the coast to the interior, as some individuals and families acquired greater wealth and political power.

Further inland, salmon runs are less bountiful. People had to rely on more meager, widely scattered food resources in an increasingly arid environment. Their toolkits, with notched and stemmed projectile points and plant processing gear, resemble those from the Great Basin and further afield. These were highly mobile hunter-gatherer populations in regular contact with others living long distances away. As a result, artifacts, ideas, and geographical information passed over enormous areas of the ancient west.

The California coast

California's later cultures were remarkable for their intensive and often highly specialized hunting, gathering, and fishing activities. After 3000 to 2000 BC, the climate was essentially the same as today. Acorn crops were important everywhere, on the coast and in the interior. Shellfish played a major role in the San Francisco Bay area, while the peoples of the Santa Barbara Channel region and further south exploited mollusks, sea mammals, and fish. The intensive exploitation of acorns and marine resources coincided with an elaboration of technology, art, and social organization in some areas, especially in the Santa Barbara Channel and the San Francisco Bay–Sacramento–San Joaquin Delta regions. These groups also developed complex social mechanisms to regulate long-distance exchange and the redistribution of resources: political alliances, kin ties and ritual obligations, and formal banking of resources. Intricate coastal and riverine adaptations gave rise to societies that reached the effective limits of social complexity without adopting agriculture. They were still flourishing in constantly changing forms along the Pacific Coast at European contact.

The California coast was a high-risk environment, affected by constant and often severe drought cycles, with dramatic short-term fluctuations in precipitation and sea-water temperatures over the past 5,000 years. In summer, most of the time a combination of a persistent high pressure off-shore and northwesterly winds caused warm surface water to move offshore. Much colder water from the depths of the ocean rose to the surface, bringing nutrients that fed zooplankton. Each summer, billions of spawning sardines moved inshore in the Santa Barbara Channel, quarry for both humans and larger fish. If the upwelling died down, fish catches suffered dramatically. This happened when major, unpredictable El Niños brought intense storms and epochal rainfall. El Niños occur when a huge accumulation of warm water builds up in the central Pacific and moves east, slackening the prevailing northeast trades and bringing warm, humid air to the South American coast. These irregular global events, caused by still little-understood interactions between the atmosphere and the ocean, trigger droughts, heavy rains, and other climatic anomalies throughout the tropics. They also bring warmer sea temperatures and above average rainfall to California, and cut off the natural upwelling of nutrients for the fish that were a staple of coastal groups. El Niños (and their opposites, La Niñas, with their cold water and dry conditions ashore) triggered unpredictable environmental and cultural stress.

Earlier human societies along the California and Oregon coast encountered easily accessible, abundant sea-lion and fur-seal rookeries. As these colonies succumbed to overhunting, so the coastal people of most of northern and central California and the extreme south near San Diego lived off terrestrial foods and never developed sedentary settlements. In contrast, at some unknown point in the past, the groups residing near offshore rocks or islands in northwestern California and the Santa Barbara Channel region developed watercraft capable of navigating rough seas and intensified their exploitation of offshore marine mammal populations. Sedentary villages developed in these areas, where dried fish and acorn stores became vitally important.

The cost of building canoes was so high that wealthy headmen were the only individuals who could pay for boats. Thus, they controlled the resources obtained from the canoes, a development that led to greater social complexity. We know that sea-otter hunting and fishing increased dramatically during the later Holocene in many coastal locations. People may have responded to stress by widening the kinds of foods they foraged and obtaining them with reduced efficiency as rising populations depleted edible resources of all kinds over many generations. Thus, a shift to more intensive fishing came about because this was the only major subsistence activity that could be intensified with greater labor investment. Large sea mammals and shellfish could produce no more.

Acorns were an important, if labor-intensive food because they were highly productive and nutritious, with good storage qualities for the winter months. Acorn consumption rose dramatically in California after about 2,000 years ago, perhaps because of rising populations and food shortages. In focusing on acorns, people exploited smaller territories, moved around less, and claimed specific landscapes, all behaviors which could lead to greater organizational complexity in local societies.

The Medieval Warm Period

Sea temperatures were a major factor in the development of coastal societies. For example, giant kelp beds edge many miles of the California coast. Kelp forests with their rich inshore fish populations are sensitive to warmer-than-average sea temperatures – above 68°F (20°C) – and can vanish or thin out during major El Niño events. Such thinning could have had a severe effect on nearby coastal populations, whereas cooler conditions would have enhanced marine productivity. Kelp beds may have responded to short-term temperature changes, but deep-sea cores also suggest that ocean temperatures were warmer than today for more than 50 percent of the past 8,000 years, meaning the kelp forests were often diminished.

Sea-temperature variations in the Pacific stem from three causes: the short-term effects of winter and summer climate, periodic El Niño events of varying severity, and longer-term fluctuations measured in centuries. A deep-sea core from the Santa Barbara Channel provides a high-resolution portrait (derived from radiocarbon-dated marine foraminifera) of maritime climate change over the past 4,000 years. Despite long-term fluctuations, climate conditions were more stable from the end of the Ice Age up to about 2000 BC. Then the climate and sea surface temperatures became more variable. A combination of sea core data and tree-rings document warm and stable water conditions between 1050 BC and AD 450. From AD 450 to 1300, sea temperatures dropped sharply to between 48 and 56°F (9 and 13°C). For three-and-a-half centuries from AD 960 to 1300, marine upwelling was especially intense, and fisheries were very productive as a result. After 1300, sea temperatures stabilized and became warmer. Upwelling subsided and fisheries became less productive. The period of increased upwelling and cooler sea temperatures, associated with prolonged La Niña conditions, coincides in general terms with major regional droughts known from tree-rings from about AD 500 to 800, 980 to 1250, and 1650 to 1750. These droughts, known from many locations throughout the west, coincide with the well-documented global Medieval Warm Period of about AD 800 to 1250.

Northern and central California

The north coast is isolated and relatively mountainous, but its sparse populations interacted with people in neighboring areas. The Yurok, from the extreme northwestern California coast, came under strong influence from coastal peoples in Oregon and Washington, while groups living to the south were open to ideas and contacts from their California neighbors. However, each local group had its own distinctive adaptation. Most of them formed "tribelets," small groups presided over by a local chief or headman, each with their own territory, often a local river drainage area. Isolated tribelets often came together, usually in the fall, and cooperated with others in catching and smoking salmon, or when netting enormous numbers of smelt on the fringes of sandy beaches each autumn. Come winter, most groups resided in base camps, relying heavily on foods stored during the summer months. This general form of lifeway thrived throughout the north coast region, albeit with considerable local variation.

The Gunther Pattern (?150 BC to recent times) of the Humboldt Bay area, and of the lower reaches of the Eel and Mad rivers, was a specialized riverside and coastal adaptation brought into the area by ancestors of the

Wiyot and Yurok peoples who lived there at European contact. Gunther sites with their distinctive barbed projectile points lie along rivers like the Klamath and Trinity, also at strategic lagoons. The inhabitants relied heavily on seasonal salmon runs and other predictable marine resources, using mountainous areas for hunting and seasonal acorn harvesting. They traded obsidian from sources at least 250 miles (400 km) away.

Further south, the Eel and Russian river areas are less mountainous, with some large coastal lagoons, especially to the south. With offshore marine-mammal rookeries, seasonal fishing, some mollusk collecting, and inland foraging, the different bands adjusted their annual rounds and settlement patterns to ever-changing distributions and availabilities of animals and plants.

Around 2500 BC, Windmiller people, well adapted to riverine and marsh-land environments, settled in the Sacramento Delta region. These Penutian speakers may have originated in the Columbia Plateau or western Great Basin, settling in a bountiful, low-lying area where their successors were to flourish for more than 4,000 years. Windmiller groups fished for sturgeon, 109 salmon, and other fish with spears, nets, and lines, as well as harvesting storable plant foods such as acorns. Many groups also hunted in the nearby Sierras during the summer months. Windmiller burials and cemeteries show evidence of ceremonial, including the use of red ocher, with many bodies commonly oriented toward the west with their faces down. Related groups spread widely in the Central Valley, also westward into the Bay area, forming the foundations of a cultural tradition that was to survive into recent times.

Soon after 2000 BC, Berkeley Pattern peoples, Utian-speaking with a basically Windmiller culture, moved into the Bay area. This movement may have coincided with a great expansion of bayside and coastal marsh-lands that supported fish and shellfish, large waterfowl populations, also game and many edible plant species. By AD 1, numerous Berkeley Pattern villages flourished throughout the San Francisco Bay area, along the central California coast, and in the Monterey Bay area. In the Bay itself there was a veritable landscape of mounds and villages set among flat marshlands and inhabited for many generations.

Many Berkeley Pattern settlements lay near freshwater streams and marshlands. By settling in such locations, the people could exploit both inland and bayside environments. The earliest settlements were in these prime sites, where there were few gaps in the annual "harvest" of different resources. Later, increasingly dense populations split off to form satellite communities in more marginal lands. The result: more formal social and political relationships, the emergence of important kin leaders and greater social complexity.

Between AD 300 and 500, the Berkeley Pattern gradually evolved into the Augustine Pattern, with technological innovations such as the bow and arrow, harpoons, and tubular tobacco pipes, and an unusual custom, that of

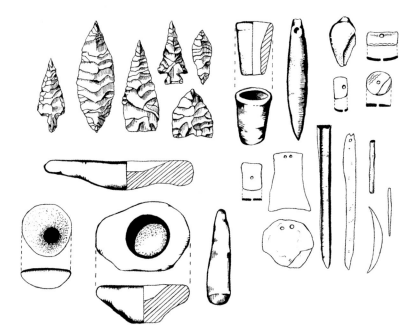

109 Windmiller pattern artifacts, including a–f, projectile points, g–k, milling, grinding, and pounding stones, and l–x, ornaments and bone implements. The same basic technology, with changes such as bows and arrows and different projectile points, continued into historic times.

burning artifacts in a grave before the body was interred. Later, during the drought-plagued Medieval Warm Period, people from the interior moved toward the more temperate coast in search of food. Environmental barriers and high population densities nearby prevented them from moving into unexploited territories. So they exploited foods like acorns, which, as we have seen, were expensive to process on a large scale.

After AD 1400, the number of Augustine settlements proliferated dramatically, many founded by kin leaders who maintained constant ties with neighboring communities. An elaborate ceremonial involving secret societies and cults came into being. Inter-community exchange assumed such importance that clam-shell disk "money" came into widespread use. This increasingly complex cultural system survived until European contact and beyond, finally to disintegrate in the face of inexorable Spanish missionary activity.

Southern California coast

The Santa Barbara Channel and other parts of the southern California coast supported sophisticated hunter-gatherer societies at European contact. They faced stressful environmental conditions, including food shortages caused by intense human predation of individual fish species. Between 1000 BC and AD 1300, coastal Chumash people depended ever more heavily on the ocean. By this time, fishers sought deepwater fish, including swordfish, off-shore, using distinctive planked canoes, known in later times as *tomols*

111 (see box p. 171). Beads and other ornaments now became status markers in society, also perhaps a form of storable wealth. Some Chumash villages in the Santa Barbara area housed as many as 1,000 people and were centers for important ceremonies and trading activities. They served as political "capitals" over several lesser villages, even small "provinces," loose political confederations of lesser communities.

110 A hereditary chief (*wot*) ruled each village. They served as war leaders and patrons of ceremonial village feasts. Once during the fall and at the winter solstice, outlying communities near and far flocked to major settlements for ceremonies that honored the earth and the sun. Chumash villages and provinces quarreled with one another constantly over food supplies and territory. Disputes over wives, social insults to chiefs (such as not attending a feast), and blood feuds were commonplace.

The Chumash were artists, too, their petroglyphs and pictographs the most spectacular north of the Mexican border. Chumash shamans and 112 specialists served as the artists, painting the walls of remote inland caves and PL. XIV rockshelters with abstract representations of the sun, stars, human beings, birds, fish, and reptiles. The meaning of the art is unknown, but at least some of it is connected with astronomical observations, and to a calendrical system. Some painted sites may have served as solstice observatories, like Condor Cave in the coastal mountains. Here, the rising sun shines through a hole carved by a shaman in the cave wall onto a sun stick set in the floor. Later, the shaman painted his spirit helper, a red-legged frog, on the wall.

Chumash groups maintained exchange contacts with other coastal communities to the south, also with peoples living far in the interior. The

110 Artist's reconstruction of a Chumash village by A.E. Treganza, 1942.

Chumash *tomols*

The coastal peoples who crossed open water to the offshore islands of southern California were consummate seamen. The Chumash and Gabrieleño on the mainland made use of planked canoes constructed from driftwood and small trees. The Chumash planked canoe, the *tomol*, was up to 30 feet (9 m) long, large enough to carry as many as six people and a heavy load. A canoe builder would take up to six months to build one, splitting driftwood into planks with whalebone wedges, then thinning them with sharp tools and dried sharkskin "sandpaper." A single heavy plank with a dished surface served as the keel, set upright on the beach with forked timbers. Then the builders would bevel, align, and fasten a patchwork of planks to form the sides, the seams caulked with a mixture of heated bitumen and pitch called *yop*. Finally, they sewed the planks together with waxed fiber twine from native grass. A central crossbeam braced the hull amidships; stout washboards deflected surf and rough seas. Once the hull was faired with sharp abalone shells, the builder would seal it with a mixture of red ocher and pine pitch, which prevented the wood from becoming heavy and waterlogged at sea.

Tomols were light, but carefully ballasted for stability. A skilled crew kneeling on sea-grass pads could make between 6 and 8 knots with a following wind, paddling at a constant rate for hours on end. However, most passages were made during early morning hours when winds were calm.

111 A reconstruction by Travis Hudson and Peter Howorth of a planked canoe (*tomol*), used by the both the Chumash and Gabrieleño groups for fishing, sea-mammal hunting, and transportation.

Gabrieleño occupied the Pacific Coast areas now under the urban sprawl of Los Angeles and Orange County. They controlled valuable steatite outcrops on Catalina Island offshore. This was a soft stone ideal for making stone griddles and pots, which they traded widely. Further south, the Luiseño and nomadic bands of Diegueño peoples moved seasonally

113 Chumash baskets.

between coast and interior harvesting acorns, seeds, shellfish, and marine mammals, as well as fishing.

Short-term climatic shifts such as El Niños played a significant role in triggering periods of rapid cultural change. Those who rely heavily on intensive exploitation of relatively few foods like nuts or acorns and store their harvests are highly vulnerable to longer-term drought cycles, such as those that had descended earlier on the west during the Medieval Warm Period. The droughts arrived as coastal populations were on the rise, when larger settlements and more densely packed settlement resulted in higher incidences of disease and malnutrition. The well-documented response along the coast was to exploit a much wider range of marine habitats, to elaborate fishing and sea-mammal hunting technology, and to invest much greater amounts of labor in such activities. The increasing complexity of coastal populations may have resulted not from bounty, but from severe drought, movements of inland groups nearer more reliable food supplies at the coast, and from the necessity to maintain territorial boundaries and regulate food supplies and exchange.

Biological anthropologist Phillip Walker studied Channel Island skeletons during the Medieval Warm Period and believes that chronic anemia, manifested by a condition called *cribra orbitalia*, was caused by high nutrient losses resulting from food shortages. Thus, severe drought, chronic illness, and, above all, water shortages may have caused widespread distress, the abandonment of many island settlements, and violence stemming from competition for scarce and dwindling water supplies. At the same time, wounds caused by projectile points increased dramatically until about 1150, when they declined again, for reasons that are unclear.

A complex interplay between ocean temperatures, rainfall, and other environmental conditions, whether natural or humanly induced, was but one factor in an intricate equation that affected the complexity of hunter-gatherer societies along the coast over more than 3,000 years.

112 (*Previous pages*) Chumash rock art: painted cave in Pleito Creek, Kern County, California.

10 · The Southwest: Villages and Pueblos

You feel overwhelmed by the complexity of the "Great House," the serried rooms pressing on the open plazas, all in the heart of an arid landscape. At Pueblo Bonito in Chaco Canyon, it's best to enter through the east wing, where the quiet rooms are carefully preserved, the veneered masonry seemingly as fresh as the day it was laid. Close your eyes and you can imagine them occupied – stacks of maize cobs along the walls, women weaving in the shade, the murmur of voices from the terraces and plazas, and an undercurrent of scents and odors, of sagebrush, human sweat, and rotting garbage. Then the image fades in the warmth of the afternoon and you're back to the reality of an intricate complex, still largely undeciphered archaeological jigsaw puzzle.

Pueblo Bonito flourished a thousand years ago, long after agriculture had become well established in the Southwest. This site, along with many similar pueblos all over the Southwest, raises important historical questions. Why did such large pueblos come into being? Why were the societies that built them so volatile? What institutions in Ancestral Pueblo society helped Southwesterners cope with the challenges of unpredictable rainfall and drought? (Ancestral Pueblo are the forebears of historic [and living] Pueblo communities that we know about in some detail.)

As we have seen, maize agriculture did not bring about dramatic changes in Southwestern life. Permanent pithouse villages appeared gradually in northern areas and increased in number until about AD 700. The next three centuries saw a change from pithouse villages to settlements of multi-room buildings constructed from adobe clay or masonry. In some areas, like Mesa Verde, Colorado, the change was a gradual one, the first rooms being storage areas built behind pithouses. Later, people moved into surface rooms, turning their old pithouses into kivas or ceremonial spaces (kivas are subterranean chambers, roofed with stout wooden beams, where secret societies met and performed important rituals). In other places, the shift was a rapid one. Why the changeover took place is a mystery, for there are no obvious causes like climatic shifts (see chronological table on p. 70 and map on p. 92).

Between AD 750 and 900, village settlement expanded greatly throughout the northern Southwest, and especially on the Colorado Plateau. Some of the largest settlements of the period in southwestern Colorado and northwest New Mexico were home to as many as 100 to 120 households. It was at this point that Chaco Canyon, New Mexico, came into prominence.

Chaco Canyon   before AD 900 to 1150

114   Chaco Canyon is a dramatic place, set in a stark landscape. The huge cliffs of the canyon glow yellow-gold in the sun, contrasting with the softer tones of desert sand, greasewood, and occasional willow trees. Shadows fall across the canyon as the sun sets, the grandiose landscape dwarfing the walls of the great pueblos that are camouflaged naturally against the high cliffs. Between AD 700 and 800, the few people living at Chaco largely abandoned pithouses and moved into masonry dwellings. The clusters of rooms, known as pueblos, lay in small arcs, so each room was equidistant from the circular pithouses in the center. These pithouses gradually developed into kivas, the focal points of ceremonial life.

Pueblo Bonito

In its eleventh-century heyday, Pueblo Bonito had at least 600 rooms and could have housed about 1,000 people, but by no means all of the rooms were in use at any one time. Tom Windes, who has studied the site for many years, believes that no more than 100 or so people ever lived there, with the largest amount of residential debris accumulating in the ninth and tenth centuries, and in the early twelfth century. The two Great Kivas at Pueblo Bonito lie on either side of a line of rooms that divided the complex into two areas.

Unquestionably, Bonito was an important ritual center, especially during the eleventh century, when construction activity intensified. Like historic Pueblo society, Ancestral Pueblo life and ritual must have revolved around the changing seasons, the solstices, equinoxes, and routine of the agricultural year. And like later Puebloans, the people who gathered at Pueblo Bonito must have nurtured corn, which pervaded every aspect of their lives with its planting, growth, and harvest. Important seasonal ceremonies involved exchange and distribution of food and other necessities brought to the canyon from some distance. The office holders who organized these ceremonies were the guardians of ritual knowledge and political acumen, gaining social recognition by redistributing commodities to people near and far.

Who these office holders were, we don't know. Some of them were buried at the pueblo at a time of enhanced ritual activity. Pueblo Bonito has yielded at least 130 burials, mainly dating to after 1000. The Chaco pueblos generally are remarkable for the small number of burials found within their precincts, probably of important leaders. These burial clusters are associated with very large numbers of cylinder vessels, wooden staffs, and other artifacts associated with important individuals. A recent discovery has established that some cylinder jar fragments bear traces of cacao, a prestigious beverage with strong Mesoamerican associations. The people buried in these clusters were also taller, suggesting a better diet.

114 Chaco Canyon, New Mexico, with Pueblo Bonito and the Chaco Wash.

115 Pueblo Bonito, showing the semicircular layout.

During the ninth century, summer rainfall was highly variable. Groups from the north, primarily from the Montezuma Valley in southwestern Colorado, migrated into the Canyon, forced from their homeland by a period of somewhat colder climate that shortened the growing season. These groups brought an early version of Great House architecture and erected the first four such houses at the junctions of major drainages in Chaco sometime after AD 850: Penasco Blanco, Pueblo Bonito, Kin Nahasbas, and Una Vida. The largest of these, Pueblo Bonito, near the northeast wall of the Canyon, stood three, and later five, stories high along its rear wall and remained in use for more than two centuries (see box p. 176). They, along with the local inhabitants, adopted two forms of agriculture, one using natural seeps, the other canal irrigation.

By the eleventh century, great houses dominated Chaco Canyon. Chaco expert Gwinn Vivian has calculated the potential carrying capacity of the canyon soils and believes no more than about 5,500 people ever lived there (estimates of carrying capacity differ considerably, however). The Chaco people took advantage of long-standing kin and trade links with groups living elsewhere and became the hub of a much wider world. Thus was born what is sometimes called the Chaco Phenomenon, a number of dispersed communities that interacted constantly with one another, linked by regular exchanges of a variety of commodities. Tree-rings show that the next eighty years were ones of generally good rainfall, a weather cycle that may have meant the system kept going longer than it might otherwise have done.

By AD 1115, at least seventy communities scattered over more than 25,000 sq. miles (65,000 sq. km) were linked through socioeconomic and ritual networks centered on Chaco Canyon. The activities of the Chaco Phenomenon were probably controlled by a small number of people. But whether these individuals formed a social elite with special privileges reserved to them, and them alone, or were simply members of an important kin group, is still uncertain. Outlying great house sites contain much Chaco pottery and share architectural features such as Great Kivas with Pueblo Bonito and other large Canyon centers, but with considerable variation. Some also had surrounding communities. An elaborate road system radiated out from the Canyon, a web of tracks that run straight or bend abruptly, use stairways

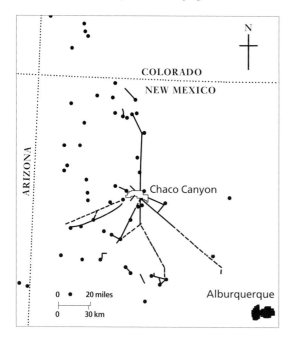

116 The Chacoan road system and outlying sites.

117 The Jackson Stairway at Chaco Canyon.

and ramps, and extend over more than 250 miles (400 km). The roads 116
did not link places as modern ones do; they were probably a powerful ideological spider's web that symbolized the ties between different parts of 117
the Chaco world. Perhaps they were ritual pathways set on a physical and
symbolic landscape.

The center of the Chaco Phenomenon shifted northward in the early
1100s. The Salmon Ruin near Bloomfield, New Mexico, is a 290-room
pueblo in a slightly modified 'E' plan with a Great Kiva (a subterranean
chamber of unusual size) and tower kiva (a circular tower which served as a
ceremonial structure). It was constructed in three planned stages between
AD 1088 and 1106. The distribution of local and Chacoan vessels through
the pueblo suggests that Salmon was founded by both local San Juan people
and migrants from Chaco itself.

118 Aztec: a Chaco outlier and major ritual center. The western part of the site is a classic Chaco great house, a D-shaped structure with twelve kivas and an enclosed plaza. People settled in the northern parts of the site by 1050, but the site was abandoned *c.* 1268.

Between 1050 and 1130, the rains were plentiful. Building activity continued in the Canyon as the Great Houses expanded. Chaco's web of interconnections prospered. The Chaco population rose steadily, which was not a serious problem as long as winter rainfall fertilized the fields. Then, in 1130, tree-rings tell us that fifty years of intense drought settled over the Colorado Plateau. Soon the outlying communities ceased to trade and share food with the Great Houses, which forced the Canyon's inhabitants to rely on their own already overstressed environment. Dry year followed dry year. Crops failed; game and wild plant foods were increasingly sparse in an area that was relatively marginal for agriculture at the best of times. An inexorable population decline set in.

The only recourse was deeply ingrained in Ancestral Pueblo philosophy: movement. Within a few generations, the pueblos stood empty, as well over half Chaco's population dispersed into villages, hamlets, and pueblos far from the Canyon. Those who remained were gone by the early 1200s. The emptying of a site like Pueblo Bonito seems like an epochal event at a distance of 900 years, but it was merely part of the constant ebb and flow of Ancestral Pueblo existence.

The Chaco system collapsed, in the sense that the people either moved to other, more productive areas where they maintained long-term alliances, formed independent, highly scattered communities, or simply remained in environmentally favorable areas. Throughout the region once integrated by the Chaco Phenomenon, the reorganized society that emerged from the prolonged drought cycle probably bore some resemblance to Pueblo Indian society immediately before European contact.

The Chaco Phenomenon was by no means the only centralized political and social system that flourished in the ancient Southwest, for there were other complex societies living in sharply contrasting ecological zones.

Hohokam: the desert irrigators   *c.* AD 450 to 1450

Hohokam (a Native American term of uncertain origin meaning "something that is all gone") was the ancient farming tradition of the southern deserts, known from its buff- to brown-colored pottery. If we use such vessels as markers, we can trace the Hohokam over more than 30,000 sq. miles (78,000 sq. km) of southern Arizona – an area larger than South Carolina. In general terms, Hohokam groups shared a common identity as farmers, a talent for irrigation agriculture, and an architecture of adobe dwellings. They also shared profound values of mutual obligation.

Hohokam culture appeared around AD 450, as new maize strains arrived   119, and farming populations rose. The first irrigation canal systems developed   123 along the Gila and Salt rivers in the modern-day Phoenix area. The Salt River Valley was the most populous and agriculturally productive valley in the Southwest before AD 1500. The land looks barren and utterly dry, yet it has fertile soils and lies near major drainages. Between about AD 450 and 1450, the Hohokam living near the river adapted brilliantly to this seemingly

119 Irrigation systems and major settlements along the Salt River in the Phoenix Basin.

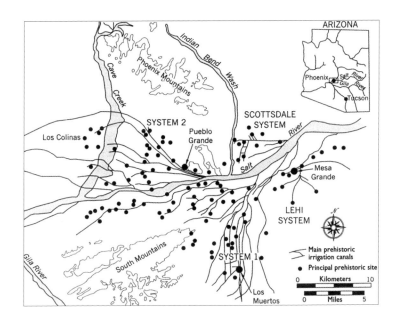

Mogollon and Mimbres

The Mogollon tradition of the ancient Southwest is an entity of the uplands and deserts that separated the Ancestral Pueblo and Hohokam, and is not described fully here. Its most spectacular expression is Mimbres, located along the river of that name in southwestern New Mexico. Between AD 1000 and 1130, Mimbres potters created magnificent painted ceremonial bowls adorned with geometric and pictorial designs. These superb examples of ancient artistry are usually found in burials, inverted over the head of the deceased and ceremonially "broken" by a small hole in the base.

120 Mimbres bowl painted with enigmatic human figures, possibly representing the contrast between life and death, or male and female. The hole through the base "killed" the object, helping release the vessel's spirit into the next world. Diameter *c.* 11.8 in (30 cm).

The Mimbres people lived in settlements of up to 150 rooms that consisted of single-story, contiguous and rectangular spaces built of river cobbles and adobe. At the well-known NAN Ranch and Galaz sites, the pueblo clusters grew according to household needs, rooms sometimes being subdivided and remodeled. Ceremonial structures included large, rectangular, and semi-subterranean kivas, sometimes with entry ramps and ceremonial offerings under the floors.

There are few signs of the long-distance trading contacts found at Chaco Canyon or in major Hohokam settlements. Most ceremonial activities appear to have taken place at the community and household level, reflecting a relatively isolated, egalitarian pueblo society.

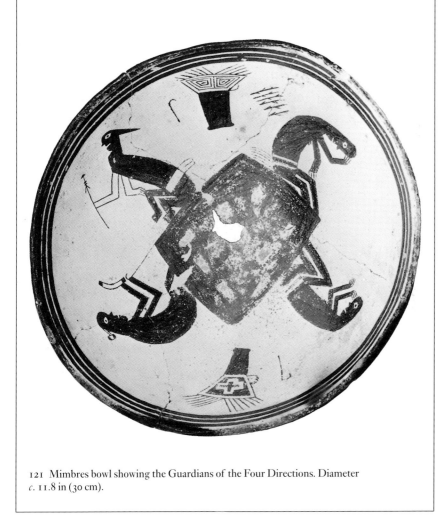

121 Mimbres bowl showing the Guardians of the Four Directions. Diameter *c*. 11.8 in (30 cm).

desolate environment, building individual canal networks up to 22 miles (35 km) long and irrigating up to 70,000 acres (c. 28,000 ha).

Most people lived in small, single-room houses built of pole and brush and covered with hardened clay. Groups of dwellings lay around small courtyards, as if extended families lived close to one another. The size of Hohokam courtyard groups varied considerably, with one of them at the Grewe site in south-central Arizona having as many as twenty-four houses, covering an area of 6,500 sq. ft (600 sq. m). Households, in the wider sense of an extended family, were the primary mechanism for controlling land ownership and the use of irrigation water.

At Grewe, a community founded as early as the sixth century AD and occupied until the fourteenth, the largest houses, presumably those of the wealthiest families, clustered in a few courtyard groups and were occupied much longer than surrounding smaller dwellings. Here, archaeologists Douglas Craig and Kathleen Henderson unearthed a communal cooking area with dozens of pit ovens cut into the soil. This lay on one side of a crowded residential zone. On the other side was a public plaza with a ball court. Craig and Henderson think that the nearest courtyards, which include the largest and wealthiest, controlled activities in the cooking area and sponsored the feasts that were prepared there, a way of acquiring prestige and social status. At the same time, the events reaffirmed property rights held by the wealthiest households as well as fostering a sense of communal identity. There are signs, too, that the same households also subsidized the manufacture of items like shell jewelry, pottery, and cotton textiles, which were traded to other groups in the region.

The Hohokam exchanged foodstuffs and utilitarian raw materials, ceremonial objects and ornaments like macaw feathers and shells, and prestige items, as well as information. Controversy surrounds the relationship between the Hohokam and cultural groups in Mesoamerica far to the south. Some scholars believe capped platform mounds, clay figurines, certain forms of polished and painted vessels, and ball courts show strong Mesoamerican influence. Most, however, argue that the Hohokam was a distinctively Southwestern culture. Certainly Hohokam communities traded with the south for copper bells, mosaic mirrors, and tropical birds, items also found in Chaco Canyon. They were middlemen in the sea-shell trade from the Gulf of California and the southern California coast (where some Hohokam sherds have been found). Between AD 800 and 1100, the Hohokam traded through a network of ball-court communities between the Little Colorado in the north and the Mexican border in the south.

By AD 1100, larger communities comprised a prominent village with communal structures such as a ball court, a plaza, or a platform mound, with outlying smaller settlements and farms, the whole surrounded by carefully laid out and intensely cultivated farm land. Since there are no signs of prominent, authoritarian rulers, it seems that close-knit economic, political,

122

XV Overhead view of Pueblo Bonito, Chaco Canyon, New Mexico. The circular structures are kivas. At top center, a rock fall that crushed part of the pueblo in 1941.

XVI The Cliff Palace, Mesa Verde, Colorado.

XVII The Mug
House, Wetherill
Mesa, Colorado.

XIX Burial mounds and earthworks at Hopewell National Historic Park, Ohio.

XVIII The circular and octagonal Hopewell earthworks near Newark, Ohio.

XX Ritual structures, such as this so-called "woodhenge" at Cahokia in Illinois, lay on higher ground above a swamp, close to the central precincts. The large wooden posts were erected by sliding them into deep pits with a sloping side, then pushing them upright.

XXI Clay figurine depicting a man, possibly a shaman, with a topknot hair style. From an unknown Ohio location.

XXII A bird of prey in copper plate from Mound City, Ohio. Length 12 in (30.6 cm).

XXIII Chiefs used ceremony and ritual to validate their power. A cedarwood mask from Spiro Mound, Oklahoma, perhaps worn by a shaman, with shell inlay and antlers carved in imitation of those of a deer. Height 11.4 in (29 cm).

XXIV Human effigy vessel with weeping eyes.

XXV Shell gorget depicting a flying shaman with a death's head in one hand and a ceremonial mace in the other. Diameter 3.9 in (10 cm).

XXVI ʻA human head cut out of a copper plate from the Craig Mound, Oklahoma. The feather was then riveted on. Length 9.4 in (24 cm). The forked eye design is thought to be derived from the markings on a peregrine falcon.

and ritual bonds provided the basis for communal actions and for creating and maintaining irrigation systems.

Snaketown on the Gila River was one of the largest Hohokam communities, a pithouse settlement with a ball court 195 ft (60 m) long and 15 to 20 ft (4.5 to 6 m) deep. Ball-court communities flourished at relatively even intervals along major canal networks. These basin-like ball-court structures were arenas where people from the surrounding countryside would gather for feasts, trading activities, and all kinds of social interaction, as well as ball games between different villages. We know of more than 200 Hohokam ball courts, large and small, shallow depressions with plastered or stamped earth floors, surrounded by sloping banks, where experiments show that up to 700 spectators could witness the games. The largest are up to 250 ft (75 m) long and 90 ft (27 m) wide, dug up to 9 ft (2.75 m) into the subsoil. Quite what form the ball game itself took remains a mystery, but there is no question that it originated in Mesoamerica, where commoners played a version of the contest that required each side to cast a rubber ball back and forth without it touching the ground. Three such balls have come from Southwestern sites. Judging from historical analogies, the contests were the culminating event of days of feasting, trading, and social interaction that enhanced a sense of communal identity.

Ball courts gave way to platform mounds after AD 1150, earth-filled structures that formed elevated places. Some are over 12 ft (more than 3.5 m) high, built within an adobe compound, with as many as thirty rooms on the summit. The platform-mound complexes symbolize a major shift in Hohokam society: the emergence of a small elite. Ball courts were open depressions, accessible to large numbers of people. Platform mounds reached for the sky, stood out on the landscape, and were only accessible to a few. It is as if some members of society now elevated themselves both in material and spiritual terms above everyone else, whereas in earlier times the relationship between the living and the ancestors, with the underworld where humans originated, was more important. The larger the platform mound, the more labor required to build it, and the greater the status of the individuals or group responsible for its construction.

As the social order changed, so environmental pressures intensified from drought and catastrophic river floods. Hohokam irrigation systems no longer produced the food surpluses to support a now more elaborate culture. The collapse came around 1450, probably a rapid dispersal, household by household, as people moved away to settle with kin or farmed on a much smaller scale.

Mesa Verde   AD 500 to 1300

With the abandonment of Chaco Canyon, the center of Ancestral Pueblo power passed north to the Four Corners Region, notably to the Montezuma Valley and a wider area north and west of the San Juan Basin – the Mesa

124

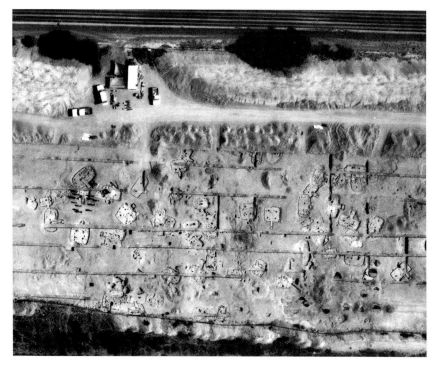

122 Aerial view of pithouses and courtyards at the Grewe site, Arizona.

123 Southwestern archaeologist Emil Haury stands in an excavated Hohokam irrigation canal, part of the elaborate irrigation systems based on the Gila and Salt Rivers that watered surrounding fields.

124 The Hohokam ball court at Snaketown, excavated by Emil Haury, is the largest such structure known in the Southwest. The court may also have served as a dance arena.

Verde area. This was a slightly wetter environment than much of the Southwest, with juniper and piñon cover and many natural water sources.

During the twelfth century, hundreds of Ancestral Pueblo households moved from dispersed communities into large pueblos by rivers and in sheltered valleys. Some populations lived in pueblos built into natural rockshelters in the walls of deep canyons, with one concentration in the Mesa Verde area. At the Mummy Lake location on Chapin Mesa, there are some thirty-six separate sites situated close to an artificial water supply. A series of ditches brought water from a nearby catchment area through a feeder canal 2,637 ft (804 m) long.

Between AD 1200 and 1300, the focus of settlement moved south from the area around Mummy Lake to Cliff and Fewkes Canyons. Fewkes Canyon supported at least thirty-three habitation sites with between 530 and 545 rooms and sixty kivas. The Cliff Palace, with its 220 masonry rooms and twenty-three kivas, has a spectacular setting but actually differs little from large pueblos elsewhere. People had moved from living in open locations to shelters and ledges in canyon walls, perhaps as a defensive measure. Only a few precipitous trails led from the canyon to the plateau farmlands above.

Not that Mesa Verde was the main center of settlement. The nearby Montezuma Valley supported eight pueblos larger than the Cliff/Fewkes

125 Artist's reconstruction of Sand Canyon Pueblo, southwestern Colorado, by Glen Feltch.

Canyon villages. One of them, Yellow Jacket, contains about 1,800 rooms and probably housed some 2,500 people, more than all of Mesa Verde. Another large settlement, Sand Canyon Pueblo in southwestern Colorado, boasted about 700 inhabitants. Sand Canyon surrounded a large spring, as did other major towns in the area. Around 1250, the residents-to-be erected a huge enclosure wall, which may have taken thirty to forty people two months to build. Over the next thirty years, they added over twenty separate room blocks, which incorporated at least ninety kivas and about 420 rooms. However, every household maintained its own identity in its cluster of structures – a living space, storage room, place to eat, and a kiva – just as they had in their original dispersed settlements. At the same time, multiple households dwelt within a single architectural complex, as if the wider ties of the kinship group had become more important than in earlier times.

Everywhere the emphasis appears to have been on individual communities, not on the kind of larger-scale regional integration so characteristic of Chaco and Hohokam.

The twelfth and thirteenth centuries saw the culmination of four centuries of rapid social and political development in the Mesa Verde region. Then, in about AD 1300, the Ancestral Pueblo abandoned the entire San Juan drainage, including Mesa Verde, perhaps because of prolonged droughts. Archaeologist Carla Van West has reconstructed the severity of June droughts between AD 900 and 1300 in the Sand Canyon area. Her figures show that the twelfth-century drought which caused the Ancestral Pueblo dispersal at Chaco had little effect in regions like Sand Canyon where there was still enough land to support the dispersed farming population. The people had enough room for the movement that was central to their survival.

Furthermore, potential agricultural productivity varied considerably from place to place and from year to year. The farmers tended to locate near consistently productive soils. They could survive the harshest of drought cycles if there were no restrictions on mobility or on access to the best soils, and if they could acquire food from neighbors when crops failed. However, their ability to move was severely restricted once population densities approached the carrying capacity of the land and the people had cultivated effectively all the most productive soils. At that point, surviving extreme short-term climatic change was much harder, especially when longer-term climatic cycles happened to coincide with a serious drought cycle, as happened during the major drought of AD 1276 to 1299. Pueblo construction slowed and ceased altogether by the 1290s.

By 1300, the great pueblos of the Four Corners were silent. The Ancestral Pueblo dispersed widely and joined distant communities in less-affected regions. They moved south and southeastward into the lands of the historic Hopi, Zuñi, and Rio Grande pueblos, where they retained the same basic community organization, with villages and larger communities, perhaps better called towns. They developed new social and religious ideas over many generations of cultural uncertainty, until stability returned with improved environmental conditions after AD 1450.

Shorter-term, high-frequency changes were risks that were readily apparent to every Ancestral Pueblo community: year-to-year rainfall shifts, decade-long drought cycles, seasonal changes, and so on. These required flexible adjustments, such as farming more land, relying more heavily on wild plant foods, and, above all, movement across the terrain. Such risk-reduction strategies worked well for centuries, as long as the Ancestral Pueblo farmed their land at well below its carrying capacity. When the population increased to near-carrying capacity, however, as it did at Chaco Canyon in the twelfth century, and in the Four Corners region a century later, people became increasingly vulnerable to drought cycles, which could stretch the capacity of a local environment within months, even weeks.

Their vulnerability was even more extreme when long-term changes – such as a half-century or more of much drier conditions – descended on farming land already pushed to its carrying limits. Under these circumstances, a year-long drought or torrential rains could quickly destroy a local population's ability to support itself. Ancestral Pueblo households in this situation had few options left to them but to disperse. Archaeologist Steven LeBlanc has drawn attention to the links between surges in warfare and periods of drought and other climatic stresses in the Southwest. Such events may have been a catalyst for increased violence throughout much of Southwestern society, and, also, for occasional cannibalism.

Katcinas and warriors   AD 1300 to European contact

The abandonments of the late thirteenth century changed the social landscape of the Southwest. The focus of human settlement moved south and east to areas of greater summer rains such as the Rio Grande Valley, and the Zuñi region of west-central New Mexico. More people moved from villages into bigger communities, some of them much larger than the greatest pueblos of earlier times. Not that these aggregations were permanent, for, as in earlier centuries, local populations fluctuated and pueblos rose into prominence, then were abandoned or became a shadow of their former selves.

The pueblos of the Rio Grande Valley, one of the few perennial rivers in the Southwest, epitomize this constant change. Until the twelfth and thirteenth centuries, relatively few people lived in the valley. Then the population swelled rapidly, both as a result of local growth and from migration into the valley from the north and northwest. Several pueblo sites, notably *126* Arroyo Hondo, just south of modern-day Santa Fé, reflect not continual growth but the characteristic ebb and flow in and out of Rio Grande settlements. A single-room block rose at Arroyo Hondo by AD 1315. Within fifteen years, about 1,200 two-story rooms arranged over twenty-four blocks centered around thirteen plazas. Just as quickly, the huge pueblo emptied; it was almost deserted by the mid-1330s. A second cycle of growth followed in the 1370s and 1380s with the building of 200 rooms, but these were destroyed by a fire in 1410.

The history of Arroyo Hondo reflects a remarkable social fluidity, marked by repeated movements of entire groups, some of whom traveled over distances of several hundred miles from the Mesa Verde region and elsewhere. One reason for this fluidity lay in the larger size of these growing settlements in an unpredictable environment where maize cultivation was at best chancy. At Arroyo Hondo, for example, even the best agricultural land could feed no more than 400 to 600 people in an average year, making it hard to accumulate adequate food reserves against drought years. The farmers tried to minimize famine by irrigating river lands and also planting better-watered fields at higher elevations. Sites like Arroyo Hondo and others

126 Aerial view of Arroyo Hondo Pueblo, New Mexico.

across much of the Southwest represent what have been called "persistent places," that is, they were used over long periods of time.

By the fourteenth century, there was frequent warfare. Pueblos now rose in easily defended locations. Sometimes, groups of settlements clustered together for protection, as they did in the Rio Grande Valley and the Hopi–Cibola region, with long distances between them. There were also major changes in Pueblo ritual, marked by new styles of kiva murals, pervasive decorative styles on ceramics, and much larger plazas. The plazas became important settings for public ceremonies, especially katcina (katchina) dances. Katcinas play a prominent role in modern–day Pueblo belief and ritual. They are ancestral spirits that serve as intermediaries between the living and the deities of the supernatural world, as well as bringing rain in clouds that they summon to the pueblos. Katcinas are present on earth from the winter to summer solstice. For the other half of the year they live in the San Francisco Peaks, to which they return through the *sipapu*, the entrance

127 to the lower regions. Katcina dancers, male impersonators who assume the sacred powers of the spirit, wear costumes and masks that impersonate the ancestral spirits during their stay on earth.

Perhaps the elaboration of katcina rituals was a way of binding together the inhabitants of much larger, more densely populated pueblos. Everyone in the community was part of a katcina society, whose membership cut across potentially divisive kin and lineage lines while ensuring that public ceremonies were conducted properly. Cooperative behavior was vital for survival and katcina rituals, with their emphasis on rainmaking (as well as warfare), provided important social guidelines and validation for the community as a whole.

Paquime (Casas Grandes)   Fourteenth century AD

Long-distance trade flourished throughout the Southwest, even in troubled times, as commodities such as turquoise, tropical bird feathers, cotton, tool-making stone, and buffalo hides passed along ancient trade routes. 128 The Casas Grandes area of Chihuahua in northern Mexico lies in relatively high-altitude basin and range country and is centered on a wide, fertile valley long inhabited by an indigenous farming population. By about the fourteenth century, the inhabitants of this valley congregated in a large settlement known as Paquime (or Casas Grandes). Initially, Paquime consisted of twenty or more house clusters, each with a plaza and enclosing wall. The people lived in single-story adobe houses, with a single water system for the entire settlement. One compound contained rows of rectangular adobe boxes apparently used for breeding macaws for their colorful feathers – pollen analyses have yielded traces of the nesting material, even eggshell fragments, skeletons, and traces of wooden perches. Paquime may have been one of the sources of macaws for Ancestral Pueblo communities far to the north. Macaw feathers were widely used in Pueblo rituals and were attached to ceremonial regalia and prayer sticks. They served as conduits to the supernatural.

During the fourteenth century, as many as 2,240 people lived in what was now a thriving town, with multi-story dwellings, I-shaped ball courts, stone-faced platform

127 Hopi artisans carve wooden dolls to teach their children about the many katcinas that are important in Pueblo ritual.

128 Aerial view of Casas Grandes, Chihuahua, northern Mexico, showing a ball court, lower right, and excavation of room blocks, lower left corner.

and effigy mounds, a market area, and elaborate water-storage systems. At the height of its power, Paquime lay at the center of a small region, its influence perhaps extending about 18 miles (30 km) from the town. Like the earlier Chaco Phenomenon, Paquime did not flourish for long, gradually falling into disrepair and being abandoned in the fifteenth century. The large towns of the southern desert were vacated, as simpler social institutions prevailed in another cycle of abandonment and downsizing. The Zuñi and Hopi pueblos endured, together with those of Acoma and the Rio Grande Valley, and others to the east, to witness the arrival of Spanish conquistadors in the sixteenth century.

Chronological table for the Eastern Woodlands

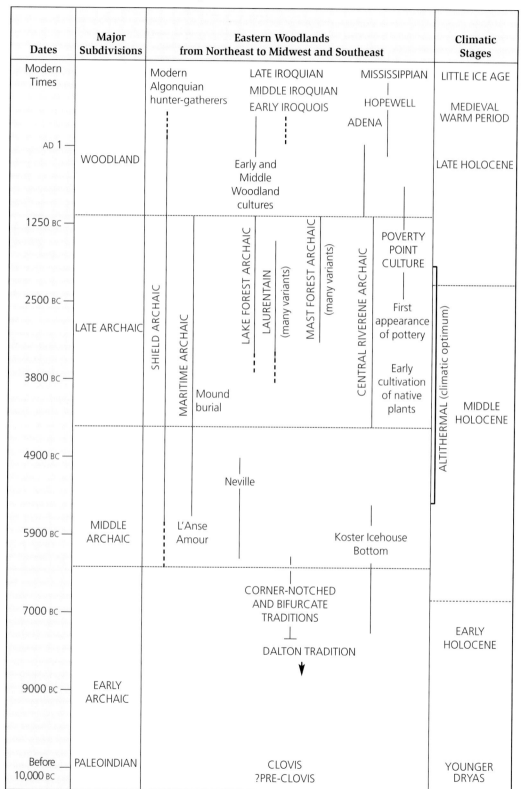

Dates	Major Subdivisions	Eastern Woodlands from Northeast to Midwest and Southeast	Climatic Stages
Modern Times	WOODLAND	Modern Algonquian hunter-gatherers — LATE IROQUIAN / MIDDLE IROQUIAN / EARLY IROQUOIS — MISSISSIPPIAN / HOPEWELL / ADENA — Early and Middle Woodland cultures	LITTLE ICE AGE / MEDIEVAL WARM PERIOD
AD 1			LATE HOLOCENE
1250 BC	LATE ARCHAIC	SHIELD ARCHAIC / MARITIME ARCHAIC / LAKE FOREST ARCHAIC / LAURENTAIN (many variants) / MAST FOREST ARCHAIC (many variants) / CENTRAL RIVERENE ARCHAIC / POVERTY POINT CULTURE — First appearance of pottery — Early cultivation of native plants — Mound burial	ALTITHERMAL (climatic optimum) / MIDDLE HOLOCENE
2500 BC			
3800 BC			
4900 BC	MIDDLE ARCHAIC	Neville / L'Anse Amour / Koster Icehouse Bottom	
5900 BC			
7000 BC	EARLY ARCHAIC	CORNER-NOTCHED AND BIFURCATE TRADITIONS ⊥ DALTON TRADITION ↓	EARLY HOLOCENE
9000 BC			
Before 10,000 BC	PALEOINDIAN	CLOVIS ?PRE-CLOVIS	YOUNGER DRYAS

11 · The Eastern Woodlands: Moundbuilders

Eastern Woodland societies embarked on a complex, multi-faceted trajectory of change and elaboration after 1000 BC. With much better-defined territories and rising populations, elaborate burial rites and interment under burial mounds and earthworks became a near-obsession. Thus were born what are sometimes called the Moundbuilder cultures, defined not by their daily lifeways – which remained little different from those of earlier times – but by embankments and tumuli. How did these Moundbuilder societies develop and why? What social and political institutions supported them? Some fascinating answers are coming from state-of-the-art multidisciplinary research.

Burial mounds and the Adena complex
before 1000 BC to AD 200–250

The idea of building earthworks was nothing new: witness mounds in the South that go back in time some thousands of years, such as Poverty Point in Louisiana and earlier shell midden earthworks of the Middle Archaic. But after 500 BC, burial mounds were an important part of mortuary ceremonialism from the western Appalachians to the Mississippi Valley, and north into Wisconsin and Michigan. The earliest marked ceremonialism of this sort manifested itself in the Adena complex of the Ohio Valley.   129

"Adena" is a convenient archaeological term that covers dozens of local Early and sometimes Middle Woodland cultures that were contemporary, often close, neighbors, and interacted with one another continuously. Such societies were remarkable for their diverse artifacts, widespread trading contacts, and burial ceremonialism. However, despite increasingly elaborate burial practises, most settlements were still small, often no more than one or two houses.

Adena was a series of mortuary rituals and spiritual beliefs that have come down to us in the form of hundreds of burial mounds in its Ohio Valley heartland alone. We can trace Adena from Indiana's Whitewater River Valley in the west to Pittsburgh in the upper Ohio Valley in the east, and from the Blue Grass of central Kentucky north to the upper reaches of the

129 The Adena Mound in Ross County, Ohio, excavated in 1901.

Scioto and Muskingum of Ohio. Mounds and Adena artifacts also occur elsewhere, as far away as the Canadian Maritimes and Mid-Atlantic states.

Specific burial customs varied greatly from simple to complex. Sometimes people started with a small mound that covered the burial of a single person in a shallow, elliptical pit lined and covered with bark. A mound could also be erected over what had been a circular structure, more likely an enclosure than a roofed house, often associated with human remains. The mound rose steadily as more and more burials joined the sepulcher. Some interments were entire bodies, perhaps wrapped simply in bark, while others were cremated remains. Occasionally the mourners simply deposited a bundle of bones, as if the body had been exposed on an open platform until the flesh decayed – or perhaps the dead person died away from home and the bones were brought back for burial. Some important burials lay with a long-defleshed skull placed on the lap. One such find at the Cresap Mound in West Virginia bore a slight polish, as if it had been treasured and handled regularly for some time.

130   The most impressive tombs, however, were built with large logs lining the sides and floor, and making up the roof. The mourners often sprinkled the dead with powdered red ocher, sometimes with yellow ocher, graphite, or manganese dioxide in small amounts. Grieving relatives occasionally painted the corpse with red ocher paint as well. They prepared the paint on crude stone tablets, convenient thin slabs of limestone, sandstone, and other rocks. Some tablets are deeply grooved by the rubbing of pieces of hematite (used as coloring pigment). Other than the burials, there are few signs of any social distinction between individuals in these societies.

130 Excavation of the much reduced Crigler Mound, Kentucky, exposed the original ground surface, also paired posts and four internal supports for a structure.

Many mounds were used again and again, with more log tombs and other burials being added to an existing tumulus. Burial areas can be thought of as stacked cemeteries, such as the Robbins Mound in northern Kentucky. Some of the largest and most elaborate mounds lie in the central Ohio Valley, like the famous Grave Creek Mound at Moundsville, West Virginia, which was originally over 65 ft (20 m) high, with a volume of nearly 2.47 million cu. ft (70,000 cu. m).

The Adenans sometimes built circular earthen enclosures, consisting of shallow ditches and adjacent embankments, near their burial mounds. These "sacred circles" may have been the meeting places for the kin group using the associated tumulus. Perhaps the individuals buried in log tombs in the mounds were important kin leaders. Sometimes, the sacred enclosures occur in groups of two to eight, as if the people from different social units were congregating at the same location.

Adena burials carried a rich variety of grave goods with them, especially the individuals interred in log tombs. Many distinctive ornaments appeared in the graves. These included

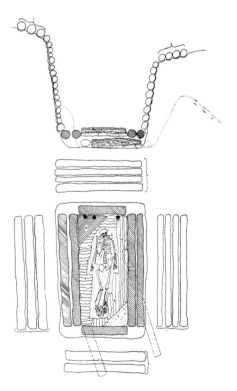

131 Cross-section and plan of an Adena burial from the Wright Mound, Kentucky.

132 The Grave Creek Mound at Moundsville, West Virginia.

copper bracelets and finger rings. There were crescents and sheets fabricated from North Carolina mica, some marine shells, and bracelets, axes, and other items from Lake Superior copper. There were many forms of gorgets (neck ornaments) and distinctive atlatl weights. Pipe designs 134 included carved animal effigies. Tubular Ohio pipestone pipes, used to generate kinnikinnick smoke, traveled through exchange networks as far away as Ontario, New England, and Maryland. Some other characteristic grave goods included large, leaf-shaped spearheads and knives, often made of bluish gray hornstone from Indiana or Illinois, artifacts sometimes found in caches. Perhaps such point collections were exchanged as gifts. Other 133 points made of local materials also often occur in Early Woodland cemeteries, and some of these artifacts were apparently exchanged over long distances. They have been found from Wisconsin and Illinois all the way to New England. Carved effigies long known as "birdstones" and "boatstones" replace the bannerstones of the Late Archaic. Birdstones are not, in fact, bird effigies, but composite animals, sometimes shown with four feet, perhaps depicting a divinity associated with sky and earth.

Several Adena mounds have yielded wolf palates, each carefully trimmed,

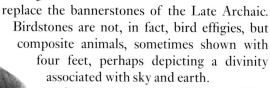

133 Birdstone from Flint County, Georgia.

with the upper and lower incisors removed, so that they could be worn in a man's mouth. At least one human skull with the front teeth knocked out long before death has been found associated with a wolf palate. Presumably this was done so the palate could be inserted into the person's mouth, the skin of the wolf head fitting over the head. Some of these artifacts may have been shamans' masks, or were used in rituals that depicted the symbolic relationships between familiar animals and different clans.

Everyone agrees that Adena burial traditions developed from Late Archaic roots in the Ohio Valley. There were Adena sites along every major tributary stream of the Ohio River from southeastern Indiana to central Pennsylvania by 2,000 years ago, with great concentrations of burial mounds in some well-defined areas – the Scioto Valley of south-central Ohio, the Kanawha River in West Virginia, and around Cincinnati, Ohio, to mention only three. Perhaps these reflect a tendency toward concentration within tribal territories.

Why did Adena and other mortuary complexes develop? Early Woodland burial complexes were highly localized – Adena was one, Red Paint, marked by promiscuous use of ocher, in the Northeast another. They flourished alongside dozens of Late Archaic communities that still lived as they had done for centuries. Perhaps, as territorial boundaries became more marked and interaction between neighbors

134 Stone effigy pipe in the form of a human, from the Adena Mound, Ohio. Height 7.9 in (20 cm).

increased, so membership of social groups assumed much greater importance, for it was these lineages and clans that controlled access to food and other resources. It is probably no coincidence that the Early Woodland sees a continuing trend toward at least semi-sedentary settlement, with people living at one base location for many months on end. This may have helped foster a growing sense of corporate identity, reinforced by regular burial ceremonies at earthworks. And in areas where the food situation was often precarious, different groups were probably careful to maintain rights of access to resources located outside their own territories, as a form of "insurance" in lean years when frosts or other natural phenomena seriously depleted local foods. People used social processes to maintain exchange networks not only to handle food, but to maintain access to resources of restricted distribution at a distance.

Judging from living societies, the main participants in such exchange systems would have been lineage leaders, individuals honored at death with special artifacts and funeral ceremonies, and adorned with the ceremonial items that recognized their social roles. Thus, burial rites validated not only group identity on a regular basis, but also commemorated the status of prominent kin leaders. These individuals were those who organized community work efforts by clan members when needed – to erect burial mounds, construct earthworks, and carry out other projects that were to the collective benefit. Everyone who participated received gifts of redistributed food and other goods. And the prized high-status goods such as mica sheets, copper ornaments, and carved pipes buried with clan leaders not only proclaimed their social standing, but maintained their high prestige by vanishing below the ground when their owner died.

As archaeologist David Brose argues, such mechanisms provided increasing social and economic stability, reinforced trends toward sedentary living and specialized exploitation of local resources, and probably led to population growth. This growth in turn triggered additional responses – more-ranked and better-integrated social systems that replaced the more flexible ones of earlier times. Brose believes that there was what he calls a "trajectory" of long-term cultural change. These changes first developed in areas where there was maximal pressure or very low potential carrying capacity. The more closely integrated social systems emphasized rank within individual lineages, validated by exotic objects of great prestige from afar and by seasonal ceremonies when all the members of lineages, from near and far, came together to reinforce their social identity and common goals. About the time of Christ, this trajectory of cultural change led to far more elaborate social institutions and ceremonial life, which culminated in the spectacular Hopewell tradition.

Hopewell *c.* 200 BC to *c.* AD 400

Hopewell, named after a mound complex on a farm in Ross County, Ohio, is famous for its earthworks, its flamboyant burial customs, and its complex interaction networks that traded raw materials and finished artifacts over enormous areas. Hopewell is a "great tradition" or an ideology in the spiritual sense, a set of understandings, as it were, shared by numerous small regional societies over much of the Midwest, accompanied by distinctive artifacts and mortuary rituals. These permitted trade and communication over long distances. The Scioto Valley-Painted Creek area near Chillicothe is the center of Hopewell development in Ohio. Elaborate mounds and spectacular geometric earthworks enclose from ten to hundreds of acres (four to many hectares). Other centers of Hopewell earthworks lie near Marietta and in southwestern Ohio. Hopewell influence extended far from its Midwestern homelands, into the Havana region of Illinois, and to Marksville in the Lower Mississippi Valley. Many contemporary societies in the East and Southeast shared mortuary customs, ritual and religious beliefs, and artifact styles.

Hopewell people lived, for the most part, in small, isolated communities, sometimes comprising no more than one or two extended families. These households were stable settlements, occupied perhaps for as long as a decade by people who not only foraged, but also cultivated indigenous domesticated plants. There are signs that some people took extended foraging trips between spring and fall. Hopewell settlements in Illinois endured for longer periods, with greater residential stability. Many communities lay in areas defined by local drainage systems, with household sites, specialized camps, and ritual precincts, normally close to the center of the community and the focus of local life. For example, the Tunacunnhee site in northwestern Georgia lies on a natural corridor connecting the interior highlands with the flatter country to the east and southeast, now occupied by a modern Interstate highway. This would have been a strategic location for many social transactions, often accompanied by prestigious gifts. More Hopewell fine objects came from the Tunacunnhee excavations than from any other site in the Southeast, testifying to its important position. The constant hiving off of new generations made for a dynamic settlement pattern, where different settlements were occupied for shorter or longer periods, with the number of settlement clusters increasing through time. Ceremonial precincts also changed continually over the generations, with the building of new burial mounds, fresh earthworks, and other features.

This was a world of intimate kin relationships, where people from neighboring groups came together to harvest nuts and hunt, and for other activities. Social and spiritual alliances ebbed and flowed; people learned and shared basic values, supernatural beliefs, and rituals common to an entire society. These mechanisms found mates and arranged marriages, and exchanged food, raw materials, and ritual objects. Larger social groupings and alliances crafted religious paraphernalia, built ceremonial centers, and performed communal rituals that revolved around healing, death, and the ancestors. Numerous leadership positions arose within these various groups, which provided the context for satisfying both prosaic daily needs and social and spiritual obligations, which were often fulfilled at ceremonial centers – complexes of one or two burial mounds, sometimes earthen enclosures covering as much as 80 acres (32 ha). These special gathering places were the spiritual core of Hopewell life.

Within the Scioto-Painted Creek area, and probably elsewhere, households formed part of about three local communities, well separated across the landscape, perhaps 7 to 12 miles (11 to 20 km) apart. Each probably comprised at least a hundred people and maintained several ceremonial centers. On a larger scale, such local communities formed close alliances 135 with others to form much bigger encompassing groups, up to 19 miles (31 km) in diameter. These larger groupings exchanged labor to build earthworks, and provided husbands and wives as well as food and commodities, thereby protecting everyone from food shortages and other challenges. Each alliance had strong social and spiritual underpinnings.

The religious beliefs that sustained Hopewell communities originated for the most part in Adena thinking. Within a relatively restricted area, groups elaborated upon, and changed, already commonplace ritual and ceremonial themes to form the distinctive Hopewell cults, many of which celebrated

135 Middle Woodland village farmers, *c.* AD 300.

ancestors. Some highly characteristic exotic artifacts such as copper ornaments and pipes were common to all. Some of these exotica passed from hand to hand via complex interaction networks, while others came directly from distant places and peoples – a suite of interregional linkages of multiple kinds that flourished from about 200 BC to between AD 300 and around 400.

Hopewell interaction networks covered most of the Eastern Woodlands, from the Southeast into southeastern Canada. The most active ones lay along major waterways like the Ohio River. The range of artifacts and materials is astonishing – native copper from the Lake Superior region, and silver from the same place and from deposits near Cobalt, Ontario. Mica and chlorite came from the southern Appalachians, quartz crystals from caverns near Hot Springs, Arkansas. The networks handled 136 large marine shells from the Gulf of Mexico as well as smaller species from both the South Atlantic and Florida Gulf Coast. Galena cubes came from northwestern Illinois and Missouri, and colorful flint from central Ohio. Neutron activation studies on Hopewell obsidian reveal sources as far away as Yellowstone Park in the Rocky Mountains, while flint came from the Knife River area of North Dakota. Characteristic Hopewell platform pipes were fabricated from Illinois and Ohio pipestone.

Large concentrations of Hopewell-style artifacts are found in two core areas – the Mississippi and Illinois River valleys in Illinois, and the Scioto and Miami valleys in southern Ohio. Each of these two areas, the one to the west, the other to the east, stands at the center of a large, interregional network. In time, they overlapped with one another, but they never lost their own identities. The intensity of exchange drops off sharply outside the Illinois/Ohio area, but it's clear that some ceremonial artifacts and beliefs spread much further afield into the Southeast. Such contacts, perhaps in person, were between individuals living at some distance from

Deciphering Hopewell

Hopewell archaeologists face a grim reality. Almost all major burial mound and earthwork excavations took place before the days of rigorous field investigation. Many of them were little more than glorified treasure-hunting expeditions. As a result, today's researchers spend their careers piecing together Hopewell society from a complex jigsaw puzzle of both spectacular and prosaic finds often made generations ago. They have done so with excellent results, in a process that archaeologists Christopher Carr and Troy Case call "thick pre-history," an attempt to describe in rich, ethnographic-like detail the environment, life ways, and history of Hopewell people.

Today's synthesis of Hopewell society is a triumph of multidisciplinary research that combines fieldwork with laboratory work, meticulous inventories of old excavations, and both ethnographic and historical records. Archaeology provides the chronological backbone, data on changing settlement patterns over many centuries, and analyses of artifacts, food remains, and other clues to ancient human activity. Biological anthropology has yielded information on the people themselves, through their anatomy and DNA.

A major component of today's Hopewell research has been the compilation of massive databases and inventories from past, hitherto unpublished excavations, unstudied burials, and other supporting information. The resulting data have made unprecedented reconstructions of Hopewell life possible, for they come not from a single location, but from entire regions like the Scioto Valley. Thanks to the recently compiled huge databases, one can examine an individual and his or her role in a much broader society.

Much effort has gone into making this information available to researchers, so that they can embark on in-depth, empirical studies of Hopewell social and personal lives, religious belief, and rituals. This is far from easy, and involves leaving behind personal and Western preconceptions as one peers into a totally different ancient world.

Fortunately, Hopewell societies left expressive statements about the intangibles of their lives behind them in their art and exotic artifacts. For example, claws, teeth, jaws, and other crafted body parts reveal the clan affiliations of the dead. Distinctive artifacts like quartz crystals and conch shells highlight the roles of shaman-like leaders in ceremonial life. Changes over time in the relative frequencies of metallic headdresses chronicle shifts in the style of Hopewell leadership from informal to more formal, priest-like offices.

The new generation of Hopewell research requires systematic, regional-scale archaeological collections and computerized data sets that can only be accumulated over long periods of time. This is a form of long-term, team research that is completely different from the much more simplistic, and usually more localized, researches of yesteryear. The archaeologists who carry out this kind of research have infinite patience and ability at complex, expensive teamwork that involves working collaboratively toward carefully formulated goals that may take years to achieve. The new perceptions of Hopewell described here come from many years of tedious, inconspicuous work, but the results are truly revolutionary for our understanding of a people whose society flourished 2,000 years ago.

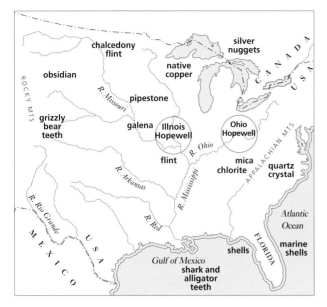

136 The far-flung sources of Hopewell raw materials.

one another, often far from rivers, a trade conducted along winding village paths. The intensity of the exchanges varied constantly, with cycles of expansion and dissolution, but the diversity and number of ceremonial artifacts passed down the networks increased over the centuries. These symbolic artifacts possessed intense ritual and social meaning. They became power symbols so important that they were buried with their owners at death.

Earthworks and cosmos

The most spectacular Hopewell burial mounds are in the Ohio PL. XIX Valley. At Hopewell itself, near Chillicothe, thirty-eight mounds lie within a rectangular enclosure covering 110 acres (45 ha). Other mound groups are as impressive. The average size of Ohio mounds is about 30 ft (9 m) high and some 100 ft (30 m) across, with a volume of about 500,000 cu. ft (14,000 cu. m). Each represents over 200,000 hours of earthmoving, all achieved using the simplest of stone-bladed tools, wooden digging sticks, and baskets.

Like their Adena predecessors, Hopewell monuments lay inside sacred 138 earthworks, but these were on a much more imposing scale. At Mound City, Ohio, for example, twenty-four mounds lie within an enclosure covering 13 acres (5 ha). A vast complex encircles the burial mounds at Newark, Ohio, PL. XVIII the entire mortuary landscape covering more than 4 sq. miles (10 sq. km) (see box p. 213).

More than 1,150 burials have been found in the major Ohio mound groups alone, interred in many different ways. More than three-quarters of scientifically studied burials were cremations. Hopewell mourners used both crypts and charnel houses. The former were large boxes constructed for the temporary storage of the dead and their grave goods until final burial in the earthen mound. They were simple structures sunk into the ground and covered with heavy roofs, often built on isolated high spots clear of the settlement. Crypts apparently served as corporate facilities for a single community. Sometimes, both cremated individuals and entire corpses lay in large charnel houses with thatched roofs and substantial post frames. Once the charnel houses had fulfilled their role, they were dismantled or burnt down and an earthen mound erected over them.

The Newark earthworks

In about AD 250, the Hopewell people living near the modern city of Newark, Ohio, embarked on a major earthwork construction project. Over several generations, they laid out an intricate maze of mounds, circles, an octagon, and a square. From the air, the Newark earthworks seem like a jumble of enclosures and earthen mounds that defies ready explanation, especially since much of the site now lies under the city streets and a golf course. Fortunately for science, journalist Ephraim Squier and physician Edwin Davis surveyed the earthworks in the 1840s, when they were still largely intact. The enclosures and mounds display an astonishing precision, with exact corners and precise astronomical orientation. For example, the Newark octagon covers 44 acres

(18 ha), with openings at each corner. A perfect 1054-ft (321-m) diameter "Observatory Circle" is attached to the octagon. This pair of earthworks is aligned with the moon, laid out with a standard unit of measurement with a remarkable knowledge of geometry and astronomy. The Newark lunar alignments were probably accurate enough to allow the prediction of years when lunar eclipses would occur near the winter or summer solstices. Some experts believe the Newark octagon and circle reflect a Hopewell concern not only with the burial of ancestors in mounds within the earthwork complex, but with seasonal rituals governed by astronomical phenomena, as if the Hopewell people arranged their earthly environment to mirror the heavens.

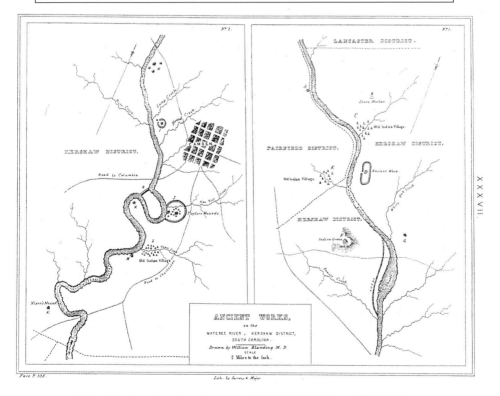

137 A plan of the Newark earthworks executed by Ephraim Squier and Edwin Davis.

138 Aerial view of the Hopewell Ohio Mound City complex, which covers areas equivalent to several New York City blocks, and has a greater surface area than the base of the Old Kingdom Pyramid of Khufu in Egypt.

Elite individuals lay in log-lined tombs within the charnel houses, accompanied by a diverse array of artifacts. A young man and woman buried together in the main mound at Hopewell wore copper ear spools, copper noses, copper breast plates, and necklaces of grizzly-bear teeth. The woman wore thousands of freshwater pearl beads, and copper-covered wooden and stone buttons. Some of the men in the mounds may have been expert artisans, like an individual from Hopewell buried with 3,000 mica sheets and 198 lb (90 kg) of galena.

Hopewell mounds contained not only richly decorated burials but caches of exotic objects. The mourners deposited copper axes, cut-out silhouettes 139 of birds, fish, claws, and human heads and hands in copper or mica, flint and chlorite disks, finely polished stone atlatl weights, and beautiful effigy pipes. 140 There were engraved human bones, painted fabrics, and occasional clay figurines depicting women in belted skirts and men in loincloths.

Dispersed Hopewell communities maintained connections with one another through a variety of social and spiritual partnerships. In Ohio, communities buried some, even all, their dead relatives together in shared cemeteries distributed between them. The intermingling of ancestral remains created powerful symbolic ties between different groups. Such ceremonial observances may have unfolded with the seasons, perhaps with different rituals performed at different earthworks in sequence, the location depending on the astronomical alignments of the earthworks.

In Ohio, everyone belonged to a clan whose members lived in different communities: far-from-local institutions that fulfilled important social and ceremonial roles throughout the year. We know, from their pendants, of at least nine clans, each with animal or totem associations, among them Bear, Canine, Felines, Raptor, and Beaver. Three or more non-kin groups organized for specific purposes flourished in Hopewell society, each identified by platform pipes, breastplates, and other artifacts. Their activities included some shamanistic duties, such as invoking the power of animals, divination, and corpse processing. No single clan dominated the others or provided supreme leaders. Hopewell was a mosaic of what one might call "horizontal" societies, without powerful chiefs or major rulers. A large number of decentralized social units complemented one another, recruited members from all parts of society, and enjoyed approximately similar levels of prestige, wealth, and access to food and other necessities. Many, usually transitory, organizers contributed to society – clan leaders, diviners, healers, people who processed the dead, and gifted men and women who were repositories of astronomical and mythic lore, for example.

139 Mica bird-of-prey claw from an unknown Ohio location. Length 11.2 in (28 cm).

Ohio Hopewell leadership was highly diversified and decentralized, with classic shamanistic and shaman-like leaders all complementing one another, all with at least some power base in the spiritual realm. Judging from art objects, Hopewell shamans impersonated animals and became them, were transformed. They were specialized practitioners, with different areas of responsibility, among them warfare and the hunt. But there were no hereditary rulers passing their office from one generation to the next. In these egalitarian societies, leaders took their regalia and ceremonial artifacts with them at death, and others took over their roles.

Hopewell art and burial customs reveal their layered cosmos of underworld and sky, defined by the cardinal directions, and by the solstices and the positions of moonrise and moonset. Hopewell astronomers balanced and combined these different realms, whose meanings and inhabitants were defined in artworks and earthwork alignments, burials and ritual deposits, also by ceremonial observance. At the core of human existence was the Center, the nexus of interaction, merging, and cooperation, of conflict and

PL. XXI

141

140 Four Hopewell clay bird-effigy smoking pipes. Locations unknown, height of tallest 2.3 in (6 cm).

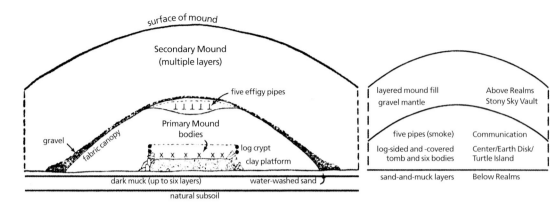

141 The Pricer-Seip mound represents the cosmos. The multiple burial was a symbol of the Center, placed on a platform: Turtle Island. Below, water-washed sand-and-muck layers depict the primordial water and the Below realm. A cache of effigy pipes above the skeletons and their smoke symbolize the Above realms, represented by the multiple mound layers.

expression of difference. Every person, every household, each pipe, every village and ceremonial place stood at the Center, a belief found in historical Eastern Woodland societies and in other groups around the world. There were wider formulations, too, such as the idea that expansive primordial waters surrounded the Center. Such was Turtle Island, a symbol of the earth disk and also the top surface of the underworld.

By the same token, earthworks rose at points in the landscape where they reiterated the importance of the multilayered cosmos, on terraces, or associated with conical hillocks that defined the Above realms. Streams defined the Below. These symbolic associations were deeply embedded in local thought right into historic times. A broad river terrace served as the place for geometric ceremonial grounds, where humans performed the ceremonies that maintained the delicate balance between the living and other beings, and forces at the Center and in the layered cosmos. Earthen enclosures served as the Center, constructed so that they had a symbolic relationship with a nearby river or stream, a form of entrance to the Below. The Scioto earthworks were aligned precisely with the point where celestial bodies such as the Sun and Moon met the horizon. Such alignments served as the benchmarks for an annual ritual calendar of gatherings for major ceremonies that could be observed both within the earthworks and from neighboring high ground. Very often, major earthworks lay close to such features

142 Composite being, associated with the Below realm, which has the horns and body of an ungulate, the legs of an aquatic mammal, and the tail of a rattlesnake.

as conspicuous cliffs, like the water-weeping shale cliff near Seip, a nesting place for vultures, perhaps an important element in mortuary rituals.

Animals played a central role in Hopewell ritual, for the people believed that some humans had the ability to transform themselves into animals and vice versa. Animals were models as leaders, symbols of clan organization, a means for achieving personal power. We see this in headdresses and a human jaw with a deer tooth replacement for a human tooth. Personal spiritual power came from trance, sometimes facilitated by smoking with pipes depicting animal guardians-cum-tutelary spirits, or by ingesting hallucinogenic mushrooms.

142

PL. XXII

Lastly, color, darkness, and light played important parts in the process of transformation, an interplay epitomized by the darkness of forests, grey skies, and open, cleared land. The raw materials like copper, mica, and some pottery clays that make up Hopewell paraphernalia can change from light to dark, from shiny to dull, or display both qualities simultaneously. The background and foreground images of their art shift and alternate, again contributing to transforming forces. Darkness, light, animals, the mysterious forces of the environment, and the supernatural world formed the central core of Hopewell life and belief.

143 Moundbuilding involved entire communities, as shown in this reconstruction set in the Upper Mississippi Valley.

144 The Great Bear Mound Group, Effigy Mounds National Monument.

The Hopewell decline and effigy mounds   AD 325 and beyond

Some time between AD 325 and 350, a three-way alliance between local symbolic communities in the Scioto region partially disintegrated. Charnel-house building slowed, earthen enclosures were no longer constructed. Ceremonial activity declined dramatically. An explanation for this sudden change eludes us. One has an impression of overall disruption that is still little understood. We know that, despite these developments, traditional subsistence activities continued almost unchanged. Climatic cooling did not play a significant role in triggering change. Rather, as the Hopewell archaeologists Christopher Carr and Troy Case argue, there is a religious explanation. The disintegrating Scioto-Painted Creek alliance broke down a powerful spiritual pact that had centered on three groups burying their dead in the Pricer-Seip charnel house. One of the three chambers in the next house was left empty. A later house at nearby Ater had but two chambers and no surrounding earthwork. A short time after, the charnel house was decommissioned and covered, as if the alliance finally had been dissolved. Some seminal, probably spiritually interpreted, event must have taken place – perhaps an epidemic that destroyed the alliance, a prophecy that failed to come true, an unexpected astronomical event, or some other happening that undermined the social and religious beliefs that had endured for centuries.

Moundbuilding continued after AD 400, but without the stimulus of Hopewell ideologies and trade networks. Numerous effigy mounds lie in southern Wisconsin, Illinois, Iowa, and Minnesota, built between about AD 650 and 1300. The tumuli depict animals of all kinds, including bears, birds, elk, turtles, panthers, and wolves. Construction began with stripping off the turf to form the outline of the effigy. Then one or more people were buried in the head or heart region before the builders piled up earth to form the mound. Many secondary interments in the earthworks may represent people who had died during the previous winter. Some of the effigy mounds are of impressive size. The Great Bear Mound in Iowa's Effigy Mound National Monument measures 137 ft (42 m) from head to tail and rises over 3 ft (1 m) above ground. It is one of 196 mounds in the park, thirty-one of which are effigies. The significance of effigy mounds is unknown, but there seem to be dualities involved, such as birds opposed to bears; duality was an important feature of later beliefs.

144

Another moundbuilding culture, Fort Ancient, centered on southern Ohio, northern Kentucky, and western West Virginia; it developed out of Hopewell and thrived between AD 1000 and 1670, with apparently few ties with the increasingly elaborate societies further south described in Chapter 12. The most famous Fort Ancient earthwork is the Great Serpent Mound in southern Ohio.

145

The centuries between AD 800 and 1200 saw maize agriculture spread from the central Mississippi Valley through the Southeast and the Eastern Woodlands. There are clear signs of gradual population growth, continued inter-community exchange, and increasing cultivation of native plants by sedentary peoples in river valleys and along coasts. The Late Woodland was a period of highly varied cultural change which culminated in a series of remarkable riverine societies after AD 800, and in the great Mississippian tradition of the South and southern Midwest.

145 The Great Serpent Mound, Ohio, the most famous of all effigy mounds.

12 · The Mississippian: Eastern Woodlands Climax

Over 6,000 years of continuous, sometimes gradual, sometimes punctuated, cultural change in the Midwest and Southeast culminated in one of ancient North America's most brilliant achievements – the Mississippian tradition. With its great centers and numerous small communities, this complex patchwork of chiefdoms of every size flourished for about six centuries, up to European contact and beyond. Its very complexity raises intriguing questions. Why and when did Mississippian society achieve such a high level of elaboration? What kind of leaders presided over the great ceremonial centers and what kind of society did they head? What was the basis of their power? It is only in recent years that we have begun to acquire some answers, thanks to research not only in archaeology, but in oral history and ethnography as well.

The origins of the Mississippian lie in Archaic and Woodland societies that flourished long before maize agriculture became widespread in the great river valleys of the East. One such culture is Coles Creek in the lower Mississippi Valley. Another is the Weeden Island culture, which arose among the ancient peoples of the deciduous and pine forests and marshy Gulf Coast plain between Florida, Alabama, and Georgia about 1,800 years ago. Weeden Island societies had both secular and sacred components, the former varying widely from one area to the next, depending on local food supplies. The ceremonial complex probably developed from earlier Hopewell practises and revolved around elaborate mortuary rituals centered on low platform mounds which served as bases for charnel houses, the residences of important people, and areas for preparing bones for burial (see chronological table on p. 202 and map on p. 126).

The McKeithen village in northern Florida is a classic Weeden Island settlement. Here, three low platform mounds form a horseshoe-shaped settlement with a central plaza. The first settlers arrived in about AD 200. Their descendants constructed the three mounds between AD 350 and 475. The structures on them burnt down in about 475. The mounds themselves formed a triangle. One supported a temple, where a priest lived and was buried. The second mound supported a charnel house, the third a pine-post screen where the dead were cleaned before being taken to the charnel house. These low tumuli formed part of a complex mortuary process, presumably supervised by the person buried in the temple.

Similar platform mounds occur over a wide area between Florida and the Mississippi River, part of a society where each village or lineage had a religious practitioner who provided a link to the supernatural. Between AD 700 and 1000, villages like McKeithen and their religious specialists assumed ever greater importance. These three centuries saw the sudden adoption of maize agriculture, also widespread political and religious changes that included the emergence of important chiefdoms and the flowering of elaborate ceremonial activities. Later Coles Creek and Weeden Island agricultural communities and their contemporaries developed into the Mississippian tradition.

A triad of cults

The term "Mississippian" defies precise definition, but what sets it apart from other cultural traditions are its social and religious institutions, defined by highly distinctive sacred artifacts.

A triad of religious cults lay at the core of Mississippian society. The first was warfare, an important power base for the elite, known from exotic motifs and symbols, and also from the use of costly raw materials like copper and sea shells. Such objects occur in elite burials, along with war axes, maces, and other weapons. Other artifacts bear strange cosmic imagery that depicts animals, humans, and mythic beasts. Some may be references to legendary warrior-heroes and their supernatural exploits, in artifacts that were perhaps part of sacred bundles kept by priests. This symbolic imagery melded warfare, cosmology, and nobility into a coherent whole. Dozens of Mississippian cemeteries and mound centers contain finely made pottery and other artifacts associated with this chiefly cult, many of them items transported over long distances. Despite local differences, themes and motifs have many features in common over a vast area, occurring not only in classic Mississippian centers like Etowah, Georgia, and Moundville, Alabama, but also in Spiro, Oklahoma, to the west, part of the related Caddoan moundbuilding culture. The artifacts include axes with head PL. XXV and shaft carved from a single piece of stone, copper pendants adorned with circles of weeping eyes, decorated clay pots and effigy vessels, and copper plates and engraved shell cups adorned with male figures in ceremonial PL. XXIV dress. Such themes as bird symbolism, circles, crosses, and weeping eyes have deep roots in more ancient societies of the Eastern Woodlands and were common to groups over a large area of the South and Southeast .

The second element, an earth/fertility cult, had close links with the earthen platform mounds so characteristic of Mississippian centers. These flat-topped tumuli may represent the Southeast Indian belief that the earth was a flat surface oriented toward four quarters of the world. The mounds acted as a symbol of renewal and fertility, the platform serving as the earth. There are historically documented connections between additions

146 Belief systems of later Southeastern peoples were closely tied to local political and social organization. Artists depicted complex symbols on clay vessels and stone, copper, and shell objects. The meanings of many symbols elude us, but they include "weeping eyes," birds, serpents, skulls, and hands. This shell head has weeping eyes and other facial decoration. Height 2.3 in (6 cm).

147 This copper head appears to have been cut out of a larger plate with the feather then riveted on. It was found in the Craig Mound at Spiro, Oklahoma. Length 9.4 in (24 cm).

to platform mounds and the communal "green corn" ceremony, which celebrated the new harvest and the fertility of the earth.

Ancestor cults were the powerful third element, for ancestors provided vital connections between the living and the land. The Great Mortuary in the Craig Mound at Spiro, Oklahoma, came into being in the early 1400s. Built on the site of earlier funerary structures, the Mortuary held clumps of human bones and fragmentary artifacts taken from sites elsewhere laid on a cane floor, with formal burials interred above them. Baskets of ceremonial artifacts such as copper-headed axes and piles of textiles lay with containers of sea shells, wooden masks, and statues. Subsequently, a set of   147 cedar poles was raised over the center of the mortuary deposit, creating both a void and a marker after the Mortuary was sealed. This Great Mortuary became a living part of the subsequent history of the Craig Mound.

The triad of Mississippian cults was each distinct. Both priests and warriors held different chiefly roles, which were confined to privileged kin groups. Elaborate ceremonial validated political power through rituals performed by the chiefs. Platform-mound cults with their emphasis on fertility and renewal were communal rites involving entire kin groups and communities that survived long after European contact. Priests, usually people with special supernatural powers, maintained temples, burial houses, sacred fires, and mortuary rituals for the ancestors. Ancestor worship cut across society, putting the priests in a powerful position to mediate disputes and competing interests.

Mississippian specialist James Knight believes these powerful cults, which defined both chiefly and communal society, transcended the South and Southeast and all their different cultural and ecological boundaries. They created a dynamic, constantly changing, and highly factionalized society with tremendous variation in social complexity. Large centers like Cahokia, near St. Louis, lay at one end of this spectrum of complexity, hundreds of small centers and minor chiefdoms at the other.

Subsistence and exchange

Mississippian societies coalesced across much of the Southeast during the eleventh and twelfth centuries, with an early efflorescence in the Central Mississippi Valley including the Cahokia region in about 1050. They developed in river valleys, often expanding up small tributaries of major waterways. For thousands of years, people had adapted to low-lying environments where locally concentrated food resources abounded. Fertile agricultural soils formed bands within these same valleys. A constant supply of water-borne nutrients helped these floodplain areas sustain high human population densities and a rich biomass of animals and plants. The Mississippians enjoyed elaborate yet very flexible subsistence patterns involving a broad range of prey. They also relied on a wide variety of plant foods, some that grew wild and others cultivated in fields. They cleared broad tracts of natural vegetation on carefully selected soils to plant maize, beans, squash, and several native plants including sunflower. Fish and waterfowl may have provided much of the protein intake of people living along the bottomlands of the Mississippi, for the river lay on a major water-fowl flyway and river meanders and oxbow lakes teemed with fish. Elsewhere, especially along narrow rivers lacking significant floodplains, there was a distinct tilt toward terrestrial animals, principally deer.

As we saw in Chapter 5, maize and bean cultivation had spread into the Southwest from Mexico during the second millennium BC. A small-cob, twelve- and fourteen-rowed race of maize was probably the first to arrive in the Southeast, about 2,000 years ago. At first, cultivation was sporadic, but it became much more commonplace during the late first millennium AD. Beans, which were to become an important protein source, arrived in the Eastern Woodlands by about AD 1000, but were not commonly cultivated until after 1300. In time, maize, and later bean, agriculture became so important that hunting and foraging provided less food than before. Nevertheless, fall nut harvests were always of vital importance, since maize yields without plows provided only a fraction of a household's yearly needs at the subsistence level. Eventually, with larger fields resulting from political or social stimuli, quite large food surpluses could have been manipulated for political ends.

Yields from both fields and nut harvests varied dramatically from year to year. Major floods could inundate agricultural soils for months, ruin pit-stored food, and disrupt fishing. Many Mississippian communities and their gardens lay on fertile, well-drained ridges or on nearby terrace soils that never flooded, even if the risk of drought was higher. Short-term climatic shifts could trigger prolonged droughts: some are well documented in tree-ring records, especially during the Medieval Warm Period of AD 800 to 1250. Everywhere, individual communities tried to minimize the risk of starvation by cultivating a mosaic of gardens located in different environmental zones. They must also have relied heavily on reciprocity, on kin in neighboring communities, who would provide food or grain in times of stress. In all communities, storage pits and granaries assumed central importance, so much so that archaeologist Jon Muller has argued that elite leaders emerged as a result of efforts to mitigate risk for households and entire villages. These leaders were those who oversaw the stockpiling of food supplies and ensured that cultivated lands thrived in different environments. At a certain level, kin ties would have been adequate for these purposes, but occasional food shortages may have been such that entire regions had to cooperate with one another, a process requiring more formal leadership.

The entire fabric of Mississippian society depended on the household, a self-sufficient unit. Thousands of them were grouped together into larger communities, with both mound centers and settlements linked to them. The most famous such regional center was Cahokia along with its immediate support area. Societies composed of a single mound center with affiliated smaller settlements are often called simple chiefdoms; when several of them are linked together, with one being dominant, they are known as complex chiefdoms. This form of segmental organization, with a great deal of local variation, survived the rise, apogee, and decline of Mississippian societies across the Eastern Woodlands. The same setup was typical of historically known societies in the region.

Wide-ranging exchange networks lay at the core of Mississippian society. The production of artifacts of all kinds was widely dispersed through the Mississippian world. For example, sea shells passed from hand to hand over vast areas of the Southeast. Specialists turned these into ornaments, often engraved with distinctive designs that included flying figures (shamans, warriors, or mythical heroes) and abstract faces. Experts can often identify motifs executed and repeated by individual artisans. Chert from Mill Creek, Illinois, was a hard material ideal for making hoes, and was widely traded after AD 900, traveling up to 430 miles (700 km) from source. Salt production assumed great importance, as maize farmers had to supplement their diet artificially with salt.

Cahokia: a great chiefdom   AD 1050 onward

Person-to-person bartering and kin-based formal redistribution were the most common ways of exchanging goods and commodities in Mississippian society. The processes of exchange were now highly politicized, often taking place at major ceremonial gatherings of a kind that still flourished in historic times. These occasions involved feasting and dancing, the sharing of food, exchanges, and the reaffirmation of ties with other villages and individuals.

There were some Mississippian centers that nurtured more complex social and political structures, most famously Cahokia in the American Bottom on the Mississippi River opposite St. Louis in Illinois. These centers raise important questions about the political organization of the most elaborate of all ancient North American societies.

The American Bottom is a pocket of low-lying floodplain along the Mississippi, the widest portion of which extends downstream from the confluence of the Illinois River for about 25 miles (40 km), with a maximum width of about 11 miles (18 km). Meanderings of the Mississippi over the flatlands formed swamps and oxbow lakes in abandoned channels. The American Bottom environment was exceptionally diverse, with fertile soils lying on the margins of several ecological zones. It was here that Cahokia flourished, with what was probably the highest population density north of Mexico.

Sedentary villages prospered at or near Cahokia after AD 600. Then, apparently within a few decades around AD 1050, a great center emerged at Cahokia, surrounded by several smaller administrative and political centers, and rural homesteads. Cahokia's population rose dramatically. Hundreds of people were resettled in small and large villages, even at some distance from Cahokia itself. These moves must have involved complex political negotiations among kin-based social groups, and the exploitation of religious beliefs that linked chief and villager. Imposing public structures and shrines, sweat houses, common art traditions, and the promotion of carefully chosen community traditions – all may have been symbols that linked elite and commoner in displays of common cultural meanings and values. The result: a regional chiefdom that melded Cahokia's authority with ancient community interests. But Cahokia was a short-lived polity. Competing factions and periodic inabilities to mobilize community labor helped fashion an inherently unstable chiefdom that appeared and dissipated with bewildering speed. After AD 1250, Cahokia's population gradually tapered off over the next 150 years, as people migrated outward from the American Bottom and more dispersed settlement patterns again prevailed. By the latter half of the thirteenth century, there were few Mississippians left in the American Bottom. This may be connected with the arrival of hardy *Maiz de Ocho*: adaptable to many conditions, eight-row corn when combined with beans allowed farming on higher ground and in other, less favorable environments.

At the height of its power between AD 1050 and 1250, Cahokia extended over an area of more than 3.8 sq. miles (10 sq. km). Dwellings covered some 2,000 acres (800 ha). The population may have been as low as 3,000, perhaps as high as 16,000 – estimates are hard to come by. Many people lived elsewhere on the floodplain and in the surrounding uplands. (Three of the largest Mississippian centers in the entire Southeast and Midwest lie next to one another in the central portion of the American Bottom – Cahokia itself, another in East St. Louis, and another across the river under St. Louis itself.) More than 100 earthen mounds of various shapes, sizes, and functions, many of them along the dry, central ridge of the site, cluster

148   around a series of open plazas. The most extensive grouping lies around Monk's Mound, the largest earthwork built by ancient North Americans. The 100-ft (30-m) high tumulus covers 16 acres (6.5 ha) and rose in four stages, beginning before AD 1000 and ending some three centuries later. A stairway once led up the south side to the first level, perhaps higher, and it faced the main plaza, the central focal point of the site. The third and fourth levels rose after AD 1200 on the northeast quadrant of the earthwork. A large building measuring 100 by 40 ft (30 by 12 m) stood on the summit of the highest terrace with a large wooden post in front of it, apparently a temple with a thatched roof. Teams of villagers supervised by expert moundbuilders erected the mound by heaping up 21.7 million cu. ft (615,000 cu. m) of earth basket by basket. In places, the architects alternated layers of sand and clay, perhaps in an effort to stabilize the structure and prevent slumping. The entire earthwork would have taken a theoretical 370,000 workdays to complete, with additional days for contouring and finishing.

148 Monk's Mound, Cahokia. The mound as seen today is a much eroded version of an imposing stepped structure, which rose in four stages beginning in AD 1000. There was a thatched wooden temple at the summit of the mound.

Some of the largest Cahokia mounds lie in two rows on either side of Monk's Mound. Most were platform mounds topped with important public buildings or elite dwellings. Some of these structures may have been charnel houses for the corpses of prominent ancestors. A log palisade with watch-towers and gates surrounded the entire 200 acres (80 ha) of the central area. We know the defensive wall, studded with bastions, was rebuilt at least four times, perhaps as a result of factional warfare.

149

PL. XX

High-status individuals lived in larger houses and were buried in great splendor. In Mound 72, an important man lay on a platform of 22,000 marine shell beads. A few other high-status men and women, perhaps close relatives sacrificed at the funeral, were interred nearby. About 800 arrowheads, copper and mica sheets, and fifteen polished disks (used in a spearthrowing game) lay close by. More than fifty young people aged between eighteen and twenty-three, apparently strangled as sacrifices, came from a neighboring burial pit. There were also other pits containing victims killed at different times elsewhere in the mound. The Mound 72 mortuary complex may have served as a kind of theater where certain mortuary narratives were performed by a high-status kin group using human bodies and ritual objects. Human sacrifice apparently played a major role in Mississippian ritual, as it did among societies in Mesoamerica far to the south.

149 Monk's Mound, 100 ft (30 to 40 m) high, dominated Cahokia's central precincts, with many smaller mounds and houses surrounding it. Trading and major public ceremonies took place in the main plaza. A log stockade protected the central precincts, with a solar calendar at far left. Maize gardens surrounded Cahokia; water came from Cahokia Creek and clay borrow pits, dug to quarry clay for moundbuilding.

Moundville   AD 1250 to c. 1500

150   Cahokia's power declined after AD 1250, when other large centers rose to prominence. Moundville, by the Black Warrior River in west-central Alabama, flourished between AD 1250 and c. 1500. The site, with its twenty-nine or more earthen mounds, covers more than 185 acres (75 ha). The larger mounds, the biggest about 56 ft (17 m) high, delineate a quadrilateral plaza of about 79 acres (32 ha); some support public buildings or the dwellings of important people. A bastioned and much rebuilt palisade protected the three sides of the site that faced away from the river. Hundreds of people lived within the general site area, perhaps as many as 1,000 souls. Altogether, 3,051 burials have been excavated at Moundville. Leaders were interred in the mounds, people of lesser status in major village areas along the northern boundary of the site.

Back in AD 900, a time of considerable political unrest and increasingly circumscribed territory, a relatively small number of people lived in the Moundville area. Maize production intensified between AD 950 and 1000, at a time when settlements grew larger, production of shell beads increased, and warfare became more commonplace. Between 1050 and 1250, maize and bean agriculture provided as much as 40 percent of the diet as the Black Warrior Valley became an important farming area. Moundville became an important ceremonial center in a process that culminated with the creation of the highly formalized, fortified town. The earthworks and plazas became a symbolic landscape, oriented from east to west, with pairings of residential and mortuary mounds and a well-defined ranking of social spaces within the site. The center assumed an importance outside its own boundaries. Tribute from perhaps 10,000 people, scattered through the surrounding area, supported the elite, who engaged in long-distance trade. The formal layout of the public architecture in the heart of the site probably reflected the status relationships of different kin groups set in the context of a sacred landscape. The paramount chief derived his position both from his supernatural authority and the power conferred on him by the sacred landscape.

For a century and a half after 1300, a firmly entrenched chiefly dynasty ruled Moundville and its environs, as we see from the lavishly adorned burials in its funerary mounds. Effectively the site became a necropolis, used by people from considerable distances away, and conceivably a location where priests with connections to the supernatural world beneath dwelt. It may also have been an entry point for the pathway that took the dead to the spiritual realms. As the dynasty became increasingly powerful and more isolated from its subjects, the population moved away from the center into the surrounding landscape. Perhaps the nucleated population left to join

150 Aerial view of Moundville Archaeological Park, Alabama.

coalitions of chiefly competitors occupying new mound centers built a short distance away. Moundville went into decline after AD 1450, when the center became a shadow of its former self. Even at the height of its power, Moundville was never a large polity, drawing labor and tribute from at most 45 miles (72 km) away. Large-scale tribute gathering may never have extended more than about 9 miles (14.5 km) from the site, simply because of the difficulty of transporting supplies and enforcing assessments.

At the height of their powers, Mississippian centers like Cahokia, Moundville, and others were large, complex communities, ruled by high-status individuals of great political, social, and religious influence. Both peace and war chiefs presided over a patchwork of smaller chiefdoms, not over sovereign states, as some claim. As time went on the power of the paramount chiefs declined except, perhaps, for some nominal allegiance. The Mississippian society centered on Moundville, like so many others – always volatile, always riven by factions – became entirely decentralized before the first contacts with Spanish explorers in the mid-sixteenth century. Other centers which did survive, especially in the Lower Mississippi Valley, were large enough to impress the Spaniards, although they lasted little more than a century following first contact, and sometimes only a matter of decades.

151 An artist's impression, based on excavations, of a palisaded Mississippian settlement at the Rucker's Bottom site in Georgia. Many villages were palisaded for defense against neighbors and enemies.

What were these complex chiefdoms?

What exactly was the nature of these complex chiefdoms? The simplest chiefdoms are single-level societies in social terms, where the chief is still a farmer, his household self-sufficient. He is expected to be a generous kinsman who redistributes goods and commodities to other members of society. More complex chiefdoms like those of the Mississippians have two or even three tiers of political hierarchy. Nobles are clearly distinct from commoners: they do not produce everything they need to support their households, but consume tribute such as food and exotic artifacts; they confine their reciprocity to ritual and secular services that only they can perform. Such societies depend on the paramount chief having power over lesser-ranking nobles, each of whom controls specific territories. The overall leader's power hangs on his ability to access large quantities of tribute passed up the line by his subordinates and their subjects. In the case of the Mississippians, the move toward greater political complexity may have come partly from control of long-distance exchange, especially in exotic goods, also in the use of this wealth to control local labor. These exotic artifacts became symbols of chiefly legitimacy, of a special relationship with the supernatural world. Centers like Cahokia were the settings for the great ceremonies that linked the commoner and the elite. Judging from historic Southeastern Indian institutions, major Mississippian centers may have had both peace chiefs and warrior chiefs.

Mississippian leaders never exercised strict control over commoners. Rather they drew them in with compelling religious ideology and distinctive cult items. They headed chiefdoms in a constant state of flux, fueled by intensely competitive political dynamics – just as was the case with ancient chiefdoms everywhere. With their regular feasts and elaborate ceremonies, Mississippian chiefs validated their authority in vivid, symbolic ways, well aware that their powers depended on negotiating the fine line between coercion and reciprocity and on the balance of the powerful cults that defined human existence over a wide area.

PL. XXIII

Fertility and duality

Thanks to a combination of archaeology and studies of historic Southeastern groups, we can begin to piece together the ancient cosmology and religious beliefs of the Mississippians. The layout of Cahokia and other great centers reflects a traditional Southeastern cosmos with four opposed sides, reflected in the layout of platform mounds, great tumuli, and plazas. Four-sided Mississippian platform mounds may portray the cosmos as earth-islands, the earth being flat-topped and flat-sided. The north–south axis of Cahokia echoes observations of the sun. Perhaps its rulers used the sun to schedule the annual rituals that commemorated the agricultural cycles of the year.

Funerary rites of a Natchez chief

In 1720, French explorer Le Page du Pratz spent time among the Natchez of the Lower Mississippi, one of the last remnants of the Mississippian way of life that had held sway over such a large area. He befriended a war chief named Tattooed Serpent. Under the chief were his kin, who served in various official capacities, Honored Men (nobles), and "Stinkards" (commoners). When the chief died unexpectedly, his hearth was immediately extinguished. He lay on his bed, dressed in his finest clothing, moccasined as if to go on a journey, and wearing his crown of white feathers mingled with red. His arms and pipes of peace lay by his side. A large wooden pole commemorated his victories.

The French sat at the side of the temple as the corpse of Tattooed Serpent was carried on a litter to the shrine, followed by sacrificial victims with red daubed hair and their executioners. The victims included the chief's two wives and his chief counselor, doctor, and pipe bearer. At the temple, the victims sat on assigned mats, their heads covered with skins. They chewed tobacco pellets that numbed their senses and were strangled swiftly. Then the chief's body was placed in a trench with his wives, and his hut was burnt down. The other victims were either buried with the chief or in their own villages. Du Pratz's account of the elaborate Natchez burial rituals, written at a time when Cahokia and Moundville were long abandoned, is the only eyewitness testimony of the use of North American platform mounds.

152 In 1720, the French explorer Le Page du Pratz depicted a dead Natchez chief being carried on a litter to his temple atop an earthen mound. Sacrificial victims kneel in wait, their executioners behind them.

As with the Hopewell, Southeastern cosmology revolved around dualities; at Cahokia these included the upper- and underworlds, also a powerful fertility cult linked to commoners and a warrior cult associated with the nobility. At first, settlement layouts reflected kin groups that controlled fertility rituals in villages divided into symbolic quarters. Later centers displayed more formal layouts with central plazas, elaborate sacred buildings, and storage and ritual pits filled with pots and other offerings made during fertility ceremonies that symbolically renewed the world. These changes reflect profound shifts in Mississippian society as power passed to an elite based at major centers. By AD 1050, carefully laid-out centers brought together two themes – the spiritual realm of fertility and life, and the validation of living rulers, who served as intermediaries with the supernatural realm.

Distinctive Mississippian artifacts offer some clues as to specific religious beliefs, notably a red softstone figurine found near Cahokia that depicts an Earth Mother associated with a serpent, itself associated with the giving of plants to humankind. She carries a sacred bundle, another gift to humanity. A feline-headed serpent monster appears widely in Mississippian art, a mythic beast that possessed the attributes of several animals and dwelt in the underworld. This world was the source of water, fertility, and power against evil, with sacred artifacts and artistic motifs creating a symbolic language with deep roots in the distant past understood by noble and commoner alike. Similar ideas and ideologies spread over an enormous area of the South, Midwest, and eastern Plains.

European contact

By the time European traders and explorers reached the Mississippi Valley in the late seventeenth century, Cahokia was long past its apogee. Moundville, though still important, was a shadow of its former self. But when Spanish conquistador Hernando de Soto and his conquistadors traversed the Southeast much earlier in 1539–41, they encountered still-powerful chiefdoms. Spanish metal, glass beads, and armor fragments have been found in several locations, notably the King site in northwestern Georgia, once a frontier village of the Coosa kingdom, a descendant of the spectacular chiefdoms of a few centuries earlier.

13 · The Northeast:
Algonquians and Iroquoians

When fifteenth-century Europeans sailed up the St. Lawrence River, they came into contact with powerful Iroquois nations and with the Huron. Less spectacular Northeastern societies flourished along the Atlantic coast, while other groups anchored themselves to interior lakes and rivers. This was an unsettled world, where farmers cultivated maize at the northern limits of its range. Much controversy surrounds the origins of two major linguistic groups: Algonquians and Iroquoians. But how and when did maize first arrive in the Northeast? What role did warfare play in the complex later history of this large region? Fortunately, a productive marriage of archaeology, ethnography, and written records provides some answers.

Algonquian and Iroquoian

People living in coastal drainages between Nova Scotia and North Carolina were Algonquian speakers. They formed the Eastern Algonquian language group, isolated from their western and northern relatives by an intrusive block of Iroquoian and other languages in the interior. The ultimate origins of Algonquian are still a mystery, but a form of this language probably goes back far into the past, to a time when ancient cultures in the Eastern Woodlands were more generalized. Both Algonquian and Gulf languages from the Southeast may, perhaps, be descended from a common group of related dialects spoken throughout the Eastern Woodlands before about 4000 to 3000 BC (see chronological table on p. 202 and map on p. 126).

The Northern Iroquoian languages form the most important barrier between the coastal Algonquian speakers and those to the west. They act as an insulating block between coast and far interior from central Pennsylvania through New York State and down the St. Lawrence Valley to the Gulf of St. Lawrence in Canada. Every linguistic expert agrees that the Iroquoian language distribution represents an ancient intrusion of a different linguistic group into the Northeast, a group later associated with the powerful Iroquois confederacies that dominated the area between the St. Lawrence and into New York State at European contact. Fierce warriors, shrewd traders, and sophisticated negotiators, the Iroquois were to play a dominant role in the Northeast to the very end of the Colonial period and beyond.

Terminal Archaic   1650 to 700 BC

Throughout the Eastern Woodlands, food-rich rivers large and small that flowed through the centers of Archaic territories provided vital communication arteries between widely scattered hunter-gatherer populations. The higher ground between the river valleys served as boundary land, sometimes remote, sometimes traversed by narrow trails often used for canoe portage. Much of the more rugged landscape was little more than a place where neighbors might hunt and collect wild vegetable foods.

Regional expert Dean Snow has estimated that no more than 25,000 people lived in New England before 8000 BC, and only between 158,000 and 191,000 in AD 1600. He calculates an average growth rate of 0.02 percent over these 9,600 years, with occasional periods of rapid increase and sometimes catastrophic decline. In contrast, the world population increase rate has been as high as 1.8 percent in recent years. This primeval population spacing lasted for thousands of years, changing only during the last six centuries before European colonization. By then, the introduction of new storage technologies and horticulture had allowed higher population densities in many parts of the Northeast.

Between 1650 and 700 BC, the Terminal Archaic communities of the Northeast enjoyed a diverse, and carefully scheduled, hunting-and-gathering lifeway. The Susquehanna tradition of New York State, Pennsylvania, and neighboring areas flourished during the earlier centuries of the Terminal Archaic (c. 1650–1320 BC). It was marked by a variety of broad projectile points that may also have doubled as knives. The Orient tradition replaced the Susquehanna in the New York region, itself characterized by long, narrow points with fishtail-shaped bases that persisted in use during later Woodland cultures as well. Oval and rectangular soapstone bowls with flat bottoms and lug handles, perhaps copies of wooden prototypes, came into widespread use by both Orient and Susquehanna people, especially in larger base camps. These heavy cooking vessels were apparently highly prized, traded widely, and long lived.

Susquehanna and Orient flourished alongside other Archaic societies in many areas, with much human settlement concentrated near rivers and coasts at a time of warming temperatures and stabilizing sea levels.

153 Orient fish-tailed point, length c. 4.3 in (11 cm).

Woodland societies   *c.* 1000 BC to AD 1000

The Algonquians of New England and the Atlantic coastal plain lived at the northernmost limit of maize cultivation and the southernmost extent of Atlantic salmon migration. Maize, an important feature of local economies at European contact, had been grown in large quantities in the Connecticut Valley and other river systems centuries earlier. People still moved to different locations according to the season, dispersing to hunt deer, and perhaps to trade or take beaver, a known historic activity. Local populations remained sparse, with the densest concentrations living in territories of widely differing size in river drainages, near lakes, and along sea coasts. Pottery appears in many local horticultural communities by at least 1000 BC, but the moment of appearance varied considerably. The increased use of pottery may signal a trend toward more sedentary settlement. Several innovations arrived during the first millennium AD, among them the bow and arrow (*c.* AD 600) and, in more northerly regions, the birchbark canoe: a light and versatile craft ideal for navigating fast-moving streams, it was made of paper birch, which flourishes in formerly glaciated terrain. Such canoes were used for gathering wild rice, which grew in dense, waterlogged stands. While one person paddled, the other would bend the stalks over the canoe and beat them with a stick, detaching the ripe seed, which could then be stored for the long winter months.

The northeast is remarkable for its ecological diversity, also its plentiful lakes and waterways, there being few significant physiographical boundaries. This meant that people moved quite freely over considerable distances, so there were frequent contacts between neighbors. Back in the 1950s, William Ritchie identified a "Meadowood phase," named after an estate of that name in Monroe County, New York. Originally, Meadowood appeared to be confined to western and central New York State, but its distinctive thin, triangular Onondaga chert blades, highly standardized projectile points, birdstones, gorgets, concoidally shaped pots, and other artifacts occur over a much wider area. The core areas are in southern Ontario north of Lake Erie and much of New York State, but Meadowood artifacts are also found along the St. Lawrence Valley and into Quebec. Now researchers talk of a Meadowood interaction sphere, a broad area over which artifacts and ideas passed among different groups between about 1000 and 400 BC.

Throughout this diverse area, large base camps anchored different territories, some of them close to rich stands of native grasses. The resulting seed caches helped tide the people over the lean months, as did squashes. Adena trade networks extended into parts of the Northeast and Meadowood country. Copper ornaments, slate gorgets, birdstones, and boatstones from Ohio – these and many other grave goods hint at an Adena cultural influence that went far beyond simple trade and exchange.

153

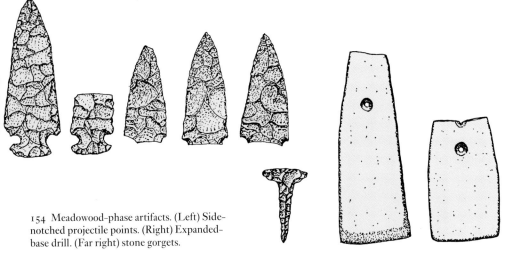

154 Meadowood-phase artifacts. (Left) Side-notched projectile points. (Right) Expanded-base drill. (Far right) stone gorgets.

Meadowood cemeteries often cluster on low, natural hills, just like burials in earlier centuries. The graves were closely packed together, the bodies usually cremated, but not always immediately after death. The mourners lined the burial pits with bark, laying out the cremated remains in red ocher-sprinkled shrouds. Later, Adena-style burial mounds with log-lined graves and exotic artifacts came into fashion across a large area from southern Ontario, through New York State and parts of southern and western New England, and into the Delaware drainage. Many of these societies were contemporary with the Hopewell tradition of the Midwest.

Northern Iroquoian origins: Early Iroquoian   *c.* AD 200 to 1000

Where, then, did the Northern Iroquoians originate? Did they develop in place from earlier cultural traditions, or did they arrive from the south during the warmer centuries of the Medieval Warm Period? Many archaeologists would now agree that Iroquoian-speaking cultures have deep roots in ancient times. The problem is to recognize them in the archaeological record. Nor do linguistic data provide many insights, beyond a notion that Algonquian and Iroquoian languages separated during the Archaic, perhaps between 2000 and 1500 years ago. We can be certain that Iroquoian history developed along multiple paths during many centuries of fluid change, of repeated separations and fusions that reflected changing alliances and trade networks, the realities of diplomacy, and a rise in warfare.

What archaeological evidence do we have for primordial Iroquoian ancestry from archaeological sites? The Canadian archaeologist James Wright divided later cultures in southern Ontario into three useful periods, the earliest of which, the Early Iroquoian, spans AD 900 to 1275. Within this time

bracket lies the Point Peninsula culture of central and southern Ontario, southern Quebec and upper New York State, which dates from the first millennium AD. It is one of several poorly defined cultures in the region. A small, and widely scattered, indigenous population lived in compact bands, each with their own territory. The people exploited game, aquatic, and plant resources ever more efficiently. Many of them turned to at least sporadic horticulture.

Some groups cultivated squash by as early as 800 BC. Maize came into use during the first millennium AD, but the key variable here was the length of the growing season. The frontier was 120 frost-free days, a boundary that passes through the Great Lakes region and across New England. This meant that the northern frontiers of maize growing moved north and south, with individual communities testing the limits each year. During the

155 The Maxon-Derby site near Syracuse, New York: the eastern end of House C with wooden markers indicating outlines of the structure.

Medieval Warm Period, and especially around AD 1000, favorable temperatures led to fewer crop failures and rising population densities, also to competition for prime agricultural land. Most communities practiced swidden agriculture, clearing forest, then shifting their small villages when the soils became exhausted. Subsequently, the Little Ice Age shortened growing seasons by the fifteenth century, intensifying competition and leading to fortified villages and abandonment of some hitherto cultivated areas.

During spring and summer, these small groups would congregate into larger concentrations of between 100 and 300 people at river- and lake-side fishing stations. These were the times when important burial ceremonies took place in cemeteries close to the fishing camps, when marriages were held, ceremonies enjoyed, and exotic artifacts and raw materials exchanged. At Rice Lake in southern Ontario, important leaders lie under earthen mounds with Hopewellian artifacts, probably obtained from Hopewell exchange networks for silver nuggets brought to the lake from northern Ontario.

This annual pattern of establishing friendly ties with neighbors was adaptive, in that it ensured that warfare did not disrupt hunting, fishing, and foraging. It also allowed people to shift from one band to another as populations rose and fell, but it is uncertain whether men or women remained with their home bands upon marriage. There was never a sufficiency of food resources in one area to allow year-round, sedentary settlement. The congregated bands had to scatter into small family groups during the long winter months to hunt forest game.

During the centuries between AD 500 and 800, numerous local populations and kin groups shared marital ties, exchange networks, and ritual beliefs and ceremonies, also a wide variety of political and social connections. These were groups with complex internal and external relationships, sometimes shared pottery styles, even varying life expectancies.

Cultural identities changed, sometimes dramatically, in a constantly evolving world, which makes it hard for us to identify specific groups from their material remains. Many local societies developed, among them the so-called Owasco culture of the Mohawk drainage and Finger Lakes region of upper New York State, but whether such formulations will stand the text of time is questionable. Nor is the relationship between, say, Point Peninsula and Owasco at all clear. This was, however, a time when longhouses and associated matrilocal residences (meaning that a new husband moved to the wife's house) appear. For instance, the Maxon-Derby site near Syracuse, New York, lies on the terrace of a large stream and covers about 2.4 acres (1 ha). Seven houses have been excavated, one of them almost square, others more elongated; one oblong dwelling measured 26 by 59 ft (8 by 18 m). House design was far from standardized at Maxon-Derby, but was clearly evolving toward the well-known Iroquois longhouse design that was used everywhere in later centuries. Earthworks and timber palisades protected other sites with longhouses such as the thirteenth-century Sackett settlement near Canandaigua. By this time, maize, squash, and bean cultivation had assumed major importance in the subsistence economy. A much higher incidence of tooth decay occurs among local populations at about this time, perhaps as a result of a higher carbohydrate content in the diet.

We will probably never be able to trace Northern Iroquoian, and certainly specific historic nations, far back into the past from artifacts alone. Even a cursory glance at ethnographic accounts of Northeastern societies reveals cases where language-uses in different communities can shift dramatically over a few generations, as both individuals and groups make strategic use of language, culture, and ethnicity.

Middle Iroquoian   AD 1275 to 1350 or later

Throughout the Early Iroquoian period, most communities numbered only a few hundred souls even at the most favorable times of the year. Some of the people, especially the elderly, may have lived in the same settlements year-round, but society was still organized in bands and localized matrilineal clans. Each group had its own leader, married outside the group, and identified with a group of totemic animals. Intermarriage was an important way of cementing good relations with neighbors, but, by the same token, there appears to have been little long-distance exchange of ceremonial goods, perhaps in a reflection of less flamboyant burial customs.

Maize agriculture assumed increasing importance in Iroquoian society as time went on and population densities rose. The introduction of the common bean in about AD 1300 also made a big difference. Maize and bean agriculture may have been one of the factors behind the dramatic changes in Iroquoian life throughout the St. Lawrence lowlands and in the Mohawk drainage during the fourteenth century. Between 1300 and 1350, Iroquoians began living in much larger communities and became heavily dependent on maize farming. For example, two or three communities near London, Ontario, joined into a single settlement along a creek. Some of the largest Iroquoian settlements now covered more than 5 acres (2 ha). More families lived in the same dwelling, and longer houses were built closer together and sometimes parallel to one another in groups. Perhaps these groupings coincided with related matrilineages or individual clans. Placing longhouses closer together may also have been a labor-saving device to reduce the amount of palisading needed to protect larger villages. By 1400, some of the largest Iroquoian settlements regularly housed as many as 1,500 people, with elaborate village plans, large work areas, and even garbage disposal zones.

Larger settlements brought new pressures to Iroquoian society. A community of 1,500 people consumed enormous quantities of firewood, to say nothing of construction timber. Agricultural land was soon cleared and exhausted, so these large settlements had to shift location more frequently than smaller ones. The men spent more and more time clearing land or in communal construction work. Nevertheless, a few Iroquoian settlements achieved populations of more than 2,000 people, about six clan groups. But factionalism may have strained dispute-resolving mechanisms to the limit

156 Artist reconstruction of the Draper site in Ontario at its largest.

The Feast of the Dead

Early French accounts tell us that a ten-day Feast of the Dead was held every ten or twelve years, when large villages moved their locations. Over these days, all corpses from local cemeteries except the most recently deceased were stripped of flesh and skin and the robes in which they had been buried. The washed and cleaned bones were wrapped in new beaver skins and placed in decorated bags. Processions of mourners carried the dead to the village where the ceremony was to be held.

A large pit some 10 ft (3 m) deep and 15 ft (4.5 m) wide was dug close by and scaffolding erected around it. Each village and clan took its proper place and displayed their gifts on poles. The chiefs stood high on the platforms and announced the offerings given in the names of the dead. In this way, the presents were redistributed throughout the villages, while each family fulfilled its obligations within society. As twilight came, recently deceased, still-whole bodies were interred and covered with beaver robes. The bone packages and grave goods were emptied into the pit at sunrise, the bodies mingled so that the burial was truly a communal one. A shrine adorned the filled ossuary. Friendships had been renewed, social bonds strengthened, and the dead provided with a proper burial.

157 *The Feast of the Dead* from Jesuit missionary Joseph-François Lafitau's 1724 *Moeurs des sauvages amériquains* (Manners of the American savages). The drawing, with its macabre image of corpses and skeletons, is supposedly based on a Jesuit description of a century earlier.

and prevented large villages from lasting long. The largest known settlement 156 is the Draper site in Ontario, which covered 20 acres (8 ha) and housed between 2,000 and 3,000 people for a few decades in the fifteenth century.

As bigger settlements developed, hitherto dispersed clans came into much closer proximity, with a greater potential for disputes, factional quarrels, and other disruptions. The Iroquoians may now have instituted more formal village councils made up of representatives from each clan. Among the historic Iroquois, these offices were hereditary in individual families of the clans. Just as with the historic tribes in the Southeast, there may have been separate chiefs (*sachems*) for war and peace. Peace chiefs kept a pulse on public opinion, settled domestic disputes, organized community works, rituals and ceremonies, and negotiated with others. War chiefs had more limited powers. They organized and led war parties, dealt with prisoners, and killed suspected witches. Both offices were sources of prestige rather than power, for no chief had the authority to do anything more than act as a spokesman. His family had to work hard to provide the additional food that enabled him to extend hospitality to other people in the village and to strangers. Since there was no fixed law of primogeniture, relatives would compete with one another for the succession, vying to prove their prowess as generous hosts, brave warriors, and expert hunters. Among Iroquoian groups living north of Lake Ontario, the solidarity of each community was celebrated with the elaborate Feast of the Dead, a ceremonial reburial of those who had died while a village was inhabited, carried out before the settlement moved to a new location (see box opposite).

Warfare became an important factor in Iroquoian life during the fourteenth century. Many settlements were now elaborately fortified, but others were still undefended, close to navigable waters, not away from them as became the rule in later, more turbulent, centuries. Cannibalism appears for the first time – in the form of split, cut, and cooked human bones found in Iroquoian sites throughout southern Ontario. The consumption of human flesh was not a matter of obtaining extra protein, but an intensely symbolic act. The northern Iroquois waged war, at least in theory, to avenge the killing of kinsfolk by outsiders. The warriors would capture someone from the group who did the killing as a replacement for the victim. Or they would kill him, bringing his head or scalp home as a trophy. Male prisoners were often slain in elaborate sacrifices to the sun, women and children usually permitted to live.

Why did warfare suddenly assume such importance after 1300? Some theories argue that the cooler and drier climatic conditions of the Little Ice Age led to more frequent droughts and food shortages, so that Iroquoian groups living on the sand plains of southwestern Ontario and on New York State's cool Allegheny Plateau may have moved away from their homelands in search of moister, more fertile soils. The shift would have triggered more competition for prime farming land and other strategic resources. However, population densities among the Iroquoians were still low and there was

more agricultural land available than people to occupy and cultivate
it. Neighboring groups could have fought over hunting rights, but why go
to war over deer, when the game population may have, in fact, increased with
so much cleared agricultural land to graze on? Most likely, warfare was
a quest for personal prestige. As time went on, the basic tasks of hunting,
fishing, and forest clearance, once tests of a man's ability to support his
family through the winter, became collective tasks carried out by larger
groups. Women, as the farmers, were now accounting for more food and
were the dominant social lineages. Thus, men had to prove themselves and
their worth. Disputes between neighboring groups may have proliferated as
the young men sought every excuse to wage war – perhaps to the point that
every community had some enemies. Constant warfare, with its risk of pre-
mature death, especially for adults, may have caused hardship by disrupting
critical subsistence.

The late Huron expert Bruce Trigger argues that this led to a situation
where some neighboring villages combined for self-defense, resulting in
much larger settlements. Fortified Middle Iroquoian communities may have
first developed in western Iroquoian country, where the people had long

158 Iroquoian groups in historic times.

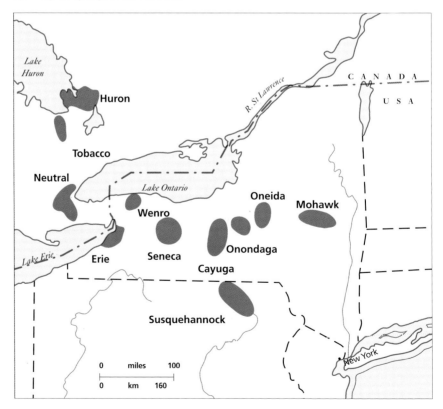

fought with the Central Algonquians, then come into use over the entire region, resulting in major changes in local society. For generations, the Iroquoians had maintained close ties between scattered communities by the practise of men and women marrying into neighboring villages. With larger settlements, the need for such marriage customs was reduced, so the ties that helped reduce conflict between neighbors evaporated. About the only alternative was to settle disputes by force. Warfare became a means, not only of acquiring prestige, but also captives, who were sacrificed to the sun, the symbol of fertility and life. Thus, argues Trigger, the men assumed a prestigious role in a society that was becoming more and more sedentary and agricultural.

To European contact and beyond   from AD 1400   158

After 1400, differences in pottery styles, burial practises, and house types chronicle major divisions between Iroquoian groups living north of lakes Ontario and Erie. South of Lake Ontario, between 1450 and 1475, a small and a much larger village near Syracuse, New York, deliberately settled within a few miles of one another to form the Onondaga nation. Canadian archaeologist James Tuck was able to show that the larger village had itself been formed by the amalgamation of two smaller ones. Similar fusions took place all over Iroquois country, with relatively dense local populations clustering in specific areas, separated from one another by largely uninhabited country. These new tribal groupings resulted in greater social complexity in Iroquoian life. Tribal councils emerged as an extension of village ones, designed to regulate life on a larger scale. Clan ties cut across village and tribal boundaries. Among the historic Iroquois, some of these clans grouped themselves into associations that organized much of ceremonial life, including funerals. There were medicine societies, too, which treated the sick and carried out curing rituals. All these complex mechanisms helped maintain links between expanding, and increasingly complex, Iroquoian societies.

Why did large Iroquoian settlements and tribes form? Some sizable communities may have controlled important resources and exchange networks. But warfare may have been the major factor in forging large communities and political alliances. And when a village reached its maximum practicable size, the inhabitants expanded into new communities, forming confederacies, tribes, and other associations. These settlement clusters depleted natural food resources more rapidly, making the people more dependent on horticulture. The constant political maneuvering and warfare led to more elaborate fortifications in the sixteenth century – villages with multiple palisades, earthworks, and massive tree-trunk ramparts.

Some time before the end of the sixteenth century, neighboring Iroquoian tribes in both Ontario and New York came together in loosely knit confederacies aimed at reducing blood feuding and warfare between close neighbors. The common link between them was an agreement to settle grievances by means other than bloodshed. A confederacy council of headmen from member tribes gathered occasionally for ceremonial feasts and conferences, and to adjudicate disputes and set reparations if called for. At European contact, the major Iroquoian tribes were the Huron, Erie, Tobacco, and Neutral in the north and, to the south, the famous Iroquois Confederacy, made up of the Five Nations: Seneca, Cayuga, Onondaga, Oneida, and Mohawk. The Susquehannocks of the Susquehanna Valley were another Iroquoian group.

When did the Iroquois League and other confederacies come into being? Bruce Trigger argued that the confederacies were a logical extension of complex, long-term forces that had much earlier replaced small hunting bands with larger groups, then with tribes. The confederacy was adaptive in that it allowed groups to legislate against unnecessary blood feuding while still maintaining individual cultural and political identity in their dealings with others. The arrival of Europeans and their fur traders created a new, highly volatile political situation, in which it was clearly an advantage for neighbors to be linked in close alliances. Since the Iroquois already enjoyed confederacies, it would have been an easy matter to strengthen them in response to new circumstances.

For generations after the Iroquois League was formed, the neighboring Huron and Algonquians greatly feared the Five Nations. The Iroquois themselves symbolized their League as a vast longhouse that stretched from west to east. The Seneca were the "Keepers of the Western Door," the Mohawk the "Keepers of the Eastern Door." The Onondaga were in the center, the "Keepers of the Council Fire." They were also "Keepers of the Wampum Belts."

Both the Iroquois and the Algonquians strung white and purple or black shell beads into strands and complex belts named after the Algonquian word "wampum," a Wampanoag Indian word meaning white shell beads. The woven dark and white designs on these belts symbolized all manner of transactions – major events, treaties, and agreements. One Onondaga chief kept the treaty wampum for the Five Nations. It was he who knew the patterns and what they meant. Wampum became a form of currency when Europeans arrived, but the beads were hard to manufacture even with iron drills and were soon replaced with cheap traded glass beads from overseas.

At European contact, all Iroquois-speaking peoples depended heavily on horticulture, with fishing also a vital part of the subsistence economy. Among the Huron of the north and the Seneca, horticulture – corn, beans, squash, and sunflowers – may have provided up to 80 percent of the diet. The northern Iroquoians lived in fortified villages, in elm tree bark-covered longhouses shared by nuclear families. They dwelt on either side of the central hearths. Unlike the Algonquians, the Iroquois were matrilineal, with the children living with their mother's clan. Each longhouse group was a subdivision of the matrilineal clan, for sisters with their husbands and

160

159 Huron Indians planting their fields, 1724, by Joseph-François Lafitau. This highly inaccurate depiction was copied from Theodore de Bry's famous drawings of Florida Indians, 1564–65.

160 Eighteenth-century Iroquois wampum belt. Location unknown.

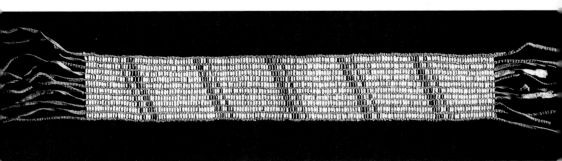

children shared a common dwelling. The men, who cleared the land, hunted, fished, traded, and built houses and fortifications, were warriors, and moved into the longhouses of their wives at marriage. The women grew, weeded, and harvested crops, and tended the children.

With its confederacies and tribes, Iroquois society was governed effectively. Their political organizations seem precarious, based as they were on decisions made by a network of tribal and community councils, in situations where consent was needed on the part of all concerned. But, in fact, they were successful in suppressing blood feuds among populations numbering as many as 20,000 souls, and at coordinating at least a degree of diplomatic policy toward outsiders.

Many common religious beliefs and ceremonial practises unified the northern Iroquoians. But, above all, they were remarkable not for their material culture, but for the sophistication and finesse of social relationships. The Iroquois respected individual dignity and self-reliance. They looked down on public displays of emotion or open quarreling, and considered politeness and hospitality toward one another and toward strangers fundamental to correct social behavior. As later events were to show, these warlike and astute people were a challenge for the European fur traders and missionaries who settled among them.

In the year 1534, French master mariner Jacques Cartier sailed past Newfoundland and up the St. Lawrence River. Bad weather forced his ships

161 Smoking native tobacco in a zoomorphic pipe. Reconstruction of Iroquois life at the Keffer site, Ontario.

162 Reconstruction of daily life at the Keffer site, Ontario.

to take shelter in Gaspe Bay at the mouth of the river, where he encountered about 300 men, women, and children. The French took the trouble to compile a word list, the earliest record of Iroquoian language ever made. From this moment on, the Iroquoians were destined to undergo catastrophic cultural change, as a result of economic factors operating far over the eastern horizons of the Atlantic, in distant Europe.

14 · Epilogue

For at least 14,000 years the Native Americans occupied the vast tracts of North America undisturbed. They developed a huge diversity of responses to a bewildering array of natural environments. The trajectory of cultural change was usually gradual, sometimes dramatically rapid, as was the case, for example, when maize and bean cultivation took hold in the Southeast. But the momentum of continual change was never disrupted. Not that the continent was completely isolated, for there were irregular contacts between peoples on the Siberian and Alaskan shores of the Bering Strait, and between the inhabitants of Mesoamerica and the Southwest. During the Medieval Warm Period, Norse colonists from Greenland traded with Inuit groups in the Canadian Archipelago and southward along the Labrador coast and into the St. Lawrence region, but they never settled permanently in North America. The seminal event came in 1492, when Christopher Columbus landed in the Indies. Now began the last chapter of Native American history – five centuries of catastrophic and disruptive cultural change in the face of an inexorable European presence. We can but summarize some of the major issues here.

The holocaust of disease

The most devastating legacy of European contact was what the Mayanist Michael Coe calls "a holocaust unparalleled in the world's history:" the fatal consequences of the introduction of hitherto unknown diseases. In epidemiological terms the turning point was 1519, when a Spanish conquistador infected with smallpox landed at Vera Cruz, Mexico. The Spaniards had some immunity to the disease, but the Indians did not. In months, smallpox spread like wildfire from the coast to the highlands. The first pandemic hit the Aztec capital, Tenochtitlan, in 1520. Indians died by the thousand. Other unfamiliar diseases, including influenza, measles, and typhus, ravaged Mexico during the next century. The Mexican population has been estimated at 11 million in 1519. A mere twenty years later, it was under 6.5 million, by 1607 less than 2.5 million. Similar massive demographic catastrophes occurred throughout the Americas. For example, more than 310,000 Indians lived in California at the time of Spanish colonization in 1769. By 1900, the total number of California Indians was 20,000, less than 7 percent of the pre-contact population.

The number of Native Americans in 1492 remains uncertain – somewhere between 2 and 18 million people, a broad range, to put it mildly. Certainly, the ravages of epidemics were catastrophic, even if the effects varied from region to region. In the Lower Mississippi, a precipitous decline followed Hernando de Soto's brutal journey across the South in 1543 and preceded French colonization in the late seventeenth century. Iroquois populations in the Finger Lakes area of New York State had fallen considerably by the same time period.

Why were there no American counterparts for European diseases? Perhaps Arctic temperatures killed off the parasites as tiny founder populations migrated into Alaska thousands of years ago. More likely, primeval population densities were too low. The survival of acute diseases depends on sustained contact between infected individuals, such as occurs in densely populated, sedentary settlements. North America lacked the densely packed, urban settlements of the Old World. It was there that bacterial and viral diseases became fixed in populations.

While epidemic diseases swept away enormous numbers of Native Americans, almost without historical trace, dealings with Europeans also took a heavy toll on Indian societies, especially those living near coasts or major waterways such as the St. Lawrence and the lower Mississippi rivers. As European settlement spread, some coastal groups were conquered or employed as agricultural laborers. On the East coast, in 1607, the English founded Jamestown, which soon became an important trading center with tentacles that stretched far into the Southeast; from it were conducted regular forays for slaves. The *Mayflower* pilgrims founded Plimoth in New England in 1620. Forty-four years later, English colonists took New York from the Dutch, ending more than fifty years of Dutch influence over fur trading in the Northeast. Even further north, the French had settled along the St. Lawrence, where they dominated fur-trading activity. By 1700, the peoples of the Eastern Woodlands were surrounded by what archaeologist Marvin Smith calls an "ever-tightening noose of the European presence." Dutch, English, French, and Spanish – each had different, competing interests that exerted severe pressure on Indian groups often hundreds of miles away from actual direct contact with the foreigners.

Furs and wampum

The interactions between Europeans and Native Americans varied greatly from one area to the next and resulted in many different transformations in indigenous societies. In the case of the Onondaga Iroquois in the Northeast, the fur trade transformed both French and Indian society. The Onondaga's first response to Europeans reflected their existing cultural beliefs and values. They craved iron axes, for example, but viewed them from their own cultural perspectives. The people were selective in their response to European culture. Initially, the Onondaga may have thought of Europeans as alien beings, as keepers of exotic trade objects such as mirrors, beads, and metal objects. These substitutes for earlier exotica such as native copper and sea shells became the substances of "power" during the sixteenth century. But as European artifacts became commonplace and utilitarian, they lost their associations of power and prestige. Such artifacts and materials were accepted, not because they were considered superior, but because they made sense in an opportunistic, flexible culture both in spiritual and utilitarian terms.

Despite smallpox epidemics and other disruptions, the Onondaga still retained their basic cultural values and beliefs in the mid-seventeenth century, living in a culture where European exotica had been grafted onto traditional society. After 1655, circumstances changed profoundly. European contacts increased dramatically: Jesuit missionaries were in residence, a French settlement was nearby, and the Onondaga's new neighbors were increasingly aggressive. The archaeological record now shows more blending of European and native culture. Wampum had become a valuable medium of exchange for use in the fur trade. The Onondaga were the keepers of wampum for the Five Nations, so it was of great importance to them as an emblem of diplomacy not only between Indians, but with Europeans as well. In the late 1660s, the Onondaga used their diplomatic talents to restructure the Iroquois Confederacy, redefining its workings so that the organization would act as the diplomatic front for all the Five Nations. This led to a series of treaties and alliances in 1677, agreements that stabilized and balanced the competing interests of the English colonies, which had supplanted French settlers to the southeast, the Five Nations, and other tribal groups. The resulting covenant, with its diplomatic expertise and treaties expressed in terms of wampum belts and intricate rituals, was a response to new external realities that, ultimately, the Iroquois were sometimes able to exploit to their advantage.

The huge profits to be made from the fur trade had a profound effect not only on the Iroquois and their neighbors the Huron, but on peoples living far inland on the plains, where fur traders introduced firearms, with devastating consequences for nomadic bison hunters. Russian, American, and European fur traders pursued otters and beavers in the Aleutians and Alaskan waters, also in the Pacific Northwest and south into California, especially after the late eighteenth century. Wealth acquired by chiefs living in strategic bays transformed the economic and political landscape of Northwest groups like the Nootka and the Haida, until land-hungry European colonists usurped tribal lands during the nineteenth century.

The Spanish borderlands

The northern frontier of New Spain (Mexico) was an ever shifting one. There was constant interaction between settlers and Native Americans along the frontier, between long-established indigenous societies and aggressive newcomers. Ultimately, the borderlands stretched from St. Augustine, Florida, in the east, to San Francisco, California, in the west. The processes of interaction and cultural change began with conquistador Ponce de Leon's expedition to Florida in 1513, with Fray Marcus de Niza's excursion into the Southwest in 1539, with Hernando de Soto's journey from Florida to the Mississippi River from 1539 to 1543, and with Juan Cabrillo's voyage up the California coast in 1542. The borderlands ceased to have importance with the Mexican Revolution of 1821. 163

Hernando de Soto's foray through the Southeast is a terrible baseline in North American history, famous not only for its brutality, but for its legacy of smallpox and other diseases that devastated Indian populations, triggered long-term massive political and social change, and undoubtedly had profound psychological effects on Southeastern society. The chroniclers of the de Soto expedition make it clear that diseases introduced by earlier coastal visitors had preceded the conquistadors into the interior. At the village of Talomeco in South Carolina, hundreds of bodies were stacked

163 The chief of Coosa in the Southeast greets Hernando de Soto and his conquistadors in this romanticized early eighteenth-century engraving. In the background, the chief arrives on a litter accompanied by trumpeters.

up in four houses. Evidence of epidemics from later decades is abundant. Sir Francis Drake's men contracted a highly contagious form of fever, perhaps typhus, in the Cape Verde Islands, and carried it ashore when they attacked the Spanish settlement at St. Augustine, Florida, in 1586. Hundreds of Indians living nearby soon died of the disease. And Thomas Hariot noted that the English settlers at Roanoke, in the colony of what was then called Virginia (now North Carolina), soon infected the local people: "Within a few days after our departure from everies such townes, people began to die very fast, and many in short space."

Inevitably, these later coastal epidemics entered the interior, resulting in massive depopulation, perhaps killing as many as 90 percent in some villages. Depopulation may have been so rapid and extreme that ancestral traditions and much of indigenous culture may have been swept away in a few short months. The loss, in particular, of religious and genealogical lore is especially devastating to a traditional society, for such elements help people adjust to a new culture. A visitor to the Arkansas people in 1698 remarked that "not a month had elapsed since they had rid themselves of smallpox, which had carried off most of them. In the village are now nothing but graves, in which they were buried two together, and we estimated that not a hundred men were left."

Political breakdown followed. The large and powerful chiefdoms encountered by de Soto fragmented into dozens of small-scale societies ruled by petty headmen. The fall of the chiefdoms stemmed not only from epidemics, but also from the severe loss of the manpower that peopled the hierarchical provinces of the Southeast. Archaeologically, the decline can be documented by a virtual cessation of moundbuilding – known to have been a chiefly activity – and a trend toward more dispersed villages. It was not until the eighteenth century that the peoples of the Southeast came together in the Creek Confederacy, a response to armed invasions by northern Indian groups, and to raids by European slave traders.

Devastated, without the support of their traditional beliefs, the societies of the interior were in a state of cultural impoverishment. By virtue of their remoteness from the coast, they had not been exposed directly to Spanish, French, and English culture and Christianity, as they were after 1673. Ultimately, the drastic cultural changes of the previous 130 years made it somewhat easier for the Indians to accept elements of European culture in the years that followed. Acculturation began in part from the spread of an extensive mission network through the Spanish borderlands. By the mid-seventeenth century, thirty-eight missions served approximately 25,000 Indians in La Florida. Some were substantial foundations. Santa Catalina de Guale, on St. Catherine's Island off the Georgia coast, was a square, fortified compound with palisades 193 ft (59 m) on a side and a central, shell-covered plaza. The compound protected the church, friary, kitchen, and garrison. The church, constructed with a single nave, was a rectangular building some 65.5 ft (20 m) long and 36 ft (11 m) wide. The wattle-and-daub façade

164

supported a pointed gable and a thatched roof. Pine planking and wattle formed the whitewashed sidewalls, which may have been adorned with ornate metal panels. The sanctuary was planked, and elevated slightly, with a sacristry on the left side facing the altar.

There were more than fifty missions in the Southwest, and a chain of twenty-one Franciscan stations in Alta California by 1830, the latter seen as

164 Santa Catalina de Guale mission church undergoing excavation, June 1982, St. Catherine's Island, off the Georgia coast. The foundations of the nave are visible as a dark outline.

a way of controlling the indigenous population along the coast in the most cost-effective manner. For instance, the Mission Nuestra Señora de la Soledad was founded 33 miles (53 km) southeast of Monterey Bay in central California in 1791, to control the Chalon Costanoan and Esselen Indians, as many as 12,500 people. The friars adopted a policy called "reduction" to achieve their goals, gathering the once-dispersed hunter-gatherers at the mission, changing their culture, and turning them into a Christian labor force. The policy failed miserably. Crowded into cramped, unhealthy quarters, the Soledad Indians died in large numbers. Even continual, often forcible recruitment failed; indeed, it weakened attempts to acculturate and convert the Indians. Most of the mission Indian population was superficially Christian and within Spanish culture, but, as excavated artifacts show, traditional culture remained strongly ingrained.

* * *

The history described in these pages is nameless and without individual faces, a story not of great statesmen and charismatic rulers but of ordinary people going about their daily lives far from the spotlight of written records. This book has chronicled broad sweeps of cultural change extending over millennia and centuries, the lives of members of numerous societies as a whole, to weave a rich tapestry of brilliant achievement.

The story began with the settlement of an uninhabited continent with harsh Ice Age landscapes by mere handfuls of hunter-gatherers, perhaps 15,000 years ago. Later their descendants adapted to dramatic climate change (far greater than anything we have experienced in modern times), to a continent of increasingly diverse and often demanding environments, with opportunistic success. They thrived in ice-girt arctic lands, developed complex foraging societies in richly endowed woodland, riverine, and coastal landscapes, and acquired a stunning expertise with edible and medicinal plants.

By 4000 BC, some eastern groups were cultivating native grasses, in one of the few independent centers of horticulture in the world. Within a thousand years, their successors enjoyed complex ritual observances and elaborate mortuary cults, epitomized by spectacular burial mounds and earthworks. At the time when William the Conqueror invaded Britain in AD 1066, many Native Americans in the Eastern Woodlands lived in powerful chiefdoms with great ceremonial centers like Etowah, Cahokia, and Moundville.

In the arid and semi-arid Southwest, maize agriculture took hold by at least 2000 BC, among people who became experts at farming in marginal environments. The Hohokam successfully irrigated the river valleys of what is now southern Arizona for a thousand years. Ancestral Pueblo peoples built the great houses at Chaco Canyon, New Mexico, after the tenth century, as ritual centers for people living for hundreds of miles around. And when the great droughts of the eleventh century AD descended on the Southwest, they moved northward to Montezuma Valley and Mesa Verde, Colorado, before drought again forced them elsewhere. The Ancestral Pueblo and the Hohokam left behind them a powerful cultural legacy: it flourishes to this day in pueblos which themselves have been occupied for many centuries.

The rich and sometimes turbulent history of ancient North America reached an apogee in the centuries before Christopher Columbus set foot in the Indies in 1492. The European *entrada* precipitated a devastating clash of cultures that left indelible scars on Native American societies everywhere. Millions succumbed to imported diseases, were forced off their lands, or were killed in desperate skirmishes with the newcomers. By the early twentieth century, the Native American population had fallen to its lowest level since 1492. Yet, quietly and triumphantly, the rich legacy of ancient Native American societies, transmitted from one generation to the next by word of mouth, survived genocide, disease, and the conquest and appropriation of Indian lands. The native population has risen steadily. In some places, it now surpasses estimates for pre-contact times. Some 2.4 million people counted in the 2000 US census stated they were wholly Native American or Alaska Natives. A further 1.9 million reported they were in the same category, at least partially, the combined total of 4.3 million representing 1.5 percent of the total US population. With this growth has come resurgence in awareness of oral histories and legends, of treasured cultural traditions; these survive for the future. Increasingly, too, Native American tribal authorities are involved in archaeological research, notably in Alaska and the Southwest, where digging for the past adds a new dimension to traditional beliefs. To a considerable extent, the future of the history in these pages lies with upcoming generations of Native American archaeologists, who will bring their unique cultural perspectives to bear on the first North Americans.

This is a tale of successful adaptations to North America's many environments, of challenges like drought and rising population densities overcome. It's an account of humans going about their business – being born, growing up, falling in love, quarreling, negotiating, going to war, and dying: in short, of human nature, which is, after all, what history is about. As the late historical archaeologist James Deetz once wrote: "look at what we have done." The story of the first North Americans gives us a wonderful opportunity to achieve a better understanding of human diversity, and of ourselves.

Further Reading

The literature of North American archaeology is enormous and growing exponentially every year. Much of it appears in obscure academic journals, edited volumes of papers, and in Cultural Resource Management reports, many of which are difficult to access. More and more reports now appear on the internet. This tidal wave of publication, good and bad, occasionally seminal and usually highly specialized, is a challenge even for specialists. The Further Reading that follows makes no claims to be comprehensive. Most entries are books, together with some journal articles. In the case of edited volumes, only a few of the papers may be relevant, but a quick search of their contents page will provide enlightenment. All of the entries feature bibliographies, which lead to the more technical literature. Websites are not cited, as they are inappropriate for basic sources such as those here.

General Works

There are few comprehensive accounts of North American archaeology. My *Ancient North America*, 4th edition, London and New York: Thames and Hudson, 2005, offers a more detailed summary of the subject covered in this volume. Sarah W. Neusius and G. Timothy Gross, *Seeking Our Past*, New York: Oxford University Press, 2006, covers the same ground. See also Dean Snow, *Archaeology of Native North America*, Upper Saddle River, NJ: Prentice Hall, 2010, and Timothy R. Pauketat and Diana Di Paolo (eds), *North American Archaeology*, New York: Wiley-Blackwell, 2005. All these are college textbooks, while Charles C. Mann, *1491: New Revelations of the Americas Before Columbus*, New York: Alfred Knopf, 2005, covers the entire Americas selectively for a general audience. *The Handbook of North American Indians,* Washington, DC: Smithsonian Institution, 1978, is a superb multivolume source, especially on ethnography. A selection of oral histories will be found in Brian Swann (ed.), *Coming to Light: Contemporary Translations of the Native Literature of North America*, New York: Random House, 1994. Finally, two crucial reference books: Paul E. Minnis (ed.), *People and Plants in Ancient Eastern North America* and *People and Plants in Ancient Western North America*, Tucson: University of Arizona Press, 2010.

ABRAMS, ELLIOT M., and ANNCORINNE FRETER. *The Emergence of the Moundbuilders: The Archaeology of Tribal Societies in Southeastern Ohio.* Athens, OH: University of Ohio Press, 2005.

ADAMS, E. CHARLES. *The Origin and Development of the Pueblo Katsina Cult.* Tucson: University of Arizona Press, 1991.

ADLER, MICHAEL A. (ed.). *The Prehistoric Pueblo World, AD 1150–1350.* Tucson: University of Arizona Press, 1996.

ADOVASIO, JAMES M. *The First Americans: In Pursuit of Archaeology's Greatest Mystery.* New York: Random House, 2002.

AIKENS, C. M. *Hogup Cave.* Salt Lake City: University of Utah Press, 1970.

ALTSCHUL, J. H., and D. R. GRENDA (eds). *Islanders and Mainlanders: Prehistoric Context for the Southern California Bight.* Tucson: SRI Press, 2002.

AMES, KENNETH, and HERBERT MASCHNER. *Peoples of the Northwest Coast: Their Archaeology and Prehistory.* London and New York: Thames and Hudson, 1999.

ANDERSON, DAVID G. and KENNETH E. SASSAMAN (eds). *The Paleoindian and Early Archaic Southeast.* Tuscaloosa: University of Alabama Press, 1996.

_____, and ROBERT C. MAINFORT, JR (eds). *The Woodland Southeast.* Tuscaloosa: University of Alabama Press, 2002.

APPELT, MICHAEL, JOEL BERGLUND, and HANDS CHRISTIAN GULLØV (eds). *Identities and Cultural Contacts in the Arctic.* Copenhagen: Danish National Museum and Danish Polar Centre, 2000.

ARNOLD, JEANNE E. *Craft Specialization in the Prehistoric Channel Islands, California.* Berkeley: University of California Press, 1987.

_____ (ed.). *Foundations of Chumash Complexity.* Los Angeles: Cotsen Institute of Archaeology, University of California Press, 2004.

_____ (ed.). *The Origins of the Pacific Coast Chiefdom: The Chumash of the Channel Islands.* Salt Lake City: University of Utah Press, 2001.

BAMFORTH, DOUGLAS B. *Ecology and Human Organization on the Great Plains.* New York: Plenum Press, 1988.

_____. "Projectile Points, People, and Plains Paleoindian Perambulations," *Journal of Anthropological Archaeology*, vol. 28 (2009), 142–57.

BENSE, JUDITH. *Archaeology of the Southeastern United States: Paleoindian to World War I.* San Diego: Academic Press, 1994.

BENSON, LARRY V., TIMOTHY R. PAUKETAT, and EDWARD R. COOK. "Cahokia's Boom or Bust in the Context of Climate Change," *American Antiquity*, vol. 74 (4) (2009), 467–83.

BIRMINGHAM, ROBERT A., and LESLIE E. EISENBERG. *Indian Mounds of Wisconsin.* Madison: University of Wisconsin Press, 2000.

BRINK, JACK W. *Imagining Head-Smashed-In: Aboriginal Buffalo Hunting on the Northern Plains.* Edmonton, AB: Athabasca University Press, 2008.

BROSE, DAVIS S., C. WESLEY COWAN, and ROBERT C. MAINFORT, JR (eds). *Societies in Eclipse: Archaeology of the Eastern Woodland Indians,* AD 1400–1700. Washington, DC: Smithsonian Institution Press, 2001.

_____, and N'OMI GREBER (eds). *Hopewell Archaeology: The Chillicothe Conference.* Kent, OH: Kent State University Press, 1979.

BROWN, JAMES ALLISON. *The Spiro Ceremonial Center: The Archaeology of Arkansas Valley Caddoan Culture in Eastern Oklahoma.* Ann Arbor, MI: Museum of Anthropology, University of Michigan, 1996.

CANTWELL, ANNE-MARIE, LAWRENCE A. CONRAD, and JONATHAN E. REYMAN (eds). *Aboriginal Ritual and Economy in the Eastern Woodlands: Essays in Memory of Howard Dalton Winters.* Springfield, IL: Illinois State Museum, Centre for American Archaeology, 2004 (Paper 30).

CARLSON, ROY (ed.). *Indian Art Traditions of the Northwest Coast.* Burnaby, BC: Simon Fraser University, Archaeology Press, 1983.

CARR, CHRISTOPHER, and D. TROY CASE (eds). *Gathering Hopewell: Society, Ritual, and Ritual Interaction.* New York: Kluwer Academic/Plenum Press, 2005.

CASE, D. TROY, and CHRISTOPHER CARR. *The Scioto Hopewell and Their Neighbors: Bioarchaeological Documentation and Cultural Understanding.* New York: Springer, 2008.

CHAPMAN, JEFFERSON. *Tellico Archaeology: 12,000 Years of Native American History.* Revised edition. Knoxville: University of Tennessee Press, 1994.

CHARLES, DOUGLAS K., and JANE E. BUIKSTRA (eds). *Recreating Hopewell.* Gainesville: University Press of Florida, 2006.

CHARTKOFF, JOSEPH L., and KERRY KONA CHARTKOFF. *The Archaeology of California.* Stanford: Stanford University Press, 1984.

CORDELL, LINDA. *Archaeology of the Southwest.* 2nd edition. Walnut Creek, CA: Left Coast Press, 2009.

DAMAD, DAVID (ed.). "Arctic," *Handbook of North American Indians.* Vol. 5. Washington, DC: Smithsonian Institution Press, 1984.

DEETZ, JAMES. *In Small Things Forgotten: The Archaeology of Early American Life.* New York: Anchor Books, 1977.

DILLEHAY, THOMAS D. *The Settlement of the Americas: A New Prehistory.* New York: Basic Books, 2000.

DIXON, E. JAMES. *Bones, Boats & Bison: Archaeology and the First Colonization of Western North America.* Albuquerque: University of New Mexico Press, 1999.

DUMOND, DON E. *The Eskimos and Aleuts.* 2nd edition. London and New York: Thames and Hudson, 1987.

DYE, DAVID H. *War Paths, Peace Paths: An Archaeology of Cooperation and Conflict in Native Eastern North America.* Lanham, MD: AltaMira Press, 2009.

EMERSON, THOMAS E., DALE L. McELRATH, and ANDREW C. FORTIER (eds). *Archaic Societies: Diversity and Complexity Across the Midcontinent.* Albany: State University of New York Press, 2009.

_____, DALE L. McELRATH, and ANDREW C. FORTIER (eds). *Late Woodland Societies:*

Tradition and Transformation Across the Midcontinent. Lincoln: University of Nebraska Press, 2000.

ENGELBRECHT, WILLIAM. *Iroquoia: The Development of a Native World.* Syracuse, NY: Syracuse University Press, 2003.

ERLANDSON, JON M., and M. W. GLASSOW (eds). *Archaeology of the California Coast During the Middle Holocene.* Los Angeles: Cotsen Institute of Archaeology, University of California, 1997.

————. *Early Hunter-Gatherers of the California Coast.* New York: Plenum Press, 1994.

————, and ROGER H. COLTEN (eds). *Hunter-Gatherers of Early Holocene Coastal California.* Los Angeles: Cotsen Institute of Archaeology, University of California, 1991.

ESDALE, JULIE A. "A Current Synthesis of the Northern Archaic," *Arctic Anthropology,* vol. 45 (2) (2008), 3–38.

FAGAN, BRIAN. *Before California: An Archaeologist Looks at Our Earliest Inhabitants.* Lanham, MD: AltaMira Press, 2003.

————. *Chaco Canyon: Archaeologists Explore the Lives of an Ancient Society.* New York: Oxford University Press, 2005.

————. *The Great Journey: The Peopling of Ancient America.* Revised edition. Gainesville: University Press of Florida, 2003.

FARNSWORTH, K. B., and T. E. EMERSON (eds). *Early Woodland Archaeology.* Kampsville, IL: Center for American Archaeology, 1986.

FENTON, WILLIAM N. *The Great Law and the Longhouse: A Political History of the Iroquois Confederacy.* Norman: University of Oklahoma Press, 1998.

FISH, SUZANNE K., and PAUL R. FISH (eds). *The Hohokam Millennium.* Santa Fe: School for Advanced Research Press, 2007.

FITZHUGH, WILLIAM W. (ed.). *Crossroads of Continents: Cultures of Siberia and Alaska.* Washington, DC: Smithsonian Institution Press, 1988.

————, and SUSAN A. KAPLAN. *Inua: Spirit World of the Bering Sea Eskimo.* Washington, DC: Smithsonian Institution Press, 1982.

FRISON, GEORGE. *Prehistoric Hunter-Gatherers of the High Plains and Rockies.* 3rd edition. Walnut Creek, CA: Left Coast Press, 2010.

GAMBLE, LYNN H. *The Chumash World at European Contact: Power, Trade, and Feasting Among Complex Hunter-Gatherers.* Berkeley: University of California Press, 2008.

GIBSON, JON L. "Formed from the Earth of That Place: The Material Side of Community at Poverty Point," *American Antiquity,* vol. 72 (3), 509–23.

————, and PHILIP J. CARR (eds). *Signs of Power: The Rise of Cultural Complexity in the Southeast.* Tuscaloosa: University of Alabama Press, 2004.

————. *The Ancient Mounds of Poverty Point: Place of Rings.* Gainesville: University Press of Florida, 2001.

GRAYSON, DONALD K. *The Desert's Past: A Natural Prehistory of the Great Basin.* Washington, DC: Smithsonian Institution Press, 1993.

GREGRORY, DAVID A., and DAVID R. WILCOX (eds). *Zuni Origins: Toward a New Synthesis of Southwestern Archaeology.* Tucson: University of Arizona Press, 2009.

GRIFFIN, JAMES B. "Eastern North America: A Summary," *Science,* vol. 156 (1967) 175–91.

HALL, ROBERT L. *An Archaeology of the Soul: North American Indian Belief and Ritual.* Urbana: University of Illinois Press, 1997.

HARP, ELMER, JR. "Pioneer Cultures of the Subarctic and the Arctic," in JESSE D. JENNINGS (ed.), *Ancient Native Americans.* Mountain View, CA: Mayfield, 1978, 303–371.

HART, JOHN P. "Evolving the Three Sisters: The Changing Histories of Maize, Bean, and Squash in New York and the Greater Northeast," in JOHN P. HART (ed.), *Current Northeast Paleoethnobotany II,* Albany: New York State Museum, 2008, 87–99.

————, and HETTY JO BRUMBACH (eds). "Cooking Residues, AMS Dates, and the Middle to Late Woodland Transition in Central New York," *Northeast Anthropology,* vol. 69 (2005), 1–33.

————, and CHRISTINA B. REITH (eds). *Northeast Subsistence-Settlement Change: AD 700–1300.* Albany, NY: New York State Museum, 2002 (Bulletin 496).

HAURY, EMIL W. *The Hohokam: Desert Farmers and Craftsmen: Excavations at Snaketown, 1964–65.* Tucson: University of Arizona Press, 1976.

HIVELEY, R., and R. HORN. "A statistical study of lunar alignments at the Newark Earthworks," *Midcontinental Journal of Archaeology,* vol. 31 (2006), 281–322.

HOFFECKER, JOHN F., and SCOTT A. ELIAS. *The Human Ecology of Beringia.* New York: Columbia University Press, 2007.

HUCKELL, BRUCE B. "The Archaic Prehistory of the North American Southwest," *Journal of World Prehistory,* vol. 10 (3) (1996), 305–74.

JABLONSKI, N. G. (ed.). *The First Americans: The Pleistocene Colonization of the New World.* San Francisco: California Academy of Sciences, 2002.

JEFFERIES, RICHARD W. *Holocene Hunter-Gatherers of the Lower Ohio River Valley.* Tuscaloosa: University of Alabama Press, 2009.

————. *The Archaeology of Carrier Mills: 10,000 Years in the Saline Valley of Illinois.* Carbondale, IL: Center for Archaeological Investigations, 1987.

JENNINGS, JESSE D. *Danger Cave.* Salt Lake City: University of Utah Press, 1957.

JONES, TERRY, and KATHRYN A. KLAR (eds). *California Prehistory: Colonization, Culture, and Complexity.* Lanham, MD: AltaMira Press, 2007.

KANTNER, JOHN. *Ancient Puebloan Southwest.* Cambridge: Cambridge University Press, 2004.

KENNETT, DOUGLAS J. *The Island Chumash: Behavioral Ecology of a Maritime Society.* Berkeley: University of California Press, 2005.

KING, ADAM. *Etowah: The Political History of a Chiefdom Capital.* Tuscaloosa: University of Alabama Press, 2003.

KNECHT, HEIDI (ed.). *Projectile Technology.* New York: Plenum Press, 1997.

KNIGHT, VERNON JAMES, JR. *Mound Excavations at Moundville: Architecture, Elites, and Social Order.* Tuscaloosa: University of Alabama Press, 2010.

KORNFELD, MARCEL, and MARY LOU LARSON. "Bonebeds and Other Myths: Paleoindian to Archaic Transition on the North American Great Plains and Rocky Mountains," *Quaternary International,* vol. 191 (2008), 18–33.

_____, GEORGE FRISON, and MARY LOU LARSON. *Prehistoric Hunters of the High Plains and Rocky Mountains.* 3rd edition. Walnut Creek, CA: Left Coast Press, 2010.

LARSON, MARY LOU, MARCEL KORNFELD, and GEORGE C. FRISON (eds). *Hell Gap: A Stratified Paleoindian Campsite at the Edge of the Rockies.* Salt Lake City: University of Utah Press, 2009.

LeBLANC, STEVEN A. *Prehistoric Warfare in the American Southwest.* Salt Lake City: University of Utah Press, 2007.

LEKSON, STEPHEN A. *A History of the Ancient Southwest.* Santa Fe: School for Advanced Research Press, 2009.

_____ (ed.). *Archaeology of Chaco Canyon: An Eleventh Century Pueblo Regional Center.* Santa Fe: School of Advanced Research Press, 2006.

_____. *The Chaco Meridian: Centers of Political Power in the Ancient Southwest.* Walnut Creek, CA: AltaMira Press, 1999.

LEVINE, MARY ANN, KENNETH E. SASSAMAN, and MICHAEL S. NASSANEY (eds). *The Archaeological Northeast.* Westport, CT: Bergin and Garvey, 1999.

LOREN, DIANA DIPAOLO. *In Contact: Bodies and Spaces in the Sixteenth- and Seventeenth-Century Eastern Woodlands.* Lanham, MD: AltaMira, 2007.

MABRY, JONATHAN B. (ed.). *Las Capas: Early Irrigation and Sedentism in a Southwestern Floodplain.* Tucson: Center for Desert Archaeology, 2008.

McCARTNEY, ALLEN P. (ed.). *Thule Eskimo Culture: An Anthropological Retrospective.* Ottawa: National Museum of Man, 1979 (Archaeological Survey of Canada, Mercury Series no. 88).

McCULLOUGH, K. M. *The Ruin Islanders: Thule Culture Pioneers in the Eastern High Arctic.* Hull, Quebec: Canadian Museum of Civilization, 1989 (Archaeological Survey of Canada, Mercury Series 141).

McGHEE, ROBERT. *Ancient People of the Arctic.* Vancouver: University of British Columbia Press, 1996.

_____. *The Last Imaginary Place: A Human History of the Arctic World.* Chicago: University of Chicago Press, 2007.

MASCHNER, HERBERT, OWEN MASON, and ROBERT McGHEE (eds). *The Northern World AD 900–1400: The Dynamics of Climate, Economy, and Politics in Hemispheric Perspective.* Salt Lake City: University of Utah Press, 2009.

MASON, OWEN K. "The Contest between the Ipiutak, Old Bering Sea, and Birnirk Polities and the Origin of Whaling during the First Millennium AD along Bering Strait," *Journal of Anthropological Archaeology,* vol. 17 (3) (1998), 240–325.

MASON, RONALD J. *Great Lakes Archaeology.* New York: Academic Press, 1981.

MAXWELL, MOREAU. *Prehistory of the Eastern Arctic.* Orlando: Academic Press, 1985.

MELTZER, DAVID J. *First Peoples in a New World: Colonizing Ice Age America.* Berkeley: University of California Press, 2009.

_____. *Folsom: New Archaeological Investigations of a Classic Paleoindian Bison Kill.* Berkeley: University of California Press, 2006.

_____. "Human responses to Middle Holocene (Altithermal) climates on the North American Great Plains," *Quaternary Research,* vol. 52 (1999), 404–16.

_____. "Late Pleistocene Human Adaptations in Eastern North America," *Journal of World Prehistory,* vol. 2, (1) (1988), 1–52.

MILANICH, JERALD T. *Laboring in the Fields of the Lord: Spanish Missions and Southeastern Indians.* Washington, DC: Smithsonian Institution Press, 1999.

_____. *McKeithen Weeden Island: The Culture of Northern Florida, AD 200–900.* New York: Academic Press, 1984.

_____, and SUSAN MILBRATH (ed.). *First Encounters: Spanish Explorations in the Caribbean and the United States, 1492–1570.* Gainesville: University Press of Florida, 1989.

MILNER, GEORGE R. *The Cahokia Chiefdom: The Archaeology of a Mississippian Society.* Washington, DC: Smithsonian Institution Press, 1998.

_____. *The Moundbuilders: Ancient Peoples of Eastern North America.* London and New York: Thames and Hudson, 2004.

MORATTO, MICHAEL J. *California Archaeology.* New York: Academic Press, 1984.

MORSE, DAN E. (ed.). *Sloan: A Paleoindian Dalton Cemetery in Arkansas.* Washington, DC: Smithsonian Institution Press, 1997.

MULLER, JON. *Archaeology of the Lower Ohio Valley.* Orlando: Academic Press, 1986.

_____. *Mississippian Political Economy.* New York: Plenum Press, 1997.

NASSANEY, M. S., and K. E. SASSAMAN (eds). *Native American Interactions: Multiscalar Analysis and Interpretations in the Eastern Woodlands.* Knoxville: University of Tennessee Press, 1995.

PAUKETAT, TIMOTHY R. *Ancient Cahokia and the Mississippians.* Cambridge: Cambridge University Press, 2004.

_____. *Cahokia: Ancient America's Great City on the Mississippi.* New York: Viking Adult, Penguin, 2009.

_____, and T. E. EMERSON (eds). *Cahokia: Domination and Ideology in the Mississippian World.* Lincoln: University of Nebraska Press, 1997.

PLOG, STEPHEN. *Ancient Peoples of the American Southwest.* London and New York: Thames and Hudson, 1997.

PLUCKHAHN, THOMAS J. *Kolomoki: Settlement, Ceremony, and Status in the Deep South, AD 350 to 750.* Tuscaloosa: University of Alabama Press, 2003.

POWELL, J. F. *The First Americans: Race, Evolution, and the Origin of Native Americans*. Cambridge: Cambridge University Press, 2005.

REID, JEFFERSON, and STEPHANIE WHITTLESEY. *The Archaeology of Ancient Arizona*. Tucson: University of Arizona Press, 1997.

RENFREW, COLIN (ed.). *America Past, America Present: Genes and Languages in the Americas and Beyond*. Cambridge: McDonald Institute for Archaeological Research, 2000.

RUSSO, MICHAEL. "Southeastern Archaic Mounds," in KENNETH E. SASSAMAN and DAVID G. ANDERSON (eds), *Archaeology of the Mid-Holocene Southeast*, Gainesville: University Press of Florida, 1996, 259–87.

SAUNDERS, JOE W., et al. "Watson Brake: A Middle Archaic Mound7 Complex in Northeast Louisiana," *American Antiquity*, vol. 70 (4), (2005), 631–68.

SCHLEDERMANN, PETER. *Crossroads to Greenland: 3,000 Years of Prehistory in the Eastern High Arctic*. Calgary: Arctic Institute of North America, 1990.

————. *Voices in Stone: A Personal Journey into the Arctic Past*. Calgary: Arctic Institute of North America, 1996.

SEBASTIAN, LYNNE. *The Chaco Anasazi: Sociopolitical Evolution in the Prehistoric Southwest*. Cambridge: Cambridge University Press, 1992.

SHAW, ROBERT D., and HOLMES, CHARLES E. (eds). "The Norton Interaction Sphere: An Orientation," *Arctic Anthropology*, vol. 19 (2) (1982), 1–49.

SIMMS, STEVEN R. *Ancient Peoples of the Great Basin and Colorado Plateau*. Walnut Creek, CA: Left Coast Press, 2008.

————. *Traces of Fremont: Society and Rock Art in Ancient Utah*. Salt Lake City: University of Utah Press, 2010.

SMITH, BRUCE D. *Rivers of Change: Essays on Early Agriculture in Eastern North America*. Washington, DC: Smithsonian Institution Press, 1992.

————. *The Mississippian Emergence*. Washington, DC: Smithsonian Institution Press, 1990.

SNEAD, JAMES A. *Ancestral Landscapes of the Pueblo World*. Tucson: University of Arizona Press, 2008.

SNOW, DEAN R. *The Archaeology of New England*. New York: Academic Press, 1980.

————. *The Mississippian Emergence*. Washington, DC: Smithsonian Institution Press, 1990. *The Iroquois*. Cambridge, MA: Blackwell, 1996.

SPETH, JOHN D. *Bison Kills and Bone Counts: Decision Making by Ancient Hunters*. Chicago: University of Chicago Press, 1983.

STRUEVER, STUART, and FELICIA ANTONELLI HOLTON. *Koster: Americans in Search of their Prehistoric Past*. Prospect Heights, IL: Waveland Press, 2000.

THOMAS, DAVID HURST. *St Catherines: An Island in Time*. Atlanta: Georgia Endowment for the Humanities, 1988.

————. "The Archaeology of Hidden Cave, Nevada," *Anthropological Papers of the American Museum of Natural History*, vol. 61, (1) (1985), 1–430.

————. "The Archaeology of Monitor Valley 2: Gatecliff Shelter," *Anthropological Papers of the American Museum of Natural History*, vol. 59, (1) (1983), 1–552.

TOWNSEND, RICHARD F., and ROBERT V. SHARP (eds). *Hero, Hawk, and Open Hand: American Indian Art of the Ancient Midwest and South*. Chicago: Art Institute of Chicago and Yale University Press, 2004.

TRIGGER, BRUCE G. *Natives and Newcomers: Canada's "Heroic Age" Reconsidered*. Montreal: McGill-Queen's University Press, 1985.

————. *The Children of Aataentsic: A History of the Huron People to 1660*. 2 vols. Montreal: McGill-Queen's University Press, 1972.

TUCK, JAMES A. *Newfoundland and Labrador Prehistory*. Ottawa: National Museums of Canada, 1976.

VARIEN, MARK D., and RICHARD WILSHUSEN (eds). *Seeking the Center Place: Archaeology and Ancient Communities in the Mesa Verde Region*. Salt Lake City: University of Utah Press, 2002.

WATERS, M. R., and T. W. STAFFORD, JR. "Redefining the Age of Clovis: Implications for the Peopling of the New World," *Science*, vol. 315 (2007), 361–365 [1122–26].

WEBB, WILLIAM S., and CHARLES E. SNOW. *The Adena People*. Knoxville: University of Tennessee Press, 1974.

WEST, FREDERICK H. (ed.). *American Beginnings: The Prehistory and Palaeoecology of Beringia*. Chicago: University of Chicago Press, 1996.

WILSON, GREGORY D. *The Archaeology of Everyday Life at Early Moundville*. Tuscaloosa: University of Alabama Press, 2008.

WITTLESEY, STEPHANIE M., RICHARD CIOLEK-TORELLO, AND JEFFREY H. ALTSCHUL (eds). *Vanishing River: Landscapes and Lives of the Lower Verde Valley*. Tucson: SRI Press, 1997.

WOOD, W. RAYMOND (ed.). *Archaeology on the Great Plains*. Lawrence: University Press of Kansas, 1998.

Sources of Illustrations

Maps drawn by Drazen Tomic, © Thames & Hudson Ltd., unless otherwise acknowledged.

Black and white illustrations

a=above, b=below, c=centre, l=left, m=middle, r=right; numbers refer to page numbers

Frontispiece Werner Forman Archive/Field Museum of Natural History, Chicago. Location: 11 **15** Denver Museum of Nature & Science **17** Drawn by Julie Longhill **18** Table drawn by Drazen Tomic **19** Courtesy J. M. Adovasio **20** Photo Jim Barlow, Media Services, University of Oregon **23** After John F. Hoffecker and Scott A. Elias, *Human Ecology of Beringia*, Fig. 3.9, p. 99, Columbia University Press, 2007 **24** Photograph by Charles E. Holmes, 1991 **25** From Brian Fagan *The Long Summer*, p. 89, Basic Books, 2006 **28** Photo Gault Project, Texas A&M University Field School Staff **29a** After Willey, 1966 **29b** Arizona State Museum, University of Arizona, Tucson **30** Guy Robinson, Fordham College at Lincoln Center, New York **34** Photo Mary Lou Larson **36** David C. Eck, Trust Land Archaeologist, New Mexico State Land Office **38** Photo Joe Ben Wheat, University of Colorado Museum **39** After Joe Ben Wheat in Fritz and Fritz (eds), *New World Archaeology*, p. 221, Freeman & Co., 1974 **40** Photo H. Drewes/USGS **41** Drawn by Eric Carlson from Steve R. Simms, *Ancient Peoples of the Great Basin and Colorado Plateau*, Left Coast Press, 2008 **42a** University of Utah Archaeological Center, Salt Lake City **42b** Werner Forman/Utah Museum of Natural History **44** Photo John Pafford **46b** Courtesy The Frank H. McClung Museum, University of Tennessee, Knoxville **49** From the Archives of the Illinois State Museum **50** Photo L. R. Binford **51** From Richard W. Jefferies, *Archaeology of Carrier Mills: 10,000 Years in the Saline Valley of Illinois*, Southern Illinois University Press, 1986 **52** Center for Archaeological Research, Southern Illinois University, Carbondale **56b** After Dumond, 1987, ill. 14 **57** *Mink Island Site and the Amalik Bay Archaeological District. A High Resolution, Long-term Snapshot of Human Maritime Adaptation*, in Francis P. McManamon (ed.), Archaeology in America: An Encyclopedia. Vol 4: pp. 294–300, Greenwood Press, 2009 **58a** From Brian Fagan, *Where We Found a Whale*, Fig. 3.8, p. 41, National Park Service, 2008 **58m** Courtesy of the Alutiiq Museum, Kodiak, Alaska **58b** Photo courtesy Museum of the American Indian, Heye Foundation **60** From Fitzhugh and Crowell, 1988. Drawn by Jo Ann Moore **61** Photo Herbert Maschner **62** After Dumond, 1987 **65** Photo Robert McGhee **67** National Museums of Canada, Canadian Museum of Civilisation, Gatineau, neg. no. 77-26 **68a and b** Bjarne Gronnow, National Museum of Denmark, Copenhagen **72** Library of Congress, Washington, D.C. **75** Roy Carlson **76** National Anthropological Archives, Smithsonian Institution, Washington, D.C., neg. no. 56748. Courtesy Dale R. Croes, Washington State University **78** G. R. Keddie, 1981, *The Use and Distribution of Labrets on the North Pacific Rim, Syesis* 14:60-80, Royal British Columbia Provincial Museum **79** From Hilary Stewart, *Indian Fishing*, Douglas & McIntyre, 1977. Reproduced with permission from the publisher **89** National Anthropological Archives, Smithsonian Institution, Washington, D.C. neg. no. 75-14715 **90** Stephen Powers, *Tribes of California* (1877) **94** After Cordell, 1984 **95–96** Courtesy of The Witte Museum, San Antonio, Texas **97l** Courtesy of The Witte Museum, San Antonio, Texas. Photo J. Zintgraff **97r** Bob Daemmrich/Corbis **98–99** Marilyn Angel Wynn, Nativestock Pictures/Corbis **100, 101, 103** Adriel Heisey **104, 106** Field Museum of Natural History, Chicago **108, 109** Photo Doak Heyser, www.singingdesert.com **113** From Wedel and others, 1968 **114** George Frison, University of Laramie, Wyoming **116** Drawn by Sue Cawood **117** Courtesy Head-Smashed-In Buffalo Jump Interpretive Centre, Alberta **119** Joslyn Art Museum, Omaha, Nebraska. Gift of the Enron Art Foundation **120** Walters Art Gallery, Baltimore **123** National Anthropological Archives, Smithsonian Institution, Washington, D.C. **124** Russ Hanson, Courtesy National Park Service **129** Drawn by Tracy Wellman **133al** Photos James A. Tuck, Memorial University of Newfoundland **133ar** Redrawn after Willey, 1966, Fig. 5.15 **133b** University Museum of Archaeology and Ethnology, Cambridge **134** Drawing by Thomas W. Gatlin from Richard W. Jefferies, *Archaeology of Carrier Mills: 10,000 Years in the Saline Valley of Illinois*, p. 84, Southern Illinois University Press, 1986 **134–35** From Theodor de Bry, *Indorum Floridam Provinciam Inhabitantium Eicones*, 1591 **136** From Kenneth E. Sassaman *Technological Innovations in Economic and Social Contexts*, in Kenneth E. Sassaman and David G. Anderson (eds), *Archaeology of the Mid-Holocene Southeast*, Fig. 4-2, University Press of Florida, 1996. Reprinted with the permission of the University Press of Florida **138** From Jon E. Gibson, *Poverty Point: A Culture of the Lower Mississippi Valley*, University of Southwestern Louisiana, 1985 **143** From Fitzhugh and Crowell, 1988. Drawn by Jo Ann Moore **144** Werner Forman Archive/American Museum of Natural History, New York **146** Werner Forman Archive/Smithsonian Institution, Washington, D.C. **148a and b** National Museums of Canada, Canadian Museum of Civilization, Gatineau **150a and m** National Anthropological Archives, Smithsonian Institution, Washington, D.C. **150b** Photographer G. S. McTavish/National Archives of Canada, Ottawa/C8160 **152** National Archives of Canada, Ottawa/PA129869 **154** Department of Ethnography, National Museum of Denmark **156** National Museums of Canada, Canadian Museum of Civilization, Gatineau **160a** After Wayne Suttles (ed.), *Handbook of North American Indians: The Northwest Coast*, Smithsonian Institution, 1990 **160b** British Museum, London **161** National Archives of Canada, Ottawa **162** Courtesy Richard

D. Daugherty **163a** and **b** Courtesy Richard D. Daugherty **164** Shirley Tewhaus, courtesy of the U.S. Army Corps of Engineers **169** After J. L. Chartkoff and K. K. Chartkoff, *The Archaeology of California*, Fig. 33, Stanford University Press, 1984 **170** Phoebe A. Hearst Museum of Anthropology, University of California, Berkeley **171** Photo Peter Howarth. Santa Barbara Museum of Natural History **172–73** William James Warren/Corbis **174** Photo William Dewey. Santa Barbara Museum of Natural History **177a** Adriel Hersey **177b** Photo O. C. Havers. National Geographic Society **178** Drawn by Tracy Wellman **179** Photo R. G. Vivian. Arizona State Museum, University of Arizona, Tucson **180** Jan Hauser/Corbis **181** Reprinted with permission from David E. Doyel, *Irrigation and Power in Phoenix Basin, Hohokam Society* in Suzanne and Paul Fish (eds), *The Hohokam Millennium*, School for Advanced Research, 2007. 2007 School for Advanced Research, Santa Fe, New Mexico **182**, **183** Werner Forman Archive/Maxwell Museum of Anthropology, Albequerque **194a** Photo courtesy the Arizona Department of Transportation and Northland Research Inc. **194b** Arizona State Museum, University of Arizona, Tucson **194** Werner Forman Archive **196** Painting by Glenn Felch courtesy of the Crow Canyon Archaeological Center **199** Photo David Grant Noble, School of American Research, Santa Fe **200** Photo courtesy the Museum of Archaeology and Anthropology, University of Cambridge **201** Courtesy the Amerind Foundation Inc., Dragoon, Arizona **204** Ohio Historical Society **206a** Photo by Michael Keller, West Virginia Division of Culture and History **206b** Photo John Bigelow Taylor/American Museum of Natural History **207** Ohio Historical Society **210** Painting by Greg Harlin reproduced with permission of The Frank H. McClung Museum, University of Tennessee, Knoxville **213** E. G. Squier and E. F. Davis, *Ancient Monuments of the Mississippi Valley*, 1848 **214** Ohio Historical Society **215a** Werner Forman Archive/Field Museum of Natural History, Chicago. Location 11 **215b** British Museum, London **216a** From D. T. Case and Christopher Carr, *The Scioto Hopewell*, Fig 2.8, p. 54 (Springer, 2008) **216b** President and Fellows of Harvard College, Peabody Museum 82-35-10/29685 **217** Drawing M. Hampshire, courtesy of the U.S. National Park Service **218** Photo U.S. National Park Service **219** Photo Tony Linck **222a** Werner Forman Archive/Museum of the American Indian, Heye Foundation, New York **222b** Photo 1985 Dirk Bakker **227** Photo David Dye, University of Memphis **228** Cahokia Mounds State Historic Site. Painting by William R. Iseminger **229** Moundville Archaeological Park **230** Painting by Martin Pate. Courtesy of Southeast Archaeological Center, National Park Service **232** From Le Page du Pratz, *Histoire de la Louisiane*, 1758 **237** From William A. Turnbaugh, *Man, Land and Time: The Cultural Prehistory and Demographic Patterns of North-Central Pennsylvania*, Unigraphic, 1977 **238–39** Division of Research and Collection, New York State Museum **241** Artist Ivan Kocsis. Courtesy The Museum of Ontario Archaeology, London, Ontario **242** "Feast of the Dead" from Jean-François Lafitau, *Moeurs des sauvages ameriquains, compares aux moeurs des premiers temps*, 1724 **247a** "Huron Planting their Fields" from Jean-François Lafitau, *Moeurs des sauvages ameriquains, compares aux moeurs des premiers temps*, 1724 **247b** Museum für Völkerkunde, Vienna **248**, **249** Artist Ivan Kocsis. Courtesy The Museum of Ontario Archaeology, London, Ontario **253** P. van Der Aa, *De gedenkwaardige Voyagie van don Ferdinand de Soto na Florida*, 1706. W. S. Hoole Special Collections Library, University of Alabama **255** Photo Dennis O'Brien. American Museum of Natural History, St. Catherine's Island Foundation

Color illustrations

Plate I Warren Morgan/Corbis **Plate II** Werner Forman Archive/University Museum, University of Alaska, Location: 16 **Plate III** Werner Forman Archive/ American Museum of Natural History, New York. Location: 21 **Plate IV l** and **m** Werner Forman Archive/University Museum, University of Alaska. Location: 12 **Plate IV r** Werner Forman Archive/Smithsonian Institution, Washington, D.C. **Plate V** Werner Forman Archive/Canadian Museum of Civilization, Gatineau. Location: 19 **Plate VI** Werner Forman Archive/Field Museum of Natural History, Chicago. Location: 21 **Plate VII** Galen Rowell/Corbis **Plate VIII** Paul A. Souders/Corbis **Plate IX** *Indians Hunting the Bison* by Karl Bodmer, from *Travels in the Interior of North America during the years 1832–1834*. Arthus Bertrand, Paris 1840–1843 **Plate X** *Interior of the Hut of a Mandan Chief* by Karl Bodmer, from *Travels in the Interior of North America during the years 1832–1834*. Arthus Bertrand, Paris 1840–1843 **Plate XI** Werner Forman Archive/Provincial Museum, Victoria, British Columbia. Location: 19 **Plate XII** Canadian Museum of Civilization/Corbis **Plate XIII** Seattle Art Museum/Corbis **Plate XIV** David Muench/Corbis **Plate XV** Henry D. Wallace **Plate XVI** George H. H. Huey/Corbis **Plate XVII** David Muench/Corbis **Plate XVIII** Richard A. Cooke/Corbis **Plate XIX** David Muench/Corbis **Plate XX** Painting by Lloyd K. Townsend. Cahokia Mounds State Historic Site **Plate XXI** Werner Forman Archive/Peabody Museum, Harvard University, Cambridge, MA. Location: 11 **Plate XXII** Photograph 1985 Dirk Bakker **Plate XXIII** Werner Forman Archive/Museum of the American Indian, Heye Foundation, New York. Location: 10 **Plate XXIV** Werner Forman Archive/Field Museum of Natural History, Chicago. Location: 09 **Plate XXV** Werner Forman Archive/Museum of the American Indian, Heye Foundation, New York. Location: 09 **Plate XXVI** Werner Forman Archive/Museum of the American Indian, Heye Foundation, New York. Location: 09

Index